BEN TILLETT

Ben Tillett

Portrait of a Labour Leader

Jonathan Schneer

UNIVERSITY OF ILLINOIS PRESS

Urbana   Chicago   London

© 1982 by Jonathan Schneer
Printed and bound in Great Britain

Library of Congress Cataloging in Publication Data

Schneer, Jonathan.
   Ben Tillett: portrait of a labour leader.
   (The Working class in European history)
   Bibliography: p.
   Includes index.
   1. Tillett, Ben, 1860-1943. 2. Trade-unions – Great
Britain – Officicials and employees – Biography.
3. Socialists – Great Britain – Biography. I. Title.
II. Series.
HD6665.T54S3   1982   331.88'092'4   [B]   82-13653
ISBN 0-252-01025-6

CONTENTS

The Working Class in European History

Editorial Advisers:

Standish Meacham
Joan Scott
Reginald Zelnick

PREFACE

The public performance of Ben Tillett is a subject which any modern British historian might examine easily enough. The numerous organizations, committees and public bodies on which he served usually left printed records of their proceedings. The political campaigns and strikes in which he participated were reported almost always in the press. Tillett himself wrote numerous pamphlets and articles explaining where he stood on questions of the day. But his private circumstances are not so readily accessible to researchers. A small Ben Tillett Collection at the Modern Records Centre, Warwick University, casts almost no light upon them. Tillett's daughter, Mrs Jeanette Davis, who died in 1976, knew little about her father's early years, and preferred not to discuss life in the Tillett household. Frank Stillwell, Tillett's son-in-law (he had married a second daughter), also died in 1976 before I could speak to him. Consequently, *Ben Tillett: Portrait of a Labour Leader* inevitably focuses upon Tillett's public career, which extended from 1887-1921. It is not intended to be a full-length biography, though I have dealt briefly with his early and late years.

Many people helped in the preparation of this manuscript. I would like particularly to acknowledge my profound debt to Professor Stephen Koss, of Columbia University, who supervised my research while I was his student, and who encouraged me with friendly criticism and suggestions at later stages of the project. Professor Robert Paxton, Professor Peter Weiler, Professor James Cronin, Professor Eugene Black, Professor Peter Stansky, Professor David Montgomery, Professor Standish Meachum and Mr John Grigg also read portions of the manuscript and offered sound advice. In addition, I owe thanks to Janet Druker and Richard Storey of the Modern Records Centre at Warwick University for directing me to much useful material, to Professor John Saville of Hull University who generously opened the files of the *Dictionary of Labour Biography* to me, and to David Barlowe, former research librarian of the Transport and General Workers' Union. To librarians, archivists and friends too numerous to list, I offer thanks as well.

INTRODUCTION

On a blustery evening in early March 1976, Lord George-Brown emerged suddenly from the Palace of Westminster to announce his resignation from the Labour Party. He had become increasingly disenchanted with the 'Labour establishment', the former Labour Cabinet Minister said, because it no longer cared about individual freedom.[1]

In the rambling talk with which he accompanied his statement of resignation, Lord George-Brown emphasized that he did not easily make the break with Labour. He had been affiliated with the labour movement since the beginning of his career. His father had been one of its pioneers. 'My dear old dad' joined the Dockers' Union in 1898; his 'membership card was signed by Ben Tillett'. Then Lord George-Brown, who perhaps had had too much to drink, fell down.[2] Tillett, who on one occasion had to be led to the TUC rostrum because he could not find it himself, would have sympathized.

The invocation of Tillett was appropriate in another respect. Like Lord George-Brown, Tillett was a man with a talent for plain speaking which often generated more antagonism than anything else. He was less at home with the politicians than with the trade unionists in the Labour Party. Above all else, he was 'labour's stormy petrel', a title which early in his career he proudly advertised, but which later he wished to renounce. And, as with Lord George-Brown, that proved to be impossible. Tillett was a weathercock during the heroic age of British labour history; where he pointed others were sure to follow, and that usually meant rough weather ahead.

The man capable of inspiring Lord George-Brown's admiration had other considerable achievements to his credit. Ben Tillett helped to lead the great London dock strike of 1889 and to found the Dock, Wharf, Riverside and General Labourers' Union of Great Britain and Ireland, of which he was general secretary until 1922, when it was transformed into the modern Transport and General Workers' Union. A prominent new unionist during the late 1880s and early 1890s, he was no less notable during the 'great unrest' of 1910-14 as a direct actionist. He played a significant role in nearly all the industrial disputes affecting British dockers between 1889 and 1921. At the annual meetings of the Trades Union Congress (TUC), as a member of its parliamentary committee between 1892 and 1895, as the leader of one of England's

1

largest unions of unskilled labourers, and as co-founder of the National Transport Workers' Federation and the Triple Alliance which contained the National Transport Workers' Federation, miners' and railwaymen's unions, Tillett proved himself a formidable figure in the trade union world. Simultaneously he was carving a niche in the political side of the working-class movement. He was a founder of the Independent Labour Party in 1893 and a member of its executive council during the following year. In 1900 he helped to establish the Labour Representation Committee (direct ancestor of the Labour Party) and served for a year on its executive council as well. He stood unsuccessfully for Parliament in 1892, 1895, 1906 and 1910, gaining national attention during the first and last of these contests. In 1917, during the First World War (which he vehemently supported), he finally gained entrance to the House of Commons as the Labour Member from North Salford, which he continued to represent until 1924, and then again from 1929-31. He was deeply involved in most of the important developments affecting the modern working class during its formative period.

Tillett is significant not only for the important role he played in the modern British labour movement, but also for the peculiar nature of that role. He was one of those fascinating figures enlivening the late-Victorian and Edwardian landscape: one part eccentric, two parts egoist, three parts crusader – though never for lost causes, if he could help it. The new unionism, socialism, syndicalism, patriotism, internationalism – at one time or another Tillett espoused them all. Consistency was never his strong suit. He began as a Lib-Lab supporter, but remarkably suggested in 1892 that Labour should ally with the Conservatives. He preached in Labour churches but denounced the 'Methodist cant' which, in his opinion, disfigured the labour movement. A teetotaller in his early days, he lived to become the scourge of the 'temperance bleating martyrs' within the Independent Labour Party. An exponent of class war, he became perhaps the primary working-class advocate of binding industrial arbitration. A leading internationalist before 1914, during the First World War he delivered himself of the chilling opinion that the only good German was a dead one. At the outset of his career a stammer so impeded his speech that he could barely speak in public; at its end, he was generally acknowledged to have been one of the labour movement's greatest orators. He was famous for putting into words what the aggrieved and downtrodden thought but could not say themselves. Pugnacious, mercurial, ambitious, he was not a representative figure, but at one time or another he represented, and was unsurpassed as spokesman for, nearly every current which moved the British working class. Thus an examination of Tillett enhances an understanding of the labour movement as a whole.

Perhaps the peculiarity of his temperament and the inconsistencies which marked his career explain the absence of a biography. After all, the study of a man who began somewhere in the middle of the political spectrum and then oscillated from one side to the other for thirty-odd years, finally ending somewhere to the right of the Labour Party leadership, must seem uninviting to the true believers of any camp. For this, Tillett has been consigned nearly to oblivion. Inevitably, however, references to him are scattered throughout the literature. The standard labour histories depict him as a socialist possessing the attitudes of a typical member of the Independent Labour Party. The Webbs, G.D.H. Cole, Henry Pelling, Phillip Poirier variously date Tillett's conversion to socialism before, during and after the great London dock strike of 1889. Tillett's middle years, 1900-10, when he was advocating industrial conciliation, are generally passed over, but he reappears during the 'great unrest' as a prominent syndicalist. George Dangerfield, Cole and even Eric Hobsbawm consider him among 'the cadre of militant leaders' at this stage. Little attention is paid to the twists and turns which, in fact, marked Tillett's career. Only the authors of *A History of British Trade Unionism since 1889*, Hugh Clegg, Allen Fox and A.F. Thompson, make note of them. They ungenerously accept the verdict of Tillett's contemporary enemy, the self-described 'apostle of free labour' William Collison, who wrote in 1913 that the dockers' leader was 'a demagogue with the taste of a sybarite, a voluptuary with the hide of an agitator'. In this interpretation, Tillett the socialist is superseded by Tillett the opportunist.[3]

This judgement is picked up and elaborated by Tom Nairn in an article written in 1964, which attempts to explain why the Labour Party has failed to mount an effective and sustained challenge to British capitalism. Recalling Tillett's infamous reference to 'chatterers and magpies of continental revolutionists' at the founding conference of the Independent Labour Party in 1893, Nairn writes:

Here was the authentic spirit of Labourism: proudly anti-theoretical, vulgarly chauvinist, totally deluded by the false social-democratic contrast between 'revolution' (conceived as 24 hours of blood red violence) and 'evolution' (conceived as a sort of arithmetic adding up of socialism by little, regular instalments).

At least Nairn's attack restores Tillett to his rightful place at the heart of British labour's experience. Whether it is fair, either to Tillett or to Keir Hardie, the founder of 'labourism', to describe the dockers' general secretary as 'labourism's authentic spirit' is another matter, however, and one of this book's primary concerns.[4]

Since Nairn's assessment of Tillett is the one which currently holds sway, it seems useful to point out that less than two weeks prior to the chauvinist declamation quoted by him, Tillett had appeared before Bristol's striking dockers to insist that they:

> must not finish at trade unionism— they must not finish until the workers of all grades and degrees commanded absolutely the whole machinery of the state, the whole machinery of government, of production, control and distribution.

Surely this classic Marxist injunction bears little resemblance to the 'authentic spirit of labourism' which Tillett is held to have embodied. It highlights a second main concern of this work: to situate in historical context the countless transfigurations which characterized Ben Tillett's career, and thereby to gain a better understanding of both the man and the movement he helped to shape.[5]

Much has been said about the perils of writing the biography of a generally unsympathetic character. This author must confess at the start to a certain ambivalence about his subject. It is easy to quote Ben Tillett against himself, for there is scarcely a position he took up which he did not later directly contradict. At times his cynicism and opportunism were transparent to the point of blatancy. Yet it is also true that Tillett could stand fast, and was capable of great courage and fire. Particularly during the late-Victorian period of the new unionism, he fought the dockers' battle against great odds with skill and tenacity. Then, and at times later, he earned the grudging respect of his opponents in and outside labour's ranks, and of his biographer as well. It seems best therefore to begin this study with a simple assertion: for good or ill, Tillett's role was a major one. By tracing and explaining it, it should be possible to illuminate the wider scene.

Notes

1. *Guardian*, 2 March 1976.
2. Lord George-Brown claimed that he had been blinded by flashbulbs and stumbled.

3. Sidney and Beatrice Webb, *The History of Trade Unionism* (Longmans, London, 1920); G.D.H. Cole, *A Short History of the British Working Class Movement* (G. Allen and Unwin, London, 1941) in which Tillett, Mann and Burns are described as socialists in 1889 (p. 244), and Tillett and Mann as syndicalists in 1911 (pp. 328-33); Henry Pelling, *The Origins of the Labour Party* (Macmillan, London, 1954), in which Tillett appears in 1890 as a 'trade union socialist', (p. 91); Phillip Poirier, *The Advent of the Labour Party* (Columbia University Press, New York, 1958), in which it is claimed that Tillett was 'an ILP man' in 1900 (p. 81); George Dangerfield, *The Strange Death of Liberal England* (Capricorn Books, New York, 1961); Eric Hobsbawm, *Labouring Men* (Weidenfeld and Nicolson, London, 1964) from which this quote is taken (p. 215); Hobsbawm also implies (on p. 221) that Tillett discovered in socialism 'a theory of industrial warfare'; H. Clegg, A. Fox, A.F. Thompson, *A History of British Trade Unionism since 1889* (Oxford University Press, London, 1964), vol. 1, p. 89.

4. Tom Nairn, 'The Nature of the Labour Party' (I), *New Left Review*, vol. 27 (September/October 1964), p. 50.

5. *Bristol Mercury*, 8 January 1893.

1 EARLY YEARS IN BRISTOL AND LONDON

Ben Tillett was born at 8 John Street, in Easton, Bristol, on 11 September 1860.[1] His mother is said to have been Irish, though she listed Bristol as the city of her birth in the 1861 census; his father, who worked at a cart factory as a polisher, was almost certainly from Bristol as well. Ben had five older sisters and two older brothers. The Tilletts also kept a lodger, and shared their house with a collier, his wife and daughter. In all, then, there were fourteen people living at 8 John Street. As the average number of residents in numbers 1-7 John Street was six, and in numbers 9-16 John Street was seven, it is safe to assume that the Tilletts were poorer than their immediate neighbours. It is unlikely that they were richer and lived in a bigger house, since there are indications that all of Tillett's brothers and sisters worked from early childhood, hardly a sign of affluence. Of the 121 children under 16 years of age who lived in John Street, 48 were designated as 'scholars' in the 1861 census. What this appellation actually signified is unclear, as it included infants who could not possibly have been attending school. In any case, none of the Tillett children was so designated. At the age of 7, Ben himself cut slabs of clay with a crescent-shaped knife at Roaches Brickyard from 5 a. m. until dark. For this he was paid one shilling and six pence per week.

The fact that Tillett's childhood was extremely unhappy was undoubtedly partly responsible for shaping his rebellious personality. His mother died within a year of his birth and a succession of stepmothers ignored or punished him in turns; his father drank to excess.[2] Tillett had run away twice before he was 7 years old. After the stint in Roaches Brickyard, he ran away with Old Joe Barker's Circus and learned to be an acrobat. One of his sisters rescued him from that exciting milieu, however, and brought him to live with her in Staffordshire, where he attended school and was taught shoemaking. Neither of these occupations seem to have pleased the boy who, on one occasion, knocked his teacher over with a right fist to the jaw, and then performed handstands and somersaults off the desks. He had learned these tricks in the circus and, not surprisingly, returned to it after this brush with the authorities. The theatre, too, appealed to him. He was, in fact, a striker of dramatic poses for as long as he lived. One evening in

1873, his father discovered him in the gallery of a Bristol playhouse, and in short order marched him to the nearest Navy recruiting station and endorsed the papers which made it possible for the boy to be signed up. He was just 13 years old at that time.[3]

Tillett learned how to read and write in the Navy. It was an accomplishment he immediately turned to advantage by charging his shipmates a fee for composing their letters. He enjoyed racing about the masts and rigging of the old sailing ships until he slipped and ruptured himself. This injury led to his being invalided out of the service. Probably he was not unhappy to leave it. Conditions in the lower decks can hardly have been much easier than in Roaches Brickyard. The food was terrible, the work back-breaking and poorly paid, and the living conditions dehumanizing. 'Some people think it a change for the good to "hammock it" ', Tillett wrote years later:

> but imagine rows of perspiring humanity within a couple of feet of the deck overhead, merely divided by the space of the body, where even to shift sideways means a narrowing of the space that is altogether insufficient to bring about comfort or health. And then there is a complete absence of ventilation.

Tillett also realized that there was little prospect for advancement. 'Once a lower deck man, always a lower deck man', he lamented in the same article. Above all, however, he objected to the manner in which the men were treated. 'I was in the Navy long enough to know that the lower deck man and boy is brow beaten and cheated out of courage and sturdy manhood . . . ' he charged on another occasion. Still, the Navy showed Tillett what disciplined men, acting together, might accomplish. In this sense, his experience was perhaps a useful introduction to the organizational work he carried on in later years. Finally, it is not impossible that the Navy also imbued him with an undying if unacknowledged patriotism which, dormant until 1914, surfaced with the declaration of the First World War.[4]

When Tillett left the Navy in 1876, he joined the merchant marine, eventually becoming an able-bodied seaman in the timber trade. He sailed to Philadelphia, the West Indies, Riga and many of the European ports. He may, at this stage, have picked up some experience as a docker, unloading cargoes in France as a member of the ship's crew. Apparently this was a standard practice in certain European ports, although local dockers objected to it.

Between sailing trips, Tillett often stayed with his sister's mother-in-law in Bethnal Green, East London. This was his introduction to the East End, to the happy family life that had been denied him during his childhood, and to his eventual wife, Jane Tompkins, who was the sister of his own sister's husband. Not surprisingly, Tillett preferred his newly adopted family to life at sea; yet between 1876 and 1882, when he married Miss Tompkins, he was forced to alternate between them.[5]

Unemployment drove him back to sea each time. Today historians and economists question whether there actually was a 'Great Depression' between 1873 and 1896.[6] For Tillett and other young men who were entering the labour force in those years such scholarly debate would appear academic, to say the least. Between 1873 and 1896 Britain ceased to be 'the workshop of the world'. Two consequences of German and American economic competition were falling prices and rising unemployment at home. Those who kept their jobs benefited, since wages did not drop so fast as prices. But those who lost them, or could not find any to begin with, suffered acutely. Compounding the problem for men like Tillett, who hoped to earn a livelihood in the city, was the continuing migration of agricultural workers to urban areas. Between 1871 and 1891, 200,000 agricultural workers were lured into towns, or were forced from the land by farmers who could not pay wages during a depression, or wanted to replace their hands with machines. Foreigners, too, particularly East European and Russian Jews, poured into Britain at the rate of almost 10,000 per year. Like Tillett, most made their way to London's East End.

What did they find there? In 1883 Andrew Mearns, a journalist, created a sensation with his pamphlet 'The Bitter Cry of Outcast London'. This was the first of a number of exposés — some fearful, others compassionate, all lurid — provoked by the combination of depression and radical revival. Mearns purported to have discovered appalling conditions in the East End; Charles Booth, a wealthy ship-owner who originally set out to disprove these allegations, was shocked to discover that many of them were true. Determined to pursue his research no matter where it led, Booth embarked upon a sociological study of monumental proportions.[7] His multi-volume work, *The Life and Labour of the People of London*, conclusively demonstrated that one-third of the East End's 900,000 inhabitants lived at or below the poverty line. About 100,000 were 'very poor', that is 'at all times in want'. Booth wrote of these people: 'their life is the life of savages . . . their food is of the coarsest description and their only luxury is drink. It is not easy to say how they live.' He estimated that another 200,000 'though they would be much better for more of everything are not "in want" . . . By "want" is here meant an aggravated form of poverty.' In money terms, this meant that 300,000 people in the East End lived on less than 18-21 shillings per week. Booth calculated that a male adult needed a minimum of 7s 4d per week: 4s 1½d for food, 2s 10½d for rent, and 4d for clothes. But it was possible to survive on 5s 11d, if one spent 3s 6½d on rent and one penny per week on clothes. Approximately 100,000 East End residents adhered to this second budget.[8] To give some idea of scale, we may note that Eric Hobsbawm has estimated £300 to be a minimal annual income for a member of the middle class in 1865-6, and £700 per year to represent a 'comfortable income in mid-Edwardian England'.[9]

For the most part, East London's inhabitants were labourers or artisans: 48.5 per cent in Bethnal Green, 58.2 per cent in Poplar and 57.6 per cent in Stepney. Among East End craftsmen in 1881, the three trades that attracted the most men aged 20 years or older were boot and shoemaking, with 10,966, cabinet-making and upholstering with 7,660, and metal working with 7,094. As might be imagined, even these 'labour aristocrats' often endured extremely primitive housing conditions. In 1883 the medical officer for Bethnal Green — where Tillett lived — reported that out of 20,000 homes which he visited, none was without:

> some grave sanitary defects; in a very large number the walls of the staircases, passages and rooms are black with filth, the ceilings are rotten and bulging, the walls damp and decayed, the roofs defective and the light most imperfect.[10]

Those men who had not learned a craft, or could not find work in it, performed odd jobs as building labourers, or at the massive Beckton Gasworks in East Ham, or they drifted to the docks. Such men, if they were unmarried, usually hired beds in doss houses by the night for two or three pence. Those with families often rented a back room, or if they could count upon regular employment as unskilled labourers, two or three rooms. Their wives worked as well, a sure sign of desperate need in Victorian England. But charring and washing were not seasonal jobs, and the women were often able to earn more on an annual basis than their husbands.

The docks were a sort of court of last resort for men in straitened circumstances; hiring practices there often seemed to correspond to the luck of the draw. For Tillett, and countless others, they acted like a magnet. He worked for a time as a laster at Markies Bootmakers in

Finsbury, but when he was dismissed from that firm, he discovered that the trade taught him in Staffordshire during his youth was over-supplied. Then he joined the throngs crowding about the dock gates clamouring for work. In one form or another his association with such men and their profession was to last for the rest of his life. Consequently it is necessary to examine the nature of the work, and the structure of the dockland labour force in detail.

II

In 1885 there were four dock companies along the Thames in East London: the East and West India Dock Company, including the Tilbury Dock; the London and St Katherine Dock Company, including both the Victoria and Albert Docks; the Surrey Commercial Dock Company; and the Millwall Dock Company. They were in cut-throat competition with each other, and had been since their inception. The West India, East India, London and Surrey Commercial docks opened during the first decade of the nineteenth century. The Surrey Docks, whose board of directors were the company's main customers and knew precisely what facilities they wanted, staked out early an exclusive claim to the grain and timber trade — which also happened to be their business. When the Millwall Dock opened in 1868, its directors arranged with Surrey to divide this trade, and between them they effected a monopoly over it. They formed, as one historian of the London docks has put it, 'a port within a port'.[11] Soon the other dock companies found it necessary to combine formally in order to survive. Thus, the East and West India Docks amalgamated in 1838, and the London Dock Company amalgamated with the St Katherine and Victoria Dock Company in 1864.[12] These two companies became the giants of the port; their rivalry remained intense.

The increasing size of ships rendered many of the older facilities obsolete. In 1870, 10,727 foreign vessels brought to London goods weighing approximately 4,031,000 tons; in 1879, 10,725 foreign vessels carried into London cargo weighing over 5,500,000 tons.[13] Docks capable of accommodating these new deeper-hulled ships were necessary. For this reason, the London and St Katherine Dock Company opened the Royal Albert Dock in 1880; six years later the East and West India Dock Company answered with the construction of an elaborate complex at Tilbury. Unfortunately there were now more facilities available than ships to use them. The result was a lowering of rates — and profits — all around.

The dock companies were not only in fierce competition with one another; from the mid-nineteenth century they faced an increasingly effective challenge from the wharfingers. A wharf is simply a structure at the river's edge to which relatively small boats may be attached, and behind which warehouses can be erected for storing goods. A dock is an elaborate system of channels and basins capable of containing many ocean-going vessels, and generally ringed with warehouses. Traditionally the wharves received those boats engaged in domestic — or coastwise — trade, whereas the docks accepted the larger international vessels. After Parliament ended the dock companies' monopoly on foreign trade in 1857, however, it became possible for the wharfingers to accept dutiable goods; although they still could not accommodate the large ocean-going vessels, they were quite capable of housing their cargoes. Private wharves sprang into existence, dotting the banks of the Thames. Since, they did not charge a quay fee, unlike the docks, it proved cheaper for shippers to have their goods discharged into barges or lighters and transferred to warehouses belonging to the wharves, while continuing to dock their vessels as usual. The result was that, although the docks received ships with more cargo than ever before, their warehouses received fewer goods in relation to the warehouses of the wharves. This fact is significant, as it was in warehousing that the dock directors had made their fortunes. Moreover, although London's proportion of ships received between 1850 and 1890 rose from approximately 15 per cent to 18 per cent in comparison with the rest of the country, her proportion of international traders received declined from 32.5 per cent to 21 per cent. This loss was born by the dock companies; the wharves, which still relied more upon coastwise shipping, lost a smaller proportion of trade. The heightened incidence of transhipment — that is, of transferral of cargo from incoming to outgoing vessels without landing any of it on the quay — contributed to a further decline in the fortunes of the dock companies.

The complicated structure of officialdom at the docks hardly facilitated business arrangements in any case.[14] It differed only slightly from dock to dock. Essentially, each dock was under the charge of a superintendent, chosen by the board of directors and often of their number. Dock police, who were supposed to check petty pilfering and generally keep an eye on the men, were responsible to him alone. Directly subordinate to him was the dock master, usually a former ship's captain, who took charge of all vessels before they entered, or as they left the dock. Under the dock master's command there were several deputies and berthing masters who were held responsible for the ships while they were inside the dock. At the same level as the dock master, and subordinate only to the superintendent, was the engineer, whose responsibility was to oversee all machinery and structures in the docks; beneath him were a bevy of artisans whose skills corresponded to the needs of the appliances in the dock. A third category of official directly responsible to the superintendent, but lower in the hierarchy than the dock master or the engineer, were the inspectors, labour masters and warehouse keepers; these, as their titles suggest, were in charge of the various stages through which the cargo passed as it was removed from the holds of the ships, on to the quays, and into the warehouses or vice versa. The warehouse keepers oversaw another small army of clerks and foremen, who in turn took charge of processing the

Figure 1.1: Structure of Dock Work-force

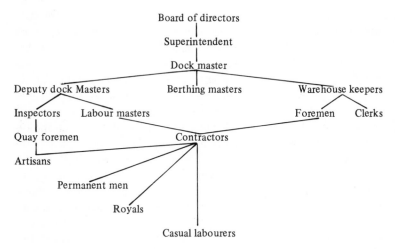

goods once they had been brought into the warehouse. Before this operation, however, the goods had to be sorted on the quay; this was the responsibility of the quay foreman. Similarly, someone had to take charge of the goods as they were moved from ship to shore; this was done by another foreman, or contractor (for further discussion about contractors, see below pp. 18-19). Usually, the latter was a permanent employee of the dock company, but occasionally he was chosen by the dockers themselves.[15]

Labourers in and around the docks were divided into two main categories: casual and permanent, though there were gradations within each.

The 'perms' as they were sometimes called, represented a small minority: Colonel DuPlat Taylor, managing director of the East and West India Dock Company, calculated that he employed three hundred such men, whom he paid twenty to thirty shillings per week.[16] Beneath these 'superior labourers' were the 'Royals' or 'preference men' (their appellation depended upon the dock, but it meant the same thing), who were chosen first in the event that there was more work than the permanent men could handle. Beneath them were the vast majority, thousands of casual labourers, totally dependent upon the vagaries of the shipping trade.

The amount of work available depended upon the number and size of ships entering or departing the dock. The fluctuation was considerable: during the week ending 17 April 1885, the East and West India Dock Company paid 2,399 extra hands and 1,266 permanent hands £5,072; during the week ending on 16 October 1885, the same company paid 1,313 extras and 1,263 'perms' £3,717 16s 4d. Colonel DuPlat Taylor stated to the House of Lords Committee on Sweated Industries in 1888 that the number of extra hands he employed on a given day might vary between 100 and 3,000 men. The number of men employed permanently by the dock companies was calculated so finely that it rarely exceeded the minimum number required on the slowest day: in 1885 the East and West India Dock Company employed 1,408 men regularly; the London and St Katherine Dock Company employed 1,070; the Millwall Docks 300; and the Surrey Commercial Docks 455.

When work was plentiful, however, the supply of labour always exceeded the number of jobs to be filled. Tillett, who also testified before the 1888 Commission, claimed that there were 'one hundred men at least for every job that would take forty', and no one contradicted him. Beatrice Potter (later Mrs Sidney Webb) estimated that in 1887 there were probably 10,000 casual labourers employed at the docks alone (that is, this figure does not include the thousands who worked on the wharves), of whom approximately 3,000 could not find work on a given day. Colonel Birt, general manager of the Millwall Docks, suggested that 50,000 men regularly sought work on the docks and wharves of the Thames; Lord Dunraven, chairman of the 1888 Lords Committee on Sweated Industries, asked at one point whether there might not be as many as 200,000 labourers who earned the bulk of their wages in dockland. The figure generally accepted, however, appears to have been 100,000, though it is difficult to conceive how it was calculated, as the figure varied enormously day by day, indeed hour by hour. There was no regular 'calling on' time, and the men were hired and dismissed depending on demand throughout a 24-hour period. For the vast majority, work on the docks was so uncertain that they were forced 'to take work costering, and if very energetic can go early to market before the docks are open and have a turn with the barrow at night or on Saturdays while the wife perhaps minds a stall', as one of Charles Booth's researchers rather optimistically explained.[17]

The man in search of work at the docks had to arrive early enough without costering, for ships were loaded or discharged at any hour. The hiring system differed according to the dock, but no matter where he sought work, the late-comer − or even the man who wandered from the place of hiring, for whatever reason − risked missing a 'calling on'. At the East and West India and Tilbury Docks, the Millwall Dock, and the Surrey Commercial Dock, men were called upon by name and then admitted inside the dock gates. However, at the London and St Katherine Docks (which also included the Victoria and Albert Docks), the system was less rational. 'I have been down at the London Docks, Number 5 Gate every morning since last Friday', James Grey, a casual labourer testified before the Lords Committee.

> Yesterday I was there from half past eight until half past eleven. At half past eleven I should say there was something like 350 men waiting for employment at this special gate. A contractor, by the name of Clemence, came to the gate for, I will not be sure, I think it was 14 men, it was either 14 or 16 men, and of course there was a struggle . . . They have a certain number of tickets to give out, and there was a struggle between us men at the gate who should be lucky enough, as it were, to gain one . . . It is a common occurrence for men to get seriously injured in a struggle like that . . . men struggle like wild beasts; we stand upon one another's shoulders.[18]

Such scenes left indelible impressions. Seventy-five years later the son of a master stevedore could still recall how 'a man used to get up on steps with a handfull [sic] of brass tickets . . . and throw three or four at a time amongst the almost starving men, and they used to fight like Ravens to pick them up'. Such hiring methods encouraged bribery, though the dock officials denied it: the man with the tickets might give one to the docker who bought him a beer, or offered him some other inducement beforehand. James Sexton, the Liverpool dockers' leader, even claimed that contractors demanded and received favours from the wives of men looking for work. Obviously it was essential for the hopeful docker to be where the tickets were night or day, in case any work turned up; and even more, to be one of the familiar faces whom the 'caller on' would recognize.[19]

Once inside the docks, the casual labourer was either put to work unloading the ship's cargo, landing it on the quay, warehousing it, or if it was destined for the wharves, loading it into barges. If he worked in the warehouse, he might weigh, mark, sample or store the goods that were brought to him. Equally, he could be set to work transporting merchandise from the warehouse to the quay for export.

These tasks required varying degrees of skill and strength. When a ship entered the dock, the men who were to work it were organized into gangs, and divided according to the number of holds aboard. Usually there were four: six men would work in the first, or fore hold; eight in the second or main hold; six in the number three hold, and eight in the number four hold.[20] In the early 1870s, men still carried the goods from the hold to the deck, but by 1887 their job was to load the sling which had been lowered into the hold from a crane on the dock, or by a winch aboard the ship itself. This was difficult, cramped work, and also dangerous: if the sling slipped from the crane, or if the goods inside were tipped out, they might crush whoever worked beneath. Consequently, on deck above each hold, a 'fender off' was stationed to watch the sling, keep it on an even keel — which required great strength — and direct its operator. The men complained that despite its manifest importance contractors often insisted that the weakest member of a gang take this job in order to free stronger men for work in the hold. As a result, accidents were common.[21]

Once the goods had been lifted by the sling from the hold to the quay, another army of men set to work sorting and piling it, and when this was done, still more labourers trucked it in barrows from the quays to the warehouses. This last task was generally considered the easiest in dockland.

Stevedores performed practically the same work in reverse. Goods were brought down to the quay from the warehouses. Stevedores put them into the sling, by which they were hauled onto the deck and into the hold, or packed into lighters which brought the goods to ships anchored in mid-stream, and then unloaded them from the lighter to the ship's deck and finally into the hold. Packing in the hold required great skill, as it was important not merely to use space economically, but to distribute the cargo according to weight so that it did not upset the ship's balance. For loading a general cargo, stevedores worked in gangs of twelve: two loaded the sling from ashore or aboard the lighter;

one, a 'donkeyman', operated the winch; one guarded the gangway as a 'fender-off'; and eight worked in the hold. Stevedores also did some unloading, but only at the Millwall Dock.

Throughout the nineteenth century, the complex hierarchy among dock officials found its counterpart in an equally stratified system among the labourers which muted, though it could never erase, the more basic cleavage between masters and men. The stevedores, lightermen and gangers who laboured on the water were considered to be an elite workforce, whereas those who worked on land, no matter what their task, were deemed inferior in status. In general, it was recognized that packing or unpacking goods in the hold required greater strength, skill and stamina than wheeling a truck along a rail on a quay, or storing merchandise in a warehouse. There were divisions as well between the workers who never set foot in a boat. Dockers who handled only certain goods would often refuse to associate with labourers who did not specialize; their wives observed these distinctions too. Above all, there remained the primary divide between the mass of dockers and the 'Royals' or 'preference men', who received more money and were employed more often than their fellows.

Two factors, however, may have worked against this atomization of the dock labour force. First of all, socialist propaganda among the unskilled emphasized the dignity of all work. In the Social Democratic Federation journal, *Justice*, a young engineer, John Burns, repeatedly warned against the 'selfish snobbish desertion by the higher grades of the lower',[22] and numerous socialist meetings at the dock gates reiterated this message. Subsequent events would indicate that such agitation was not entirely ineffective. Secondly, as the economic crisis of the London dock companies became more acute, it would seem that men who specialized in carrying crates of oranges could hardly afford to refuse barrels of tea, or anything else. Thus Jim Welsh, a docker of twenty years' standing, proudly stated before the Lords Committee on Sweated Industries that he was capable of performing any task a dock foreman set him, as were hundreds of his mates. Despite such evidence, however, fragmentation of the labour force remained a primary obstacle for those who hoped to ameliorate general conditions for the dockers.

Wide discrepancies in pay also undermined solidarity among the men. Nominally the rate of wages among dock labourers varied little: in fact, the system of contract work, in combination with the favouritism displayed by certain foremen, led to significant distinctions which gave rise to much jealousy and antagonism. Generally dockers received either four pence or five pence an hour, depending on whether they were 'Royals'. Overtime was worth a penny an hour extra to the dock companies, and began between 6 and 8 p. m. If a worker laboured through the night and into the morning, which was common, he received the regular rate of pay again after 6 a.m. 'Royals' were also entitled to a share in the 'plus' (see below, p. 18), though as the years passed, fewer of them were allowed to share it, and their proportion of it dropped.

Two factors must be borne in mind when considering rates of pay at the docks. First of all, work was episodic for the majority of dockers. At times they worked feverishly, but more often they were lucky to get a full day in a week. 'The ordinary dock labourer', Tillett stated, 'is lucky if he gets five [months' work throughout the year] .' R.G.S. Self, a docker interviewed by one of Charles Booth's researchers, reported that he had gone ten weeks at a stretch without work. Even G.E. Jarrold, a stevedore who was presumably much better off than the average docker, worked only 156 full days in 1890, and 147 in 1891. Thus the four or five penny rate, small as it was, became even smaller when viewed in terms of yearly earnings.[23]

The effects of prolonged unemployment may be imagined. Casual labourers who had not eaten for days had become too weak for work when they finally were given it. 'They have worked for an hour and have five pence', Colonel Birt of the Millwall Docks testified. 'Their hunger will not allow them to continue; they take the five pence in order that they may get food.' In 1892, Tom Mann, in his capacity as a member of the Royal Commission on Labour, interviewed Frank Brien who worked in a tea warehouse:

Mann When a man has been out of work, say two months . . . what sort of joint of meat will he get for his Sunday dinner?
    Brien A joint of meat?
    Mann Yes?
    Brien A joint?
    Mann What does he get?
    Brien I do not believe he ever sees a joint.[24]

The second major factor affecting the rate of pay in the docks during the 1880s was that time-work was being phased out, the directors having discovered a more profitable method of employing their workers, namely the contract system. At the East and West India Docks and at Tilbury, piece-work continued as the basis for calculating workers' earnings. That is, work time was estimated by the responsible official who gave the foreman a lump sum to pay the men an hourly wage to accomplish it. As an incentive to the men, they were permitted a share in the 'plus', that is, the remainder of the original sum, if they finished the work sooner than anticipated. Because the docks had fallen on hard times, however, the number of workers allowed to share this bonus had been drastically reduced: Tillett complained to the Lords that, before 1872, the 'plus' usually amounted to 40 per cent of the ordinary docker's wages; now, in 1888, he got none at all, and even the 'Royal' received a reduced amount. Moreover, the men had no means of telling whether the foreman gave them a fair share of the 'plus', since they were not told how the original sum had been calculated.

The dock companies charged the shipper for unloading his cargo, and the merchant for warehousing and delivering his goods. Out of this money they paid all salaries. But after 1872, they found it convenient to take the money from the shippers and merchants, and then allocate a portion of it to contractors who undertook to hire the men necessary for the work. The men complained that often a contract to work on a specific ship would pass through the hands of as many as seven different subcontractors, each paying the one below him a smaller sum to find the labourers for the work. In this manner, a contract for unloading sugar, worth 1s 8d per ton to the first contractor was reduced to 4d per ton to the last.[25] But whether the work was taken by the first or seventh contractor, he hired as few men as possible and usually worked them mercilessly, thereby reducing the amount he paid in wages. He could then keep any sum left over for himself.

A man became a contractor in two ways: either he contacted the dock company as an independent entrepreneur and attempted to set up a contracting business with them, as was done at the Surrey Commercial Docks, or dockers who had gained the attention of company officials were approached and asked to undertake certain jobs for a lump sum. If the result was satisfactory to both parties, the docker might become a contractor of labour on a permanent basis. By doing so he almost inevitably incurred the odium of his peers, for he made his money cutting corners wherever possible. The men also charged that the dock companies chose as contractors bullies who were prepared to drive their workers and deal strongly with those who objected. It was the prevalence of the contract system on the docks which qualified it as a 'sweated' industry in the opinion of the Lords Commission.

At the Millwall Docks, thirty contractors hired the labour necessary to warehouse and prepare for sale the goods that had been unloaded from the ships. At the London Dock, 257 contractors and 42 independents concerned solely with the wool trade were responsible for hiring labour. The men tended to view the contractors, and not the owners of the dock companies, as primarily responsible for the harshness of their lot. The contractors' reputation is perhaps best reflected in a pamphlet issued in 1888 by the Tea Operative and General Labourers' Union:

The Contractor's Petition to Starve All if they can get a Profit

We your humble and cringing servants, who are satisfied to do any dirty work you can put us to; we who have been selected because we have less heart and feeling than the rest of our class, and have been raised to the position of contractors by bribery, humbly petition you, the managers and directors of the docks, to protect all our jewelery, our private houses, our chandler shops, our gigs and trotting ponies, our best furniture, our pianos, silk dresses and etc., from the hands of those who dare to ask for food, fair treatment and fair wages; we who for greed and self have narrowed up labour so that we make two men do the work for which you used to employ four; we who often screen you from paying compensation to the widow and the tender little ones of the men who get killed by our neglect and through our hurry to make more profit; we who have brought the work that employed men for weeks and months together down to days and sometimes hours work, claim as a reward for having degraded labour, sent the labourer to an early grave, killed his wife, starved his children, and ruined the future of thousands, the right to do worse in the future — exulting while others die, and grinning while others weep.

Yours truly,

All Contractors in General[26]

In fact, the growth of the contract system was merely one aspect of a more general speed up. Work at the docks had always been irregular, but, when available, it was performed at a reasonable rate. Ships arrived depending upon the winds and tides. Their cargo was often stored in the dock warehouses for months at a time while its owners waited for prices to rise, or merely for opportunities to sell. Consequently — and with the exception of mail packets — there was no great rush to unload ships as they entered the dock. In an unpublished and undated essay,

'The Docker: His Life and Work', Tillett looked back upon the less hectic pace of the old days with obvious nostalgia:

> There was a time when vessels came in schools and fleets . . . The Clipper, the Quebec barque, the Jordie Brig, the small but swift sailing little coasters, brigantines, schooners, came leasurely [sic] into dock with song and welcome and great demonstration . . . [27]

'But that is done with now', he concluded. The introduction of steam ships and the invention of the telegraph enabled shippers and merchants to operate according to strictly calculated schedules. The huge new ships represented great investments which were jeopardized every moment that they lay idle. The intensification of international and domestic economic competition accelerated the traditional tempo of work on the docks. 'There is hurry and scurry and desperate pullings and haulings, man against man, gang against gang, to the last ounce . . . soul and body alike are killed.' Management confirmed Tillett's complaint that the pace of work had been increased. 'When I was first appointed 18 years ago', Colonel DuPlat Taylor told the Lords:

> if a West Indiaman of 300 or 400 tons were discharged in a week they thought it very good work. We now have steamers discharging 1,500 tons of sugar, and which have to be got out in seven hours; and the samples have to be in the brokers' hands the same day; very often they are working all through the night.

Some of the older skills had become obsolete. Stevedores packing goods into the holds of steam ships, for example, did not need to pay such strict attention to balancing as in the older sailing vessels. More usually, it was simply that speed rather than skill was demanded of the labourers. Colonel Birt of the Millwall Dock explained to the Lords Committee why he did not like to hire casual labour: 'The poor fellows are miserably clad, scarcely with a boot on their foot, in a most miserable state, and they cannot run; their boots would not permit them.' Nevertheless, when a steam ship needed to be discharged at great speed, dock officials overcame such scruples, and hired whoever was available. That was why they encouraged the men to wait all day by the dock gates. When there was work to do, labour was never in short supply.[28]

The dockers objected both to the intensification of their labour and to the influx of casual labour from the ranks of the unemployed. Once, Tillett reflected, 'dock work was a profession . . . [Now] two thirds of the men working at the docks and wharves are not . . . dock labourers by trade'. We 'are among the Lazaruses that starve upon the crumbs from the rich man's table', Tillett asserted on another occasion. And now 'an endeavour is being made to shorten our supply even of them'. To an increasing number it appeared that the only solution was to organize a union capable of imposing terms upon the employers. For a brief period such an organization had, in fact, existed. The Labour Protection League, established in 1870, had carried off a successful strike in 1872 at the crest of the wave of trade activity that followed the Franco-Prussian War. But with the downswing of the economic cycle later in the decade, most of the League's membership lapsed, only branches among the stevedores and corn porters surviving. These, in turn, split to form their own exclusive and essentially craft unions. Consequently, by the mid-1880s, there was no organization to represent the vast majority of port labourers; and indeed it seemed unlikely that ill-clothed, famished and dispirited as they were, it would prove possible to establish one.[29]

Notes

1. All information on John Street is taken from the 1861 census, Public Record Office,RG 9/1734. There were 151 males, 161 females living in the street, including 121 children less than 16 years of age.

2. In January 1895, Tillett's 'Ned's Christmas Eve, A Story from Life' appeared in the *Labour Prophet*, a monthly journal edited by the Christian socialist, John Trevor. Ned, an unhappy child, lives with his brutal father. On Christmas Eve, he discovers his mother's grave, falls asleep on it and dies.

3. Information on Tillett's childhood is sketchy. I have mainly used his own reminiscences in *Memories and Reflections* (J. Long, London, 1931) and various obituary notices printed at his death in 1943. In addition, I am indebted to Mrs Jeannette Davis (1890-1976), Tillett's daughter, who kindly consented to an interview on 19 January 1976.

4. *Daily Herald*, 14 August 1912; 11 September 1912. Tillett was attacking the Admiralty, and especially Winston Churchill, its First Lord, in the course of which he mentioned his own experiences in the Navy.

5. Tillett first worked in the London docks in 1876. See his testimony before the 1888 Select Committee of the House of Lords on Sweated Industries, *Parliamentary Papers* (1888), vol. XXI, p. 111.

6. See, for example, S.B. Saul, *The Myth of the Great Depression* (Macmillan, London, 1969).

7. For more on the middle-class discovery of poverty in the East End, see Gareth Stedman Jones, *Outcast London* (Clarendon Press, Oxford, 1971), pp. 280-3.

8. Unless otherwise noted, all figures in this section come from Charles Booth, *Life and Labour of the People of London*, vol. 1 (Macmillan, London, 1892).

9. Eric Hobsbawm,*Industry and Empire* (Penguin, Harmondsworth, 1975),

pp. 156-7.

10. Quoted in Paul Thompson, *Socialists, Liberals and Labour: The Struggle for London, 1885-1914* (Routledge and Kegan Paul, London, 1967), p. 9.

11. John Lovell, *Stevedores and Dockers* (Macmillan, London, 1969), p. 24. For more on the early days of the London docks see also Sir Joseph Broodbank, *History of the Port of London*, vol. 1 (Daniel O'Connor, London, 1901); David J. Owen, *The Port of London, Yesterday and Today* (Port of London Authority, London, 1927); and H.L.L. Smith and Vaughan Nash, *The Story of the Dockers' Strike* (Fisher Unwin, London, 1889), chapter 1.

12. The chrononology of dock openings and amalgamations before 1889 is:

1802	West India Dock opened
1805	London Dock opened
1806	East India Dock opened
1807	Surrey Commercial Dock opened
1828	St Katherine Dock opened
1838	East and West India Docks opened
1855	Victoria Dock opened
1864	St Katherine and London Docks amalgamate
1880	Royal Albert Dock opened
1886	Tilbury Dock opened

13. London County Council, Royal Commission on the Port of London, 1900. Statement of Evidence by the Clerk of the London County Council, 3 December 1900, table 3. He got his information from the *Annual Statements of Navigation and Shipping*. Unless otherwise noted, all figures cited in the following pages are from the same source.

14. See Figure 1.1, which shows the dockland hierarchy.

15. This description of the structure of dock officialdom is largely taken from Tillett's testimony before the Select Committee of the House of Lords on Sweated Industries, *Parliamentary Papers* (1888), vol. XXI, p. 180.

16. *Parliamentary Papers* (1888), vol. XXI, p. 238.

17. Charles Booth Collection, London School of Economics and Political Science, Group A, vol. 24, numbers 10 and 67; Booth, *Life and Labour of the People of London,* vol. 4, p. 25; *Parliamentary Papers* (1888), vol. XXI, p. 277.

18. *Parliamentary Papers* (1888), vol. XXI, p. 207.

19. Ben Tillett Collection, Modern Records Centre, Warwick University, MSS 89/2: James Sexton, *Sir James Sexton, Agitator* (Faber and Faber, London, 1936), p. 72.

20. Charles Booth Collection, Group A, vol. 24, number 86. This is a hand-written essay by Booth himself on the history of waterside labour in London.

21. This extract from the *East End News* of 30 October 1888 is typical: 'Martin Kummerow, aged 32 years . . . has just died in Poplar Hospital from injuries caused while at work on the SS *Albatross*. A stupendous log of timber was being raised, when a part gave way, and the log fell upon the deceased, inflicting such serious injuries that he died from shock.'

22. *Justice*, 24 January 1885.

23. *Parliamentary Papers* (1888), vol. XXI, p. 119; Booth Collection, Group A, vol. 24, numbers 10 and 58.

24. *Parliamentary Papers* (1888), vol. XXI, p. 279; Minutes of Evidence taken before the 1892 Royal Commission on Labour, *Parliamentary Papers* (1892), vol. XXXV, p. 6.

25. *Parliamentary Papers* (1888), vol. XXI, p. 116.

26. *Parliamentary Papers* (1888), vol. XXI, pp. 256, 481, and 500.

27. From its style, the pamphlet would appear to have been written before

A Dock Labourer's Bitter Cry, which Tillett had printed in 1887. It survives in fragmentary form in the Tillett Collection, MSS 74/7/6/6.

28. *Parliamentary Papers* (1888), vol. XXI, pp. 238 and 279.

29. *Parliamentary Papers* (1888), vol. XXI, p. 121; *A Dock Labourer's Bitter Cry*, an address delivered by Ben Tillett on 27 July 1887 at the St Mary's School in Whitechapel and printed as a pamphlet soon afterwards.

2 THE LIBERAL WORKING MAN, 1887-8

I

Between 1882 and 1887 Tillett personified in many ways the ideals of respectability, thriftiness and prudence extolled by such Victorian working-class leaders as Henry Broadhurst and George Howell.[1] He lived with his wife in his mother-in-law's flat at 19 Huntslett Street in Bethnal Green. He read voraciously, later claiming acquaintance with the works of Lamb, Hazlitt, Wordsworth, Huxley, Spencer, Carlyle, Ruskin and Darwin among others. A Congregationalist (though much impressed by the secularism of Bradlaugh and the agnosticism of Huxley — with whom he is supposed to have corresponded in *The Times*),[2] Tillett became the librarian for his local church. In an attempt to overcome a stutter with which he had been afflicted since childhood, he read aloud at night to his wife from Dickens. Because he harboured the secret ambition to become a barrister, he attempted to teach himself Latin and Greek. In addition, he attended the Bow and Bromley Institute, where working men could listen to lectures free of charge on such subjects as the distance in miles from the earth to the sun. He also joined a Good Templars Lodge and, appropriately, the Cobden Club. At this early point in his career, he belonged neither to the dying world of radical artisans nor to the apolitical, jingoistic, but closed-in, working-class culture which Gareth Steadman Jones believes to have replaced it.[3] Rather, he typified the respectable Victorian working-man, a supporter of the Liberal Party who hoped to improve his lot through self-discipline and hard work.

None the less, two factors caused Tillett to stray from the narrow path of self-improvement. The first was his own temperament, partly shaped, no doubt, by his difficult childhood. He was constitutionally incapable of keeping quiet about things that troubled him. Even in the mid-1880s, when he was brought by consumption to what he thought was his deathbed, he found breath to rail against the inadequacies of the medical treatment he received. His combativeness carried over into political and industrial matters as well. During his days in the merchant marine he had become involved in disputes between masters and men. In one case he had brought the complaints of his mates about accommodation in the forecastle of a ship bound for the West Indies to the attention of the Bristol Port Authority, an intervention requiring not a little courage given the strict discipline maintained on ships.

During his stint at Markies, he had joined the Boot and Shoe Operatives' Union and had become friendly with its London secretary, Charles Freak. His pugnacious disposition often prevailed over his better judgement. Consequently, in 1882, when he finally found regular employment in dockland, conditions there were likely to provoke him to resentment and revolt. His job carting barrels up and downstairs at the Monument Quay Tea Warehouse, a medium-sized firm employing 120 men, during the busy summer season, was not designed to cool his temper either. As Frank Brien, a tea porter there explained to the 1892 Royal Commission on Labour:

> A chest [of tea] will weigh 1 cwt and 8, 9 or 10 pounds, about 1 cwt 5 pounds is the usual weight . . . it is extra-ordinarily heavy for one man. Picture to yourself a man with 2 cwt in a narrow alley . . . he can just get up the alley . . . and he has to do it with a chest on his head.[4]

The men were not allowed to leave the warehouse during the day, even for lunch, and according to Brien the lavatory was particularly malodorous. It could only be a matter of time before Tillett protested.

The ferment of radical ideas and social agitation which increasingly marked the East End scene during the 1880s no doubt also encouraged rebelliousness. For this was the beginning in England of the era of the great socialist revival. And if the impact of the Fabian discussion group, founded in 1884, was still limited exclusively to the upper reaches of the middle class, the agitation of other socialist societies found a more heterogeneous audience. In the East End, the most important socialist organization was the Social Democratic Federation, also established in 1884, by Henry Hyndman. Hyndman was one of the more peculiar figures inhabiting the labour and socialist worlds. A former stockbroker, independently wealthy, he had been converted to Marxism after reading *Das Kapital* in the original, and reportedly had attempted to convert the retired Disraeli as well. Rebuffed by the erstwhile Tory democrat, Hyndman received only a marginally warmer personal reception from the English proletariat to whom he lectured, while invariably decked out in frock coat and top hat. Yet he attracted to his organization many restless workers impatient with Gladstonian liberalism, among them some extremely talented young trade unionists. Of these, the most immediately important for our purposes were John Burns and Tom Mann.

Burns was already in the process of establishing an independent reputation. A skilled engineer, he was an autodidact intent upon teaching others the lessons of political economy as he understood them. Possessed of a masterful presence, a booming voice which could hold enthralled a mass audience out of doors, and an acute strategic sense, he had given up his craft to devote himself to full-time labour and socialist organizing. His signed articles appeared frequently in *Justice*, where, undoubtedly, another young engineer, Tom Mann, read them with agreement. A less flamboyant personality and personally less ambitious, Mann became a committed socialist in a way that Burns never did. He spent his lifetime in the service of ideals learned in his youth, following them out of the Social Democratic Federation, first into the Independent Labour Party, then into the syndicalist movement, and finally into the Communist Party, and died in poverty. Burns gradually modified his views while climbing the social and political ladders, becoming eventually a Liberal Cabinet Minister in the governments of Campbell-Bannerman and Asquith.

In 1886, however, both still belonged to the Social Democratic Federation, whose East End activities included the sponsorship of rallies for the unemployed at the various dock gates, and at Beckton Corner in Canning Town and Dodd Street, Limehouse. On one occasion 50,000 people attended. When such meetings were proscribed by the authorities, the focus shifted for a time to the issue of free speech. This movement reached a climax on 13 November 1887, 'Bloody Sunday', when police killed a man and injured hundreds attempting to assemble in Trafalgar Square. Burns and Hyndman were among the leaders of this demonstration who were arrested; the former took the opportunity afforded by his day in court to deliver an oration (later printed as a pamphlet entitled *History Will Absolve Me*), which further heightened his reputation. A funeral procession for Alfred Lynell, the unfortunate man who lost his life during the police charge, was 'the most enormous crowd of people I ever saw', according to the great socialist poet William Morris. It took forty-five minutes for the crowd to file past Aldgate, and then they listened reverently as Morris intoned the *Death March* he had composed for the occasion:

Not one, not one, no thousands must they slay,
But one and all if they would dusk the day.

It was demonstrations such as this which moved even the pessimistic Friedrich Engels to comment that 'the labour movement is starting here, and no mistake'.[5]

Whether Tillett took part in these and other demonstrations is impossible to tell. That he remained ignorant or unaffected by them is doubtful. He belonged to the Victoria Park Lodge of the International Order of Good Templars, an organization of teetotallers which Clement Edwards, the future lawyer and Liberal MP, had recently joined. 'Among other members present at my first meeting', Edwards recalled afterwards:

> was a sickly looking young man with a cadaverous face and stubbly light brown beard. He irritated me unbearably. He tried to make a speech, but he stammered so badly that he could not utter more than ten words a minute. I heard him called 'Brother Tillett' . . . I found that never a night passed without his rising and making the same futile effort to speak.

The subject of these utterances went unrecorded, but in all probability they concerned social and topical questions. As would soon become apparent, he had already begun to consider the broad issues affecting his class. Tillett was regarded as 'something of a crank by his fellow workers', William Collison, the self-appointed 'apostle of free labour', was later to record.[6]

When, in the spring of 1887, a dispute broke out at the Cutler Street warehouse, it was Tillett to whom the men turned for advice. His membership in the Boot and Shoe Operatives' Union gave him more experience in such matters than they had, and he may have been able to call upon Charles Freak for guidance. Appointed to the negotiating committee which represented the men in their disagreement, he pressed for the formation of a union, and was one of the leading spirits behind a wider meeting of warehousemen held on 13 July at the Royal Oak, a public house in Hackney Road. It was there that the Tea Operatives' and General Labourers' Association was founded. 'Speak to them you little devil', an Irishman is supposed to have said, lifting Tillett to a table top. Ben, who had already thought the matter through, obliged. 'My stammering lips tripping me the more rapidly I spoke urged the methods of organizing – a committee, power to bring up rules, to call on the organized workmen of the country . . . I was asked to be Secretary of the Committee . . . '[7]

At a salary of £2 per week he plunged into organizing activity with feverish intensity. He spoke every Sunday at the dock gates, urging his listeners to join the union. Three branches were established in

Canning Town, Poplar and Tilbury, and a social club in Tabard Street, south of the river. The first *Quarterly Report* of the new society reveals that it had already held four public meetings by 28 September 1887, at which £2 9s 14½d was collected; that £5 3s had been spent printing bills and cards, and another £2 5s on pamphlets. Tillett wrote the pamphlet, cannily entitled *A Dock Labourer's Bitter Cry* (hoping by his title to appeal to the Liberals whose consciences had been stirred by Mearns's earlier piece), made the arrangements for its publication, hired a brass band on the occasion of a 'monstre' (sic) demonstration, and tallied accounts at the end of each week. He seized all opportunities to publicize the miserable conditions in dockland as well as the methods and aims of the new organization, corresponding with Beatrice Potter (later Mrs Sidney Webb), Annie Besant (editor of a radical newspaper, the *Link*, and a member of the Social Democrat Federation), Charles Bradlaugh (the famous radical MP and notorious atheist), George Howell (old-time trade unionist and Liberal MP for Bethnal Green) and a host of others. His diary reveals that he petitioned Lord Dunraven for permission to testify before the 1888 Lords' Commission on Sweated Industries almost a year before he was eventually allowed to do so.[8]

Tillett also appealed for aid to the Members of Parliament for East End constituencies. 'It is needless for me to remind you of the class of men who constitute the [dockland] capitalist', he wrote on the evening of the union's formation.

> Their power and wealth can be measured by their commodious warehouses and wharves, their magnificent suites of offices and palatial residences, men who are called the merchant princes of our realm. Contrasting the splendour and luxury of their living by [sic] the miserable existence eked out by those who help to make their wealth, we feel still more the bitterness and degredation of our position as we view with the gravest alarm the steps being taken to further intensify the struggle for existence. To remedy this condition of affairs we have banded together and started a society for our mutual protection.[9]

This was a bold stroke for the self-taught 'dock rat'. One may imagine him at this point, seated perhaps at a table in grimy Huntslett Street, laboriously spelling out his message to the distant figures in Parliament. Their initial response was disheartening. Tillett had invited the East End MPs to a public meeting on 27 July (the union's first) at St Mary's School in Whitechapel. In the event, none appeared, though a few sent

sympathetic messages, and it was Tillett himself, therefore, who alone
addressed the gathering.

The note he struck was moderate from the outset. He pictured life
for waterside labourers as it was and then as he thought it should be,
but hastened to assure his audience that 'We want a bloodless victory;
no strikes; no violence; these can be avoided . . . We want our position
so adjusted that by arbitration we shall prevent conflict with our employers.'[10] And when the time came to compose the 'General Laws' of
the new union, these reiterated the desire to avoid confrontation.

> The Assn. shall endeavour to form Boards of Conciliation and Arbi-
> tration for settlement of disputes. The decision of the Board and its
> referee shall be final. Should any branch refuse to accept such a de-
> cision, the Council shall have power to refuse the Assn's support.

The stated objectives of the union were equally mild in tone and
limited in scope: 'Objects: to reform the present system of contract and
sub-contract upon a basis conducive to greater regularity of employment.'[11]

At this stage, then, Tillett was far from accepting the views of
socialists like Mann or Burns. His strategy and goals stemmed from the
Liberal-Labour world view to which he genuinely adhered. His restless
and rebellious nature drew him into the labour movement; but neither
experience nor education had provided him yet with an alternative to
the reformist appproach against which the socialists were reacting.
Tillett appears, at the outset of his career, as a typical young Lib-Lab
activist.

Accordingly, it is not surprising that his efforts met with a warmer
reception from the Liberals than from the socialists. Burns scornfully
rejected his request for aid, whereas the Liberals seemed prepared to
support him. 'I should have considered it a duty to take the chair at
such a meeting in my constituency and if you can postpone it for a
week or a fortnight I could do so', Samual Montagu, the Liberal
Member for Whitechapel, had written in reply to Tillett's invitation.
And George Howell, the Lib-Lab MP for Bethnal Green, helped draft
the union's rules, registered it with the authorities and spoke on its
behalf: 'I will gladly say a word or two to encourage your efforts to
improve your conditions', he wrote in a friendly letter to Tillett.[12]

The Conservative Party rejected the union's overture outright. 'There
always will be . . . great competition for such [dock] work', N. Herbert
wrote on behalf of C.T. Ritchie, President of the Local Government

Board and a Conservative East London MP:

> and there is danger that in taking steps which are intended to dimi-
> nish the competition the amount of employment available may be
> seriously diminished, which would aggravate the evil. It is for these
> reasons Mr Ritchie has not felt justified in subscribing towards your
> association.

Tillett's revealing response disclaimed any revolutionary intent:

> it has often been said by yourself that any effort on Constitutional
> lines made by the lower classes to raise themselves would be assisted
> by the upper classes to a successful issue and that no anarchical or
> socialist roit [sic] and violence could ever do for the toilers what a
> peaseful [sic] and persistent effort would eventually accomplish.

His tone betrayed an increasing confidence in his powers of persuasion
and a developing talent for public disputation. No doubt, he asserted,
Ritchie's charitable efforts on behalf of workers had 'met with the
same clogging, paralysing cukoo [sic] cry' as the Conservative MP had
used in response to Tillett. 'What have we before us?' Tillett then
demanded:

> Does the dark vista open up any promise of brightness to you that
> we cannot see, or are you trying to advise us to keep our arms by
> our side, our voice silent and our greifs [sic] suppressed? That as we
> are God forgotten and world foresaken so we must sink deeper in
> the social mire.

Tillett's most significant words, however, were penned at the letter's
end: 'I have spoken with several of your voters,' he warned, 'and they
could hardly believe you would treat us so coldly.' Politicians who
failed the cause of labour could not count on labour's support at election time. Here were the first glimmerings of the course Tillett would
later take. For, Conservatives aside, the party of Gladstone must continue to outbid the socialists if it wanted Tillett's vote.[13]

Certain problems which Tillett faced as the leader of an unskilled
union, however, had the potential for driving a wedge between him and
the Liberals. He knew from the outset that it was futile to limit his
organizing to tea workers, or even warehousemen. During a strike,
companies have great difficulty in replacing skilled workers; they have

less, but still considerable, difficulty in finding blacklegs for 'specialized' labourers such as grain porters or coal whippers, who have learned their business over a period of years; but it is an easy matter to replace casual labourers who have no special qualification except their availability.[14] In order for Tillett's new waterside union of casual labourers to be effective, it had to include at the very least all casual labourers on the London Thames. It was a 'general union' in conception from the beginning.

The old guard of craft unionists, however, vehemently opposed such efforts. The fact is that such men looked upon Tillett's activities and aspirations with some suspicion, not to say hostility. Their own views on trade unionism had been formed earlier in the century, when skilled craftsmen dominated the organized labour movement. Greatly influenced by Gladstonian liberalism, they tended to accept the hierarchical world view implicit in the nineteenth-century English liberal consensus. In their opinion, semi-skilled workers might imitate the labour aristocrats, and successfully establish unions (as miners, textile workers, railwaymen, and other 'operatives' had done), but such achievements were beyond the capacities of the unskilled, of whom the dockers were considered to be quintessential representatives. It followed that trade union membership should be exclusive, high dues making the intrusion of the lower paid difficult if not impossible, and that the societies themselves should be concerned less with combating the employers than with building up funds to pay for sickness, burial and unemployment insurance. Above all, old-style trade unionists accepted the gospel of self-improvement, and abhorred any attempt to appeal to the state for aid. Given such attitudes, it is not surprising that the London Trades Council, which was dominated by George Shipton, founder and secretary of the craft union, the Amalgamated Society of Housepainters and Decorators, refused Tillett's repeated applications for assistance.[15] Despite his traditional and generally moderate outlook then, Tillett found himself on a collision course with old-style labour leaders, many of whom had long-standing connections with the Liberal Party.

The obstacles to his success may also have contributed to Tillett's radicalization. Company thugs broke his nose, cracked his ribs, ruptured his hernia again. Such tactics did little to weaken his resolve — friend and foe alike agreed that he did not scare easily. In fact, Tillett later claimed his response to intimidation was 'to inflame, to plan a social war'. He began a study of Napoleon's campaigns. But which Liberal would help him to launch an insurrection?[16]

In fact, there is no evidence — except for Tillett's nostalgic reminiscence – that he believed in revolution at this early date. As an organizer of the unskilled, however, he was beginning to meet socialists who did, or claimed to. He had already approached, and been rebuffed by, Burns. Also, at about this time, he made the acquaintance of Tom Mann, a connection which was later to ripen into the sort of friendship which survives all vicissitudes. Another lifelong tie was established during this period with the young Will Thorne. Like Tillett, he too had experienced a childhood of extreme poverty and hardship. Like Tillett, he was also a casual labourer with hopes of improving the lot of his mates, though at the gasworks rather than the docks. Unlike Tillett, however, he joined the Social Democratic Federation, where he came under the influence of Eleanor Marx, who taught him to read and write. It was through Thorne that Tillett now began to meet the leading figures, both working and middle class, in England's reviving socialist movement. These included Hyndman himself, and other organizers in the Social Democratic Federation, organizers like Jack Williams and Harry Quelch, who were both dockers, and Thorne's tutor, Eleanor, and her brilliant but deeply flawed paramour, Edward Aveling, the man who eventually drove her to suicide. Tillett must also have come into contact with the great socialist luminaries, William Morris and Engels himself, 'the grand lama of Regent's Park Road', as Hyndman jealously called him.

Tillett's most important contact at this point, in terms of his own development, was probably Tom McCarthy, leader of the Amalgamated Society of Stevedores. McCarthy was a small man with a militant spirit and big ideas. Descended from a long line of stevedores, he had come to believe that 'the excommunication of the unskilled by the skilled', as Burns described it in *Justice* with regard to the labour movement as a whole, was particularly counter-productive along the Thames.[17] Despite some opposition from his rank and file, he was not averse, therefore, to allying with the fledgeling organizer of the Tea Operatives. Tillett, for his part, understood that McCarthy's experiences as a trade union leader could be a valuable resource. The two men, together with Thorne, must have discussed East End labour relations far into the night on many occasions. They were a formidable triumvirate, singly or acting in concert, as the larger world would soon discover.

Tillett himself, however, was still loathe to reject the Liberals, despite these new-found friends. The enormity of his task, no doubt, disposed him to welcome support from any quarter. This could lead him occasionally into situations where internationalist-minded allies might refuse to follow. At a meeting in Canning Town, for example,

Tillett accepted £20 from the main speaker, promising to support the donor's anti-immigration campaign (which he did in his testimony before the 1888 Lords' Commission on Sweated Industries). That Tillett would never jettison certain chauvinist views was to become apparent only much later. At the time, perhaps his unflagging devotion to the immediate task at hand, organizing dockers, made it possible for more broad-minded supporters to overlook them.[18]

As an organizer, Tillett's primary objective was to overcome the lassitude and doubts of the majority of his workmates. Their apathy stemmed from two causes: first, London's casual dockers were so oppressed, so weak from lack of food and proper housing, and felt their powerlessness so acutely, that they remained for the large part deaf to his exhortations. Twenty years later, Clem Edwards remembered how 'open mouthed and wan-eyed crowds stood before him, but no applause or approving smile came to cheer him. Many and many a time have I stood and watched, but for all the response manifested by those casual dockers his words might have been addressed to a herd of dumb, driven, cattle.' Secondly, a series of bogus unions had bedevilled riverside workers for the past decade, and before he could make any real headway among them, Tillett had to convince not merely his listeners but also his potential middle-class supporters that the Tea Operatives' was a genuine labour organization. Typical of this brand of scepticism was the letter to the editor of the *Star* (4 February 1888), charging that dues paid by members of the Tea Operatives' were 'just enough to pay the secretary a good salary, and that is about all the organization is doing'.

This was manifestly unfair. Tillett had, in fact, been working unceasingly for the union, a point which he immediately made to the subeditor of the *Star* in person, thereby establishing a connection with that newspaper which was to prove useful in the near future. More important, he was about to launch a strike, the union's first, and the first in which he himself played a leading role.

II

During 1888, Tillett had concentrated his efforts on the Tilbury docks, where the men received a penny less per hour than the going rate, and where 'preference men' received a higher wage than the regular hands although they performed the same work. It is unknown when Tillett first began to plan the strike, though he must have discussed it with McCarthy and Thorne. That it had been some time in preparation Tillett revealed in a letter to the *Star*, in which he claimed to have waited until the busy season before calling the men out, in order to maximize the impact of their ceasing work.[20] On 22 October 1888, five hundred dockers went on strike.

Tillett was aided by Annie Besant and Herbert Burrows of the Social Democratic Federation, which also sent down a contingent of speakers. Yet from the first, he assumed the leading role, and in the beginning it seemed that his efforts would be successful. On the 24th, the dock company engaged about two hundred men from the West India Dock to replace the strikers. Tillett addressed the potential blacklegs from a washstand on the pier as they were preparing to disembark from the boat which had brought them to Tilbury. He won them over, before being pulled down by a police inspector. 'Whole marched together to place of meeting. A great many of them enthusiastic over events', he recounted in his diary.[21]

He was busy, however, not only with public speaking, but the multitude of details necessary to maintain the strike. In true Lib-Lab fashion, he persuaded the Liberals Montagu and Sydney Buxton to speak to the dock directors on behalf of the men. They received the predictable reply: 'It was not', said H.H. Dobree, Chairman, 'a question of granting the men a penny more per hour but whether the Tilbury Dock could survive at all.' Meanwhile he wrote letters to the local press, composed, printed and distributed bills and posters, took up collections in support of the strike and organized a system of picketing. Tillett's diary for these weeks records his unwearying and imaginative efforts to keep up the spirits of the men. On one occasion, when prohibited from speaking in Gravesend Square, he enterprisingly 'Got up into Mr West's window and spoke from there'.[22]

Picketing, however, posed a major problem. Tilbury was 26 miles downstream from East London. The strikers had either to commute each day to man the picket lines, or to sleep out in the marshes near the docks. Continual rain made this impossible, and the union was forced to rent two houses for the men to sleep in. 'These places are destitute of furniture', a correspondent for the *East End News* observed on 9 November, 'but there is plenty of clean straw and fire which alike are paid for out of the funds.' Still, this represented a severe drain on the union's treasury, which had already disbursed about £50 in strike benefits. Successful shop-to-shop collections and free lunches of bread and cheese supplied by two sympathetic local tradesmen could not continue indefinitely. The men were driven back to work after a month's resistance. As the Social Democratic Federation journal put it: 'The pallid faces of their wives and children, and the cravings of their own stomachs were too much for them.' Yet Tillett drew a different lesson from the débâcle:

> Our union has been able to prevent their [the Tilbury dock directors] having men from London: but they have scoured the district round, and got the whole of the farm labourers; that is the reason of the failure of the strike; on account of the harvest being done for the season, the men are flocking to the docks; that has enabled them to beat us.[23]

The effect upon Tillett of the defeat at Tilbury was complex. On the one hand, it sharpened his critique not only of the master but also of the established leaders of the craft unions who had failed to come to his assistance. Where he had once been content to threaten retribution on polling day, he now conjured up more desperate images. 'The dock directors certainly hold a power and use it', he wrote as the strike entered its penultimate phase.

> The brutal condition of our class, the squalor and misery of their homes and lives, is a bitter proof of how terribly it is used. How long the aristocracy of labour will hold aloof, how long our mistaken philanthropists will ply with impracticable charity, how long the world will be dead to the wants and wrongs of a neglected class of unorganised labour – and that only so because of the general indifference – I cannot tell; but this must be patent to all, that unless combination on constitutional grounds is encouraged, the country will have to face a graver danger than bludgeons will be able to suppress.

Thus, as is often the case, defeat contributed to a process of radicalization. On the other hand, however, it also instilled in him a profound pessimism. The continuing influx of labour into the docks was beyond the power of his union to regulate. The uncertainties of casual labour made the weekly collection of dues and the accumulation of a fighting fund nearly impossible. The division of the workforce into gangs undermined solidarity. Blacklists made up by the employers intimidated the men. 'Then you think', Lord Dunraven asked, 'that owing to these causes organization is practically impossible for the dock labourers to any large extent?' 'Yes', Tillett responded, 'it is impossible.'[24]

The very weakness of his position had opened Tillett's eyes to the necessity of state intervention. Yet he was far from espousing socialism. He merely wanted the government to act as arbiter between capital and labour, an aspiration which advanced Liberals could endorse. 'It is only on Social Democrats that they can rely for any real help', a Social Democrat journalist had written of the Tilbury dockers during the strike. Yet Tillett continued to look to the Liberals. 'Our union has not the strength to maintain itself', he wrote in a letter of near supplication to Henry Broadhurst, a former leader of the skilled stonemasons who had risen to become a junior Minister in a Liberal administration.

> Help us for we are weak. Help us for our children want bread, our men work and means, our women the necessaries to live. I cannot in my present state fight on alone. Send us men to speak, or funds to maintain ourselves, or we shall fall, crushed by our burden of want and woe.[25]

The young self-improver had been rudely awakened. He now believed that conditions in dockland could not be altered by the efforts of workers alone — even acting in concert. The Tilbury strike had convinced him that his Liberal allies must put pressure on the state to intervene. Yet the seeds of future dissension between Tillett and the Liberals were already present. As an organizer of the unskilled, sooner or later he was bound to antagonize old-style labour leaders with long-standing ties to the Liberal Party. As a new unionist, he was also coming into contact with the young militants, already socialists, who were challenging not only the labour movement's old guard but middle-class radicals as well. They were demanding changes which even the most 'advanced' Liberals could not accept. 'When we can once get working men in the mass to combine, the work of amelioration will be easy, comparatively speaking', Howell had written to Tillett.[26] Given his restlessness, combative nature and the probability of future labour strife, however, it was unlikely that the young secretary of the Tea Operatives' would remain content with such formulae for long.

Notes

1. For more on Henry Broadhurst see his autobiography, *Henry Broadhurst, MP* (Hutchinson, London, 1901). For more on Howell, see F.M. Leventhal, *Respectable Radical* (Harvard University Press, Cambridge, Mass., 1971); and Royden Harrison, *Before the Socialists* (Routledge and Kegan Paul, London, 1965), ch. 3.
2. Tillett's name does not appear in *The Times* index until 1887. The

exchange of letters with Huxley is said to have occurred earlier in the decade.

3. Gareth Stedman Jones, 'Working-Class Culture and Working-Class Politics in London, 1870-1900: Notes on the Remaking of a Working Class', *Journal of Social History*, vol. 7 no. 4 (1974), pp. 460-508.

4. Royal Commission on Labour, *Parliamentary Papers* (1892), vol. XXXV, p. 5.

5. For Social Democratic Federation Rallies see, for example, *Justice*, 12 and 21 February 1885. The figure 50,000 is taken from an article which appeared in the *East End News*, 25 August 1939 entitled 'Free Speech 50 Years Ago'. For more on life in East London, see William J. Fishman, *East London Jewish Radicals, 1870-1914* (Duckworth, London, 1974); Jack London, *People of the Abyss* (Macmillan, London, 1903); E.P. Thompson, *William Morris* (Lawrence and Wishart, London, 1955), p. 579, this book gives an excellent account of the activities of the socialists during these years; Annie Besant, *Annie Besant, An Autobiography* (Fisher Unwin, London, 1893), p. 327; Karl Marx and Frederick Engels, *Selected Correspondence* (Progress Publishers, Moscow, 1953), Engels to Sorge, 29 November 1887, number 203.

6. *South Wales Daily News*, 15 January 1907. Clement Edwards, MP for Denbeigh Boroughs, recalling Ben Tillett's early days; William Collison, *The Apostle of Free Labour* (Hurst and Blackett, London, 1913), p. 12.

7. Tillett Collection, MSS 74/6/1/5; Ben Tillett, *Dock, Wharf, Riverside and General Workers' Union: A Brief History of the Dockers' Union* (London, 1910), p. 5.

8. Tillett Collection, MSS 74/4/1/7 and MSS 74/7/1 (diary).

9. Tillett Collection, MSS 74/3/1/76, Tillett to 'Sir', 13 July 1887. This is a first draft of the letter sent to all Members of Parliament for the East End constituencies.

10. Tillett, *A Dock Labourer's Bitter Cry*. His pamphlet was printed under this title.

11. Webb Trade Union Collection, Section A, volume 42, item 5, number 124.

12. Tillett Collection, MSS 74/3/1/56; Montagu to Tillett, 30 August 1887, and MSS 74/3/1/34, Howell to Tillett, 29 August 1887. See also MSS 74/3/1/ 36-37 for more on Howell's activities for the union.

13. Tillett Collection, MSS 74/3/1/70, N. Herbert on behalf of C.T. Ritchie to Tillett, 30 August 1887; MSS 74/3/1/65, Tillett to Ritchie, 7 December 1887.

14. See Eric Hobsbawm's seminal articles, 'National Unions on the Waterside' and 'General Labour Unions in Britain' in E. Hobsbawm, *Labouring Men* (Weidenfeld and Nicolson, London, 1964), chs. 10 and 11.

15. Dona Torr, *Tom Mann* (Lawrence and Wishart, London, 1944), p. 21. This is a pamphlet, not the biography.

16. John Burns Papers, British Museum, Add. MS 46285. Tillett to Burns, 12 May 1914; 'the nose business is a memorial of the two years before the Dock Strike when the Contractors set their bullies on me several times and I got smashed ribs and other luxuries, the hernia nearly killing me at times'; Collison, his inveterate enemy called him 'pugnacious', Mann described him as 'tough' and a 'force to be reckoned with'; Tillett, *Memories and Reflections* (J. Long, London, 1931), p. 113.

17. *Justice*, 24 February 1885.

18. Beatrice Webb, *My Apprenticeship* (Longmans, 1926), p. 297, diary entry 1 December 1887.

19. Clem Edwards in the *South Wales Daily News*, 15 January 1907; see John Saville, 'Free Labour and the Background to Taff Vale', in *Essays in Labour History* (Macmillan, London, 1967), A Briggs and J. Saville (eds.), vol. 1, pp. 331-5; Tillett Collection, MSS 74/7/1, diary entry 7 February 1888; for more on the *Star*, see Thomas P. O'Connor, *Memoirs of an Old Parliamentarian* (E. Benn,

London, 1929); and Alfred Havighurst, *Radical Journalist: H.W. Massingham* (Cambridge University Press, London, 1974).

20. See his letter to the *Star*, 24 October 1888: 'the step taken has been for some time in contemplation, as there is plenty of work coming in we have great hopes of our efforts being successful'.

21. Tillett Collection, MSS 74/7/1 diary entry, 24 October 1888.

22. *The Times*, 1 November 1888; Tillett Collection, MSS 74/7/1, diary entry, 27 October 1888.

23. *East End News*, 9 November 1888; *Justice*, 24 November 1888; *Parliamentary Papers* (1888), vol. XXI, p. 190.

24. *Star*, 17 November 1888; *Parliamentary Papers* (1888), vol. XXI, p. 136.

25. *Justice*, 17 November 1888; Henry Broadhurst Papers, London School of Economics and Political Science, Tillett to Broadhurst, n.d. Though the letter is undated, it was clearly written in the late winter of 1888-9 or early spring of 1889.

26. Tillett Collection, MSS 74/3/1/37, Howell to Tillett, 26 November 1887.

3   THE NEW UNIONIST, 1888-90

I

In the spring of 1889, Tillett stood upon the verge of the national stage although he could not possibly know it. The great London dock strike of that year, which he helped to lead, is generally acknowledged to be second only to the General Strike of 1926 in importance to the British labour movement and to modern British labour history in general. It marked the triumphant overture of the new unionist movement, that upsurge among the unskilled workers of labour and political militancy which led to the formation and extension of mass unions, of socialism as a popular creed, and of the Independent Labour Party itself. In all these developments Tillett was to play a major role. He was about to enter the crucial period of his lifetime.

Economic circumstances were relatively propitious. Unemployment among trade unions making returns to the Board of Trade slumped from over 10 per cent in 1886, to less than 2 per cent in 1889. Meanwhile prices had been declining steadily since 1873, which meant that workers who in 1889 were collecting wages found their purchasing power to have increased dramatically. Consumption therefore increased as well: particularly of tea, sugar, tobacco and beer, which suggests that British workers felt able to afford inessentials. The docks were particularly sensitive to the vagaries of the British economy. When it boomed, they were busy; when it was depressed, they were idle. Thus the temporary lull in the 'Great Depression' placed port workers and their aspiring organizers in a stronger position than they had occupied for decades.[1]

The Tilbury débâcle, however, had left Tillett ill, exhausted and disillusioned. At this decisive moment he seems even to have considered dropping the dockers for thè gasworkers, whose union he helped to organize and for whose leadership he unsuccessfully contested against his friend Will Thorne. He now confessed that he was 'sick to death of the movement' as a whole, and might quit altogether. He was so pessimistic about the Tea Operatives that he failed to take action when the newly organized Joint Committee of the London and St Katherine and East and West India Dock Companies ignored a letter of protest against the plus system which he had composed in early August. Yet events thereafter moved rapidly.[2]

The contemporary press reveals that Tillett's reputation at this juncture was problematic. There were two socialist newspapers in London following developments in dockland during this period: *Justice*, which belonged to the Social Democratic Federation, and the *Labour Elector*, which was edited by the enigmatic and sardonic H.H. Champion. The son of a major-general, and himself a former artillery officer, Champion had been one of Hyndman's earliest converts, and had become assistant secretary of the Social Democratic Federation before quarrelling with its leader and quitting the organization to establish a rival socialist journal. The most important former Social Democrat member to follow him was none other than Tom Mann.

During the weeks immediately preceding the outbreak of the great dock strike of 1889, neither *Justice* nor the *Labour Elector* paid any attention to Tillett. They gave extensive and sympathetic coverage, however, to the formation of a rival organization of dockers, the Amalgamated Society of Dock Companies' Servants and General Labourers, for which Tillett's friend Thorne actually spoke. Champion may have been simply fishing in troubled waters: 'they [the dockers] must show a little of the pluck displayed by the Gas Stokers', he wrote on 3 August. 'They must form their Union and state their demands.' Perhaps through Tom Mann he was aware of Tillett's depression, and considered him a spent force. That the Social Democratic Federation also ignored Tillett's activities, and that Thorne was willing to speak for his rivals, suggests other possibilities: that bad blood existed between them as a result of the contest for leadership of the Gasworkers' Union; that socialists distrusted Tillett's links with the Liberals. It took the great contest between masters and men which Tillett helped lead to lull their suspicions of him.

How the great dock strike of 1889 broke out remains obscure. Clem Edwards records being present at Tillett's home in Bethnal Green on the evening of Monday 12 August, when two dockers called to explain that they had been cheated out of their share of the 'plus' in the West India Dock and wanted the union to support a strike the next day. Tillett acceded, according to Edwards, commenting that 'we are in for a big fight'. The premier historians of the strike, H. Llewellyn Smith and Vaughan Nash, however, maintain that the complaint about the 'plus' was a pretext, the men wishing to strike in any case, the spirit of rebellion having seized them. Tillett himself claimed that the men struck after he had delivered a particularly rousing speech at the dock gates on the previous Sunday. John Lovell, in the most complete recent account of the events immediately preceding the strike, argues that the newly formed Amalgamated Society of Dock Companies' Servants and General Labourers, called for action first, and that Tillett's Tea Operatives, jealous of such 'poaching', stole their thunder by assuming leadership of the strike.[3] It has even been suggested that Tom McCarthy and Will Thorne, worried by Tillett's pessimism and torpor, and believing him capable of great things, purposely forced his hand by speaking in favour of a strike at a meeting of his rivals, thereby goading him into action.[4] In any event, the significant fact here is that Tillett's assessment of the mood in dockland was entirely off the mark. 'The men wanted to strike', he wrote later with obvious surprise. 'I could scarcely believe my ears. It had never occurred to me that they were ready for such a thing.'[5]

It has been common to ascribe the militancy of the London dockers in 1889 to the inspiring successes of Thorne's Gasworkers, who won the 8-hour day that summer without a struggle, to the Bryant and May's matchgirls, who had recently won a dramatic strike, and to the recent gains in other ports achieved by Havelock Wilson's newly founded National Amalgamated Union of Sailors and Firemen. Obviously, socialist lectures and Tillett's own efforts, perhaps even including the abortive Tilbury strike, also helped to prepare the way for what followed. Nevertheless, the high morale and militancy displayed by the hitherto despised dockers caught everybody by surprise. As Champion was to write at the height of the strike: 'If these men can combine and succeed, no class of workmen . . . need despair.' Arriving at the South-West India Dock Gate on Tuesday morning, 13 August, Tillett persuaded the men to remain at work while he despatched a 24-hour ultimatum to the Joint Committee embodying their complaints and demands, and incidentally those he had sent off two weeks before. The company spokesman replied that he needed more time to consider this document, and Tillett found himself hard pressed to keep his men at work even for the remainder of the afternoon. From Wednesday, 14 August, the strike was on.

Having learned from the Tilbury venture that success might depend upon extending the strike port-wide, rather than allowing it to be confined within a single dock, Tillett was determined to bring out as many men as possible. His demands were therefore framed to apply to dock workers in general along the north bank of the Thames. They were — as they had been when he testified before the Lords' Commission in 1888 — that both the 'plus' and contract systems should be abolished; that men should be hired for a half-day at the least; that 'calling on' should occur only twice daily: that the hourly wage should be raised to six pence for casual labourers; and that overtime should be paid two pence rather than one penny more per hour than the regular rate. Although none of these were relevant to stevedores, Tillett desperately needed their support as well; if they too stopped work, trade in the port would be almost paralysed; furthermore, their union contained experienced officials who knew, perhaps better than he, how to administer a strike.

Fortunately, the secretary of the Amalgamated Union of Stevedores was Tillett's friend, Tom McCarthy. At a tense and crowded meeting of stevedore union officials held at the Wades' Arms public house in Poplar on Saturday night, the 17th, McCarthy succeeded in persuading them to declare a sympathetic strike with the dockers. This decision presaged that of the Lightermen's Union on 21 August and almost immediately thereafter of the southside corn porters and steamship workers, as well as various wharfmen and warehouse workers who had demands of their own. By Thursday, the 22nd, Tillett's first objective had been realized; the stoppage extended throughout the port.

Once again Tillett was deeply involved in strike work. This time, however, he received substantial assistance. Tom Mann, at the *Labour Elector's* offices in Paternoster Row, was the first to respond to his appeal for help, and brought Champion with him. Other socialists rallied to the dockers' cause as well, among them R.B. Cunninghame Graham, a romantic adventurer, essayist and dandy lately turned socialist MP, the Marx Avelings, Will Thorne and, most importantly, John Burns, who with Mann and Tillett came to share the leadership of the strike. Significantly, socialists and old-style trade unionists, chiefly lightermen and stevedores, appear to have co-operated successfully on the strike committee. Despite enormous logistical problems (at its height the strike encompassed 100,000 riverside labourers), they organized an effective system of strike benefits and a network of pickets that extended from the docks in East London all the way to Tilbury. Not least, they proved expert at attracting public support and funds.

This was a crucial aspect of the strike, leading to its ultimate victory. Naturally, then, the emphasis was on discipline and order from the start. Paradoxically tens of thousands of famished, ragged casual labourers marching through the streets of the city became a reassuring rather than a terrifying spectacle to middle-class London. 'Now lads', John Burns cried to the crowd on Tower Hill:

are you going to be as patient as you have been? (Yes). As orderly as you have been? (Yes). Are you going to be your own police? (Yes).

Then now march off five deep past the dock companies and keep on
the left hand side of the street.

Such processions seemed to demonstrate that the prophets of doom,
who stigmatized East London's casual labourers as an uncivilized 'residu-
um' which might sweep westward engulfing the rest of the city, were
mistaken. Even some socialists seemed relieved. Cunninghame Graham
might threaten darkly that 'revolutions were not made with rosewater',
but H.H. Champion wrote of the strikers: 'They might have made a
revolution; instead of which they have acted as constitutional Socialists'
and have been 'orderly and quiet'.[6]

Tillett himself was eager to publicize his devotion to constitutional-
ism and moderation. 'They know', he said of the men on strike, 'I shall
have nothing to do with them if they begin to riot.' 'We want to act
without violence', he said on another occasion, 'and from the first have
tried to lead the men that way. We have got the men in a good temper
and kept them in it.' At one Hyde Park rally, when Cunninghame
Graham's rhetoric went beyond the bounds of propriety, Tillett inter-
jected that he hoped for a 'moral revolution', not a bloody one. He also
objected strongly to the 'No Work Manifesto' framed by Tom Mann
and other militants on the strike committee when funds began to run
out. This called for organized labour throughout the metropolis to
down tools in sympathy with the dockers. Contemporaries and historians alike have largely agreed that it would have failed. In the event, the
manifesto was withdrawn, an enormous subsidy from Australian resources having made it unnecessary; but there was strong opposition to it
on the strike committee even before that money became available.
Burns was probably the leading opponent of the general strike. 'Don't
be drawn by manifesto', he cabled Mann. 'All unions court defeat to
benefit one.'[7] Mann was critical of this line, but Tillett (who detested
Burns for having rejected his initial overture in 1888) nevertheless
found it convincing. Perhaps he had read 'P.W.''s letter of 31 August to
The Times explaining that the threat of a general walk-out had decided
him against sending a £50 contribution to the strike committee.
Perhaps he did not entirely believe in the men's devotion to the union.

'This strike has taken everybody by surprise', a reporter for the
Labour Elector commented, also on 31 August.

Even Mr Tillett, who for the last two years has been trying to organize these men and form them into a trade union is astonished. He
attributes a good deal of the men's strength and determination to

the encouragement they are receiving from their wives and children.

At any rate, Tillett took care to publicize his opposition to violence, to oppose the general strike, and repudiate the socialists. 'I wish to deny that this movement has anything to do with Socialism', he asserted at one demonstration. 'The Socialists only joined in when the movement was in full swing, in their capacity as trade unionists.'[8]

This strategy was finally successful. The continuing influx of contributions to the strike fund convinced the dock directors to give in. Tillett's main demands were met in a series of meetings arranged by Cardinal Manning. They were summarized in the Mansion House agreement of 4 November: henceforth, all work should be paid 6d per hour (the 'dockers' tanner') and 8d per hour overtime; all contract work would be converted to piece-work, and the 'plus', if there was any, would be determined in consultation with representatives of the men; no worker could be discharged with less than two shillings' pay, except in exceptional circumstances; overtime hours were to extend from 6 p. m. until 8 a. m.; and the men would not be penalized for having participated in the strike. The quid pro quo for this last concession was that labourers who had not observed the strike would be protected from those who had. The strike committee undertook this task, eventually offering the former blacklegs a week's wages and train fare home, or if they preferred to stay, protection from the men, provided that they joined the union.

By the Mansion House agreement the dockers had gained an enormous victory. It was, however, the product of a confluence of positive circumstances, some of which were unlikely to be repeated. First, without the temporary upswing in the trade cycle and consequent increase in the demand for labour during the summer of 1889, the strike could never have been called. After all, it is impossible for the unemployed to lay down tools. Second, the willingness of all grades of workers, including the Thames labour aristocrats, the stevedores and lightermen, to strike in sympathy with the hitherto despised casual dockers was unprecedented, and only the most idealistic believed that such solidarity would become a permanent feature of the dockland scene. Equally important, the ranks of the employers themselves were rent with divisions that time might heal. A section of the wharfingers had been prepared early on to accede to the men's demands, and led by Lafone, of Butler's Wharf, did so almost a month before the strike officially ended. The shippers, too, took advantage of the stoppage to injure their rivals, the dock directors, by coming to terms with the men who did the unloading. Most important of all, public sympathy manifested in the concrete form of hard cash had been indispensable to the dockers' cause.

The generosity of the public contrasted bleakly with the refusal of many old-style labour leaders to support the dispute. The dockers' accomplishments had not softened their attitude towards the legion of unskilled, nor did they approve of the influence of socialists like Burns, Mann, Champion and Thorne on the strike committee. The TUC, whose annual meeting occurred during the strike, sent fraternal messages, but no material report. The London Trades Council, under Shipton's hide-bound leadership, likewise remained aloof. Tillett did not hesitate to rebuke the Lib-Labs for their indifference. As he put it at one Hyde Park rally:

> The so-called labour representatives were absent while the most momentous struggle of modern times was taking place . . . The Broadhursts and Shiptons were not to be seen. They had got so used to being the lap dogs of society that they forgot the duty that they owed to the men who made them what they were.

Nor was he disposed to spare the middle-class radicals: 'Their representatives in Parliament did not seem to care for them', he asserted at another rally, 'for while the men were carrying on this struggle and their wives and children starving, those representatives were off to the country to shoot grouse'.[9]

The strike, then, represents a significant stage in Tillett's political evolution. It drove a further wedge between him and the old-style labour leaders affiliated with the Liberal Party, although, as would later become clear, Tillett himself was loathe to recognise the extent of their differences. And it demonstrated to him that the working class was capable of organization and constructive action — something he had tended to doubt since the Tilbury defeat. On 24 August, he proclaimed his new view: 'Those got most who helped themselves, and if labouring men could by their own combination show such power as they had done in this movement, they ought to use it and get their own representatives into the House of Commons.' His own name was already being mentioned in this regard. But Tillett modestly endorsed the parliamentary aspirations of another: 'he hoped that their friend Mr Burns would one day be returned to Parliament, as he would give a robust manhood to the weak-kneed radicals who said they represented the people'. This was a far cry from depending on the middle class to speak for the strikers, as he had done during the contest at Tilbury. I⁺ was, however, still one step removed from demanding the formation of an independent labour party. Despite his argument with the Lib-Lab supporters, there is no indication that Tillett thought Burns should refuse to stand as a Liberal.[10]

It would not do, however, to place too much emphasis on the strike itself as the decisive factor in shaping Tillett's evolving ideology. Rather, it was one among a series of events contributing to his making as a labour militant. The immediate aftermath of the strike was, perhaps, even more important in this respect.

II

The great victory in London did not signify the end of a chapter in British industrial relations, but rather a beginning. It represented the opening salvo in what contemporary journalists were soon calling 'the Labour War'. Tillett played a major role in this campaign. Before attempting to trace it, however, it is first necessary to examine briefly the organization he led into the fray.

Perhaps the first thing to say about it is that it was consciously organized as an alternative to the old-style craft unions. Before the great strike, its membership had fluctuated between 300 and 800 men. Now, more than 18,000 port workers flocked under its banner. The original body was hardly the proper vehicle for an organization with such a large and diverse membership. At a meeting in mid-September 1889, it was transformed into the Dock, Wharf, Riverside and General Labourers' Union of Great Britain and Ireland. Tillett was elected general secretary, Tom Mann was chosen to be the first president. As a 'fighting organization', in contrast with the more pacific, traditional trade unions, it paid strike benefits to its members, but not unemployment, funeral or sickness benefits. Dues were low, so that any man who worked on the docks could afford to join: there was an entrance fee of two shillings and six pence, weekly dues of only two pence, and a quarterly assessment of four pence.

From the beginning, the new Dockers' Union strove to centralize power in the hands of its executive. In this endeavour, it distinguished itself from the original waterside union of 1870, which had permitted its branches almost complete autonomy. This difference has been ascribed primarily to Mann who, it is said, attempted to impose his own notions upon the fledgling organization. The desire to consolidate power in the central office, however, and to control the activities of the branches had also marked Tillett's Tea Operatives' Association which, as will be recalled, had invested its executive with the power to deny funds to striking branches. Furthermore, it accorded with Tillett's attitude towards the men, which still reflected, though less starkly than before, the disillusionment engendered at Tilbury. He was a member now of the editorial board of the *Labour Elector*, which had become the official organ of the Dockers' Union, and although Tillett may not have penned the following lines, they nevertheless reflect his ideas:

> Today it [the Dockers' Union] is numerically the strongest trade organization in the metropolis. But the 18,000 men who have flocked to it are ignorant of the rudiments of trade unionism, are flushed with their sudden success, and are unaware that unless their society is at once thoroughly and closely organized every advantage they have gained must inevitably be taken from them in a few years — perhaps in a few months.[11]

In their efforts to avoid such developments, by keeping hold of the entire organization, Tillett and Mann offended many branch members. In Tillett's words, the governing body of the union was 'constituted of representative working men upon the basis of proportional representation'. The union's smallest unit of organization was the branch, which met weekly and sent representatives to a district council. It too met regularly, and in turn elected members to sit on the executive council, whose leading figures were Tillett, Mann and the two national organizers — Harry Orbell, a docker, and Tom McCarthy, who had left the stevedores. Efforts were made to assure the branches that their affairs would not be ignored. 'Local questions will be handled by district councilmen . . . each branch will be thoroughly represented.' In fact, the local branches often resented the policies of the executive, which controlled the treasury and alone decided whether to dispense strike pay. During the exceptionally turbulent years which followed 1889, this exclusive power generated much ill feeling both in and outside London.[12]

The drive for centralization in the metropolis, however, faced graver obstacles. One was the South Side Labour Protection League, a direct descendant of the original waterside union of the 1870s. The league had arisen on the south side of the river during the 1889 strike. Its nucleus was the corn porters, a surviving branch of the original organization. Its members were mainly employed at the Surrey Commercial

Docks. As certain of their grievances were being ignored by the official strike committee, which met at the Wades' Arms public house across the Thames, the South Side Labour Protection League soon found itself directing affairs on the south bank. After the strike it continued to exist as a separate body, conducting business from the Sayes Court public house. It maintained the old traditions of the early union, notably in allowing its branches complete independence of action. Its leader was Harry Quelch, a devoted member of the Social Democratic Federation, who explained in an interview with Beatrice Webb that Tillett's and Mann's insistence upon centralization guaranteed the existence of his own society. The Dockers' Union executive was simply unable to respond to the particular needs of southside dockers.[13] Even if it had been able to, Quelch might have added, his individualistic members were not prepared to accept dictation from the executive council, however democratically chosen. The South Side Labour Protection League went so far as to disrupt physically several Dockers' Union meetings on the south side. The ill feeling which marked these encounters was not dispelled until the Dockers' Union finally understood that its ambitions for the south side of the Thames would have to be postponed.[14]

Outside London the Dockers' Union experienced a similar pattern of events. Extension was rapid at first. 'Branches sprang up as in the night', Tillett later recalled of the period following the London victory. Or, as Sir Joseph Broodbank, a dock director, put it: 'for at least twelve months after the strike labour was unmanageable'. Then, however, difficulties began to appear, and the employers regrouped and prepared a counter-offensive.[15]

The London dispute had hardly finished when Tillett undertook an organizing tour of the provinces. He travelled to Hull, Gloucester, Bristol, Sharpness, Southampton, Ipswich, Liverpool, Harwich and 'many other ports'. McCarthy and Orbell covered the towns he missed. 'We scoured the country and added to our ranks port after port', Tillett recorded. Some 63 new branches were formed in the first three months of 1890 alone. Recalling the way the Tilbury strike had been defeated, Tillett advocated the formation of union branches for agricultural labourers too. Mann successfully organized some of them in Lincolnshire and Oxfordshire. The dream at this stage was for the Dockers' Union to enforce a national closed shop.[16]

Tillett excelled as an agitator. Here is a typical effort, an extract from a speech he delivered before a newly formed branch of the union in Hull :

They did not want him to talk and stir them up. They were already stirred up (cheers). A gentleman on a platform said they required a lot more of it. Well they would have it if they only wanted (cheers) . . . There was nothing like discontent. There was divinity in it, and where they saw men discontented they saw men actively at work to remedy that which was harsh and cruel.

His oratory 'created a very powerful impression', one journalist observed. 'His concluding appeal touched a chord of sympathy which electrified his hearers who gave vent to their excited feelings by ringing cheers again and again repeated.' An overt sympathizer described Tillett's 'pale face, his studious expression, his general refinement of manner', and concluded:

> he hardly seems one who could hold the rough elements of unskilled labour in command. But see Tillett mounted on a platform . . . and how changed he is. The soft features are flushed with exertion, his eyes blaze and the whole man brims over with energy . . . his powerful spirit writhes in his frail body as if it would shake it asunder.[17]

As a result of Tillett's efforts, dockers at eleven ports sent representatives to the union's first annual delegate meeting. Yet his organizing drive was not entirely successful.

Problems faced by the organization in London reappeared outside the metropolis. Just as the London branches resented dictation from the executive council, so the provincial branches objected to London's pre-eminence in the organization. Just as the South Side Labour Protection League refused to give up its separate identity and merge with the dockers, so the Liverpool-based National Union of Dock Labourers rejected Tillett's overtures. Some provincial district officers failed to keep in touch with the central office. Some local branches failed to choose representatives to attend the first annual delegate meeting. In short, London with all its problems was a microcosm of the organization as a whole; the difficulties found along the Thames were present at the national level as well. Consequently as employers across the country moved to regain lost ground, the Dockers' Union discovered itself hard pressed to resist them.

III

In London, the Mansion House agreement proved little more than a truce. The men were prepared to strike at the drop of a hat, their great triumph, perhaps, having made them over-confident. On the other side, the dock directors were determined to win back concessions so recently wrested from them. Having noted the union's failure to incorporate the South Side Labour Protection League, they were quick to help other independent labourers' associations to maintain their separate identities. They successfully encouraged the permanent employees to resist Tillett's invitation to join the union. The owners of the Victoria Dock declared a lock-out of two hundred men, thereby foiling Mann's attempt to organize the carmen there. Contractors favoured former blacklegs with regular employment at the expense of union members who had observed the strike. Yet these were all subsidiary to the main attack which London employers levelled against the union within a year of its greatest victory.[18]

The primary focus of conflict was payment at meal times, supposedly guaranteed by the Mansion House agreement. In January 1890, however, the directors of Hays' Wharf announced that their men would not be paid during the dinner hour, thereby provoking a wildcat strike. Although the union would have preferred to negotiate, it nevertheless threatened a port-wide boycott of the wharf and provided the men with strike pay. This proved to be the necessary incentive for almost the entire body of port employers to combine in an organization of their own, the Union of Dock, Wharf, Warehouse Proprietors and Granary Keepers. Of the notable Thames-side firms, only the Butler's Wharf and the Surrey Commercial Docks failed to join. On 4 February 1890, the Dockers' Union issued a manifesto directing its members to refuse to deliver goods to the Hays' Wharf. In retaliation the Employers' Union promised to fire every worker who obeyed this directive. Wildcat strikes then erupted at Olivers' Wharf, Brook's Wharf, Hirsch Oil Mills and seven other establishments. 'We are determined to fight them all', Mann bravely promised at a meeting on Tower Hill. London waited in trepidation for a renewal of large-scale conflict between masters and men.[19]

It failed to materialize. Condemnation of the dockers' militant posture poured in from all sides. Among the press, only the *Star* continued to support the union. Such former friends as Sydney Buxton publicly cautioned the men to 'slow down'. Cardinal Manning, whom many dockers venerated for having helped to settle the great strike, privately enjoined Tillett 'to postpone "the meal time" for three

months'. At a meeting on 8 February, the union withdrew its ultimatum. 'They did not dare', as John Burns put it, in language reminiscent
of his opposition to the general strike of 1889, 'to risk all their gains for
the sake of one wharf'. Instead the men at Hays' Wharf would be paid
strike benefits and the dispute would be localized. About 20,000
dockers assembled at Tower Hill to hear Tillett's explanation of the
union's conduct. It cannot have satisfied those who had hoped to hear a
fighting speech: 'We call upon the public,' Tillett declared, 'to witness
that we have deliberately changed our tactics rather than give the employers a chance of bringing about either a general strike or a lock-out,
which in our opinion would be disastrous to the best interests of the
trade of the Port of London.' Four months later the men at Hays'
Wharf returned to work having failed to win even a single concession
from their employers.[20]

The verdict from Hays' Wharf encouraged the employers to provoke
similar contests elsewhere in the port. At Hedger's, Sharpe's and Hersok's
wharves, unofficial walk-outs protected payment at meal time. At the
much larger Victoria Dock, however, when management withdrew payment for the dinner hour, prompting yet another wildcat action, Tillett
and Mann issued a manifesto disavowing the strike:

> To those who have been misled by mischief makers whose disloyalty
> and underhand work can only do harm . . . the executive instruc-
> tions are: Resume work at once, taking orders only from properly
> appointed officials.

Thus the dispute was effectively ended to the men's disadvantage. But
the union leaders were unable to cut short yet another dispute at the
Hermitage and Carron Wharf in Wapping over precisely the same issue.
As Mann explained in letters to John Burns, he did not believe the
strike to be necessary, but could not oppose it without jeopardizing his
relationship with the local leaders who had appealed for aid to the
London Federation of Trades. This organisation, which had been
founded on the initiative of Mann and Tillett to counter the employers'
Union of Dock, Wharf, Warehouse Proprietors and Granary Keepers, intended to boycott Hermitage and Carron. Neither Mann nor Tillett
wished to damage the Federation of Trades by refusing to support their
move. It was left to the stevedores, lightermen, carmen and tugboatmen
to break ranks, thus bringing the contest to a close.[21]

The leaders of the union obviously hoped to avoid a major confrontation with the employers in the Port of London. Burns explained the

strategy at the Dockers' Union's first annual delegate meeting in September, 1890. He :

> strongly urged them to be cautious in their policy, much more cautious than they had been hitherto. They had not too much money, and if they would permit him to say so, he thought they should be 'off' with strikes for a time . . . they now should have a time for building up and solidifying.

Mann agreed: 'What we as a union require at the present time is not extension but solidification.' In a startling affirmation of this policy the union announced that it would refuse to accept new members in the greater London area. Tillett had conceived this step. It signalled that the union had secured membership more than sufficient to meet the labour needs of the Port of London; indeed it was as much an offensive as a defensive move, for it constituted an assertion of the union's right to control the supply of labour at the docks. Doctrinaire new unionists who believed that the primary aim must be to recruit as many members as possible, however, condemned Tillett for betraying the movement.[22]

In reality a down turn in the trade cycle was largely responsible for the cautious policy. By 22 December 1890 Mann estimated in the *Star* that there were 8,000 union members unemployed and 3,000 working only three days a week. In a private letter to Burns, whom he meant to reassure, he confessed that the London membership had dropped by 3,000 in ten weeks: 'the men haven't got the money and can't pay [dues]'. Already the Joint Committee of Dock Directors had repudiated that part of the Mansion House agreement which bound them to hire only union members; on 28 December it laid off all its employees who had worked for them for less than ten years. The union did not protest. 'We have no money to help any strike of serious proportions', Mann wrote to Burns.[23]

The employers also had helped to put the new union on the defensive. In September 1890, they had organized the Shipping Federation, designed 'from the first as a fighting machine', its official historian wrote, 'to counter the strike'. Composed of the country's leading ship and dock owners, the federation was said to have £100 million at its disposal. It had two main weapons: 'Free labour' bureaux which undermined the closed shop by issuing tickets without which a docker could not be hired; and a reserve army of black-leg labour, which could be despatched to strike-bound firms anywhere. Armed with revolvers, the latter had helped to break the strike at Hermitage and Carron. Their efforts, however, were not to be confined to the Port of London alone.[24]

Provincial dock owners were soon probing the union for weaknesses. They had been unprepared for the new unionist advance, and during a period of full employment unable, at first, to resist it. Determined to regain lost ground, however, they had only to wait for a downward turn of the economy, while in the meantime preparing for further new unionist attacks. As in London, the militancy of the rank and file proved a mixed blessing to the union leadership, intent on consolidating its gains, and unlike London, provincial employers often had local police, or even the army and navy, behind them.

In March 1890, dockers in Liverpool demanding higher wages downed tools, and the strike spread quickly to Birkenhead. Tillett had visited the area earlier, hoping to negotiate an amalgamation with the National Union of Dock Labourers which made its headquarters there. Although he had failed, friendly relations were established eventually, and with the outbreak of hostilities he returned to participate in the struggle. Of shorter duration than the London strike of the previous summer, the 1890 Liverpool dock strike was nevertheless a major event, 'a big job', as Mann called it. By 12 March, 30,000 men were on strike; and on 15 March, despite the opposition of the mayor, the city magistrates called in the army. Thus overmatched, the union leadership was unwilling to risk a protracted struggle. The strike was officially brought to an end on 1 April, after certain concessions had been won. Thus this first conflict may be said to have ended in a draw.[25]

The dockers in the Scottish port of Leith were next to strike, but it was not until September 1890 that another major battle flared up. Unlike the struggles in London and Liverpool, the strike in Southampton was marked by violence. Serious rioting erupted after 1,000 dockers walked out. The mayor's house was attacked by a mob, his boot and shoe shop was demolished, and troops using repeated bayonet charges were needed to disperse the crowds. Gunboats were also sent to the beleaguered city. As in the Hays' Wharf dispute, the union executive disapproved of what it considered to be the precipitate action taken by the local branch. This time, however, it refused to be stampeded by the *fait accompli* which the strike represented. Only two weeks previously it had denied the Southampton leaders permission to down tools because the local owners had just conceded a wage rise. Now Mann and Burns stressed these points in personal appeals to the men to resume work. On 11 September the Dockers' Union executive, meeting in London, voted eleven to four against paying strike benefits.

Tillett refused to answer telegrams appealing to him for support. McCarthy let it be known that 'the authority of the executive must be maintained at all hazard'. As intended, this attitude resulted in the collapse of the strike. It led as well to the collapse of the local branch. Angry strikers tore up their union cards, accusing London of having betrayed them.[26]

Next it was the turn of Cardiff. The Shipping Federation, in its first major provincial intervention, provoked the dispute mainly to weaken the Sailors' and Firemen's Union which had been recently organized by J. Havelock Wilson, a labour leader of Tillett's and Mann's generation. A fiery speaker and a resourceful organizer, Wilson had given no hint of the sharp turn to the political right which he was to take in middle age. Rather, at this stage in his career, he was the *bête noire* of the employers and the darling of the militant rank and file, and not merely of his own union. When the Shipping Federation attacked his organization of sailors and firemen, the dockers of Cardiff announced a sympathy strike and put forward a host of grievances of their own (chief among them the system of subcontracting). This had already been the subject of protracted negotiation. Tillett interrupted his provincial tour and hurried to the scene, where he was joined by Harry Orbell, and later by Clem Edwards, who had followed Tillett from the Good Templars' Lodge into the Dockers' Union. On 10 February 1891, Tillett and Wilson delivered rousing speeches. 'This was a struggle for their very existence', the Dockers' Union general secretary declared, 'and they meant to fight it to the bitter end.'[27]

Again, it seemed as though the decisive confrontation was about to begin. The employers would not negotiate, or even recognize the right of the union to represent the men. In return, Tillett and Wilson speculated publicly that the strike would spread to London, Liverpool and Hull, so that the Shipping Federation could not concentrate its forces on Cardiff. They predicted that the Federation of Trade Unions in London would support the strike with sympathetic action, and indeed at least the stevedores seemed ready to do so. John Burns, however, held that the Dockers' Union had no direct interest in the Cardiff dispute. 'Went down to dockers and saw Mann', he wrote in his diary the very day that Tillett had promised to extend the strike to other ports.

> I told him to localise the strike at Cardiff, to be beaten there rather than be drawn to London to be smashed by masters . . . Predicted collapse of Unions if they did not mark time and consolidate position won by [the 1889] strike.

Burns had no official connection with the dockers except as a trustee of the union. Yet his argument proved convincing to Mann, and the dispute was not extended.[28]

Tillett remained in Cardiff to struggle against hopeless odds. Delivering an average of three or four speeches per day, his aimed to induce local unions to support the port workers. On 2 March he optimistically reported to a journalist from the *Star* that he sensed an imminent breakthrough:

> The riggers, the hobblers, the seamen, firemen, tipper, dealers, railwaymen and miners are in consultation as to some comprehensive and joint organised steps being taken which will bring about an effectual block from the mines to the docks. There will be a complete reorganisation of labour in South Wales and we shall have a unification in trade unionism.

In fact, his efforts proved fruitless. An interview with the miners' leaders produced no tangible results, and on 16 March the strike was called off. Tillett then collapsed. Exhausted and ill, he was too weak to lift a spoon to his lips. In the absence of Wilson, who was in jail for 'intimidating' free labourers, Mann made the journey to Cardiff to nurse his friend.

Eighteen months after its greatest triumph, the Dockers' Union was severely challenged at every turn. In London it had failed to protect the dinner hour, or to maintain other provisions of the Mansion House agreement. In Southampton and Cardiff it had sustained major defeats. Its great expectations for both the capital city and the provincial ports had been disappointed. In the Shipping Federation it faced an implacable and deadly enemy. The trade cycle had once again entered a downswing. Tillett, who throughout his career oscillated between moods of exultation and despair, might well have been excused for pessimism at this point.

In fact, his situation was utterly different from what it had been after the Tilbury strike. The union was much better established than in 1888. The masters had not succeeded in drawing it into a decisive battle, nor if one occurred was the outcome certain. Most importantly, for Tillett the sharpened class conflict of the previous months served an educational purpose. He could have no illusions now about compromising with the Shipping Federation, or about the sympathies of a government which had despatched gunboats to Southampton and imprisoned Havelock Wilson in Cardiff. Tillett's views developed within the context of bitter struggle. That was to make them more extreme, at least in the short term, than they might otherwise have been. The young dockers' leader was about to take his place at the forefront of the British socialist and trade union movements.

Notes

1. All figures taken from G.D.H. Cole and Raymond Postgate, *The Common People* (Methuen and Co. London, 1968), pp. 441-9.

2. Tillett, *Dock, Wharf, Riverside and General Workers' Union: A Brief History of the Dockers' Union*, p. 15; Will Thorne, *My Life's Battles* (George Newnes, London, n.d.), p. 70; John Lovell, *Stevedores and Dockers* (Macmillan, London, 1969), p. 99.

3. *South Wales Daily News*, 15 January 1907; H.L.L. Smith and Vaughan Nash, *The Story of the Dockers' Strike* (Fisher Unwin, London, 1889), p. 33; *English Illustrated*, vol. 7 (1889), p. 101; Lovell, *Stevedores and Dockers*, pp. 99-100.

4. I am grateful for this suggestion to Terry McCarthy, curator of the National Labour History Museum in Limehouse, East London, and grandson of Tom McCarthy.

5. Tillett recalling the strike fifty years later in the *East End News*, 12 August 1939.

6. *The Times*, 28 August 1889 and 2 September 1889; *Labour Elector*, 31 August 1889; for a further development of this argument see Gareth Stedman Jones, *Outcast London* (Clarendon Press, Oxford, 1971), pp. 315-22.

7. *Labour Elector*, 31 August 1889; *The Times*, 2 September 1889; John Burns Papers, British Museum, London, Add. Ms. 46285/22.

8. *The Times*, 2 September 1889.

9. *The Times*, 2 September 1889 and 24 August 1889.

10. *The Times*, 24 August 1889 and 3 September 1889.

11. *Labour Elector*, 21 September 1889.

12. *Labour Elector*, 19 October 1889.

13. Webb Trade Union Collection, Section A, volume 42, item 5, fol. 148.

14. *Standard*, 16 November 1889.

15. Tillett, *Dock, Wharf, Riverside and General Workers' Union*, p. 31; Broodbank, *History of the Port of London* (Daniel O'Connor, London, 1901), vol. 1, p. 203.

16. Tillett, *Dock Wharf, Riverside and General Workers' Union*, p. 31.

17. *Hull News*, 7 December 1889; *Treasure*, 8 October 1890.

18. *Labour Elector*, 5 January 1890; *Pall Mall Gazette*, 14 December 1889.

19. *Labour Elector*, 22 February 1890.

20. Ben Tillett Collection, MSS 74/3/1/50, Manning to Tillett, 25 February 1890; *Morning Post*, 10 February 1890; *Standard*, 10 February 1890.

21. *Star*, 2 January 1891; both letters are printed in Dona Torr's pamphlet, *Tom Mann*, (Lawrence and Wishart, London, 1944), pp. 35-7; *Trade Unionist*, 24 October 1891.

22. Dock, Wharf, Riverside and General Labourers' Union of Great Britain and Ireland, *Minutes of Annual Delegates Meetings*, 1890; idem, *Annual Report*, 1890.

23. Burns Papers Add. Ms. 46285/65, Mann to Burns, 19 December 1890; Add. Ms 46285/6, Mann to Burns, 8 January 1891.

24. L. Powell, *The Shipping Federation* (Shipping Federation, London, 1950), p. 5; for more on the 'free labour' movement, see William Collison, *The Apostle of Free Labour* (Hurst and Blackett, London, 1913); and Geoffrey Alderman, 'The National Free Labour Association', *International Review of Social History*, vol. XXI, part 3 (1976), pp. 309-36.

25. *Justice*, 22 March 1890 and the *Liverpool Post* both covered the strike.

26. A. Temple Patterson, *A History of Southampton* (Southampton University Press, Southampton 1975), vol. 3, pp. 80-94; *Morning Post*, 12 September 1890; *Daily Telegraph*, 11 September 1890; *Pall Mall Gazette*, 12 September 1890.

27. *Seafaring*, 14 February 1891.

28. Burns Papers Add. MS 46311, diary entry 11 February 1891.

4 THE SOCIALIST NEW UNIONIST, 1890-2

I

Although the new unionist era (roughly 1888-93) deserves examination
in its own right, it was also critical in helping to determine the future
shape of the British labour movement. The Independent Labour Party
and therefore the Labour Party itself have their origins in this period.
During it socialism grew from the creed of several small sects, with
little impact on the bulk of the working class, into an important
political force with broad support in the trade unions. These were, then,
the crucible years during which the British working class forged and
strengthened its modern organizational forms, and developed an
ideology which continues to inform its world view. In all these spheres
Tillett had a major role to play. He influenced the course of events; but
he was likewise influenced by them. Given both his own prominence
at the time, and the enduring significance of the period itself, the evolution of his views merits particularly careful scrutiny.

The continuing conflict between masters and men in dockland, in
which Tillett played so important a part, was typical of British industrial relations in general during the new unionist era. In the mines, mills
and factories of England's heartland, in the sweated dens and shops of
her cities, unskilled labourers, hitherto without organization, now
began combining and taking concerted action against their employers.
A new generation of labour leaders — Tillett, Thorne and Havelock
Wilson among them — emerged during these efforts and helped to give
them a programmatic basis. They were opposed not merely by the
employers, but often by craft unionists who hoped to retain wage and
other differentials which separated them from the mass of labourers.
New unionists strove to establish the identity of interests among all
workers, old unionists to maintain traditional distinctions between
them. Men like John Burns, Tom Mann and Tom McCarthy were labour
aristocrats who hoped to break down the old craft union exclusivism.
They accepted the new unionist position, indeed, in the case of Mann
and Burns, they had helped to formulate it by applying socialist theory
to British conditions.

Tillett has generally been accounted one of the leading socialists
among the new unionists. In fact, throughout 1889 he held himself
aloof from the socialist movement. The great triumph in London of that

year taught him that trade unionism alone was sufficient to reform conditions on the waterfront. Both the despair engendered by defeat at Tilbury and the plea to the Lords' Committee on Sweated Industries for state aid on behalf of dockers were forgotten in the enthusiasm generated by victory.

If all casual labourers could be organized (and with the union's rapid extension in the immediate aftermath of the strike that seemed possible), then there was nothing the dockers could not accomplish. According to Mann: 'Trade Unionism was not merely a machine for raising wages and shortening hours but . . . a power by which they could banish poverty from the land.' Tillett's message was no less inspirational. The new unionism, he maintained in a typical speech, was 'a new religion' which 'had crystallized and purified all the ideals of life . . . Trade Unionism would give them freedom'. Already he could see in London the moral revolution which unionism had set in motion. 'Why the docker now went to work with his head right up straight . . . with his labour dignified, with his manhood uplifted, with a truer sense of what was just, with a better appreciation of life and home and family, and with a stronger desire to be a better man in the future.'[1]

In fact, all casual port workers could not be organized within a single union. This became increasingly clear during the employers' counter-offensive and the various battles with the Shipping Federation. Yet Mann and Tillett remained optimistic. As consolidation, rather than extension, became the order of the day, they accordingly placed increasing emphasis upon federation with, and co-operation among, existing societies. Here, however, they came up against the hostility not of employers, but of old-style craft unionists.

The dockers' great victory had done little to change their attitudes towards the unskilled. Under the domination of George Shipton, the London Trades Council remained particularly unfriendly. Tillett and Mann hoped, however, that this body would become 'a real Labour Parliament, where Labour's grievances could really be thrashed out'. They now set about the task of converting its leadership, or replacing it with new unionists. Mann won a seat on its executive council, though as a skilled engineer, not a docker, since the council would not admit representatives of the unskilled. In the short run, his views actually gained an ascendency there, though Shipton remained as president until 1895. However, by April 1891 the whole executive, with the exception of Shipton, consisted of reformers and socialists. Here the new unionist leaders had scored an indubitable success.[2]

In other respects, however, the policy of federation and co-operation suffered grave set-backs. The advent of the Shipping Federation spurred new unionist efforts to establish an organization capable of resistance, and led to the formation of the National Federated Union of Sailors, Firemen, Dock-labourers, Wherrymen, Miners, Coalporters, Gas stokers, Flatmen, Bargemen, Carters 'and other kindred tasks connected with the Shipping Industry'. At least this body reflected the reconciliation between the South Side Labour Protection League and the Dockers' Union in the face of a common enemy. Mann and Quelch were chosen president and vice-president respectively. Unfortunately, however, no single society within the Federation wished to be drawn into sympathetic strikes in which issues not directly relevant to itself were at stake. This was made crystal clear during the battle with Carron and Hermitage, when several sections refused to observe the Federation's call for a boycott. At Cardiff too, it will be recalled, Tillett discovered the obstacles to federation and the pursuit of a common policy by otherwise independent societies.

At this stage in his career, Tillett was a militant trade unionist, but the extent of his vision must not be exaggerated. 'They did not want to fight Capital' he said at the conclusion of one speech. 'They only wanted Capital to be instead of a monstrosity and an oppressor, a servant to all equally.' That is, he wanted capital to be made available to unskilled labourers. This is what the union was for. No doubt such egalitarianism was rare in late-Victorian England. The majority of trade unionists were still imbued with patriotic and deferential attitudes. As we have seen, Tillett had partially emancipated himself from them during the great strike. He was no longer a strict Lib-Lab supporter; nevertheless, he still shared many popular prejudices. One year earlier he had demanded an end to unrestricted immigration, so that native Englishmen would not have to compete for jobs with foreigners. In this respect the London victory did not alter his view. In an article for the *English Illustrated* shortly after the 1889 strike, he attacked the government policy which permitted:

all the dregs and scum of the Continent to make foetid, putrid and congested our aready overcrowded slums . . . while . . . men who would have been good citizens, good patriots, bearing and discharging every social responsibility with credit to themselves and honour and glory to their country . . . are starved and driven to desperation.

Perhaps such attitudes were derived from his stint in the navy. Perhaps they reflected the views of those casual dockers for whom it was increasingly difficult to find work. They may be taken as a salutary reminder of the milieu from which the new unionists emerged, and of which Tillett always remained a prototypical figure.[3]

A variety of factors, however, combined to alter Tillett's views, if not about immigration, then about the potential of unalloyed trade unionism. The failure to federate with other unions was one such factor. Continuing fragmentation of the dock workforce between categories of specialized men, between labourers on the docks and in the warehouses, between all these and the Thames labour aristocrats, the stevedores and lightermen who worked on the river, likewise forced him to question the efficacy of trade unionism pure and simple. So too did the realization that without the lightermen and stevedores, who maintained their separate societies, the dockers lacked a core of skilled workers whom employers would find difficult to replace during a strike. Perhaps the decisive factor, however, leading to Tillett's repudiation of trade unionism as the sole necessary instrument of the working class was the unmanageability of the rank and file.

There was in Tillett an authoritarian streak which did not take kindly to independent rank-and-file action; hence, in part, the early drive to centralize power in the union's executive. Interestingly, the Southampton débâcle provided Tillett with an opportunity to hammer not only the government which had sent troops to break the strike, but the militants who had set it in motion. 'All who belonged to the Union . . . would have to toe the line', he stated uncompromisingly.

> The tail would not be allowed to wag the head . . . They must fall into their proper places, must await orders and be ready to fight when they were called upon to do so – and not before. There must be generals and privates in every army . . . loyalty and obedience to order were necessary, and discipline must be maintained.

Such an attitude toward the union could not fail to affect Tillett's political views. Later in his career, his opposition to rank-and-file democracy would lead him towards the right wing of the labour movement. In 1890-1, however, his authoritarianism combined with his hatred of the employers to push him to the left. That is, the struggles with the Shipping Federation sharpened Tillett's class consciousness, although the divisions among the men and their frequent rejection of his advice caused him, as after the Tilbury strike, to doubt the union's strength. Other ways of advancing the workers' cause must therefore be considered, most importantly labour's independent political representation and (once again, but more seriously) government intervention in the economy on labour's behalf.[4]

Tillett did not change his views all at once, nor may his course be charted in discrete stages. Moreover it was entirely pragmatic. By late September 1890, that is immediately after the Southampton strike, Tillett was advocating municipal workshops for the unemployed. By 9 January 1891 he had become a champion of local political action. 'If only they used their electoral power there need never be a slum in any village or town', Tillett advised the dockers of Newport. He was not suggesting, however, that the dockers send their representatives to Parliament, nor did he hope, yet, for the formation of a new political party. He had abandoned the 'Lib-Labs', but had not yet come out for an independent labour party. 'Never mind party politics, to hell with them', he exhorted another dockers' audience at Goole. Approached in early May 1891 by the Bradford Labour Council to stand for the local parliamentary seat, he declined.

> As to being sanguine of any specific good being attainable through my candidacy I am not, and see only the possibility of such good being effected when, outside the House, workmen have fully made up their minds for reform . . . To devote our energies now to municipal and local government is our first duty.

As he put it in a speech at East Bradford: 'he attached more importance to local representation than to Parliamentary representation, because the one was direct and immediate in its effects, and the effects of the other were indirect and a long way off'. True to his word, he joined the London County Council as an alderman within a year.[5]

In an address delivered to the East London Fabian Society on 24 March 1891, Tom Mann summarized the shift in the thinking of the dockers' leaders since the great strike:

> The New Unionism, like every fresh movement, exaggerated its importance. It fell into the common error of supposing that it had discovered a panacea for all the ills of social life. He had had great hopes that this year there would be an improvement in East London life, but it seemed farther off than ever . . . The only way in which he could see any remedy was in the direction of municipal workshops.

Mann was busy through the summer turning down offers to stand for

Parliament. But this was an attitude which neither he nor the other dockers' leaders could long maintain. Quite simply, once the leap to political involvement in local affairs had been made, its extension to the national scene was inevitable. Tillett had declined the Bradford nomination in May; but he had accepted it by September.[6]

II

In 1890 Tillett and Mann co-authored a famous pamphlet in which they issued a ringing challenge to the 'Lib-Lab' trade union leadership: 'Our ideal is a COOPERATIVE COMMONWEALTH.' Given his prominence as general secretary of the Dockers' Union, and its fiery spokesman in numerous strikes, Tillett's pronouncement immediately catapulted him into the leadership of Britain's developing socialist movement.[7]

There has been much recent scholarly debate over the nature of that movement's ideology during the new unionist era. It has been argued that British socialists, with a few notable exceptions, have concentrated upon knife-and-fork questions, and relegated theoretical concerns to the back burner. This, it is held, has led inevitably to the ascendancy of 'labourists', willing to sacrifice long-range goals for short-term advantages; the result being the impoverishment of the native socialist tradition. Alternatively, however, it has been suggested that the 'religion of socialism', best preached, perhaps, by William Morris, but accepted by many in late-Victorian Britain, was extremely rich, and posed even in the 1890s a direct threat to capitalist authority. Did Tillett's brand of socialism fall within either of these camps?[8]

He did not believe in violent working-class revolution. Nor for that matter did Mann or many of the other new unionist leaders at this stage. The self-conscious revolutionary left in England during the late 1880s and early 1890s seems to have been confined to a few branches of the Social Democratic Federation and to William Morris's Socialist League, which, until recently had included Eleanor Marx and the disciples of Engels. This is important to stress because many of Tillett's contemporaries considered him to be an advocate of bloody revolution, and Tillett himself added to the confusion in later years by claiming always to have been a socialist revolutionary.

Tillett's oratorical efforts were partly responsible for the contemporary impression that he believed in working-class insurrection. When he was in his 'rousing up' mood, there were few who could better move an audience. Thus he may be found at Goole, exhorting his listeners, because although 'The past had been the past of the wealthy . . . the future was the future of the toilers . . . there was a great mountain to be moved . . . Successive generations would have to work at it.' During the strike at Cardiff: 'This was a battle for posterity. They were fighting for their children, their wives and their homes . . . for the right of free men to combine . . . and they meant to fight it to the bitter end.' And after the Southampton defeat, in London where he predicted that 'the day was coming when the governing authorities of this country would adopt the Continental plan and seek to suppress the rights of labour by force of arms'. 'If this were so,' he warned:

> they would realize what they would have to face . . . They did not desire to hold secret councils, neither did they desire to act as dynamitards . . . But they told the authorities of this country that liberty and justice would prevail as eternal principles when their opponents were in their graves.

Such veiled threats, it is worth repeating, deserve to be taken with the proverbial grain of salt, although most of his contemporaries swallowed them undiluted. There is simply no evidence that Tillett ever gave serious thought to violent revolution. Rather, popular impressions to the contrary notwithstanding, Tillett, who had gone out of his way to disavow revolutionary violence during the 1889 strike, continued to do so after becoming a socialist. 'They did not want to rob anyone', he explained in another speech at Bradford. 'If they did, they would be adopting the malpractices of the people who robbed them.' Indeed, reform was in the best interests of the established order:

> The wealth of the country was due in a transcending degree to the unskilled workers . . . These men, vast masses of sullen humanity, were a real danger to every state and they would remain so until it was realized that there must be more skilled men and better paid unskilled men.

In short, Tillett argued, as he had done in the 'bludgeons can suppress' letter to the *Star* immediately after the Tilbury strike, that reform was necessary and desirable in order to avert revolution.[9]

Tillett, then, was not a revolutionary during this period. It is also doubtful whether he practised the 'religion of socialism' as historians now term it. According to its most recent interpreter, the impact of

the religion of socialism' during the 1880s and 1890s was 'so substantial' that it permanently shaped the ideology of the British working
class. Its practitioners, among whom he lists many of the prominent
socialist leaders of the period, had come to believe with great intensity
in the imminence of the socialist transformation of society. It would
be accomplished by 'the people' in order to annihilate 'the irrationality
of the world', that is the world's present unequal distribution of life's
cultural and material goods. More than this, they shared with William
Morris the conviction that socialism was 'a complete theory of human
life, founded indeed on the visible necessities of animal life, but including a distinct system of religion, ethics and conduct'. They practised
this theory daily, explained and sung its praises in the Labour churches,
their unions and the various socialist organizations, criticized the established churches and politicians for failing to live up to their own principles, and thus, it is held, constituted even then a direct challenge to
capitalist order.[10]

At first glance Tillett might seem to fall within this camp. He was a
Congregationalist who preached regularly in Labour churches (his
favourite sermon was 'Come unto me all ye who labour and are heavily
burdened and I will give you rest', Matthew 11:28) and whose articles
appeared frequently in John Trevor's Christian socialist journal, the
Labour Prophet. It is also true that his speeches during this period were
studded with biblical references and passionate excoriations of the
established churches, which, in his opinion, ignored the plight of
working men and women.

Tillett, however, did not undergo some revelatory process in order
to approach socialism. Rather, he came to advocate socialist measures
gradually and as a result of his experiences as the dockers' leader. And,
having proclaimed his socialist views, it is noteworthy how little
changed was the end he had in mind.

He remained, above all, a trade unionist. 'Workingmen ought to
demand more of the wealth which they did so much to produce.' This
was his message to the labourers of East Bradford in the summer of
1891. It recurs frequently. 'The shipowners had boasted of their
£100,000,000', he informed a meeting at the Great Assembly Hall in
Mile End, 'but they meant to have some of that money'. And in
Newport: 'Today, by the aid of machinery one man could do . . . what
twenty men could do thirty years ago. They had not advanced to
twenty times better positions so far as their wages were concerned.'[11]

Tillett's vision of the future ideal society combined the mundane
with the millenarian. 'Why the economic fulcrum is the only support

for the levers of morality, truth, justice and human happiness.' This too would seem to place him outside the 'religion of socialism'. Like most people, however, Tillett was inconsistent. 'We are not to be confined to wages alone . . . To have a high wage and still be an animal would be the worst form of poverty.'

Consciousness does not reveal itself in an instant. Tillett's continued to evolve both during and after the period under consideration here, often in unexpected directions. Nevertheless, and despite occasional rhapsodies on the coming socialist utopia which were wide ranging, most of Tillett's writings and statements at this time suggest a relatively modest vision. Socialism was not, for Tillett, a complete theory of human life. Rather, as he wrote in an article for the *Labour Prophet*: 'Socialism . . . can only be said to be a claim to that protection which the vast bulwark of the constitution affords the [capitalist] class now.' As he put it in a pamphlet of 1892: the socialist new unionists 'desire a *share* in government' (emphasis added). Or, on another occasion: 'What can give security to one class can give it to another . . . The protection that property already possesses, the toiler now seeks.' In short, he did not want to turn the world upside down with the producers of wealth on top, so much as he wanted to improve their relative position. He seems to have envisioned a future society which continued to be divided by classes, but with the working class better integrated within it.[12]

In early 1891, Tillett applied for membership and joined the Fabian Society. He must have been somewhat uncomfortable in its rarefied atmosphere of high-powered intellectualism. 'Should you ever leave the West End and come East', he wrote with the suggestion of acerbity to Edward Pease, the Fabian secretary, 'a call at our offices would oblige.' Yet certain Fabian attitudes towards the working class appealed to Tillett. 'There was no class of people whom he would fear more to have in their possession an unlimited power [than the workers]', he declared, 'because they would use it against themselves and their own best interests.' The selfishness and shortsightedness of the rank and file were a continuing source of irritation to him. 'He knew what it had been to have 100,000 men in one mind', he told the 1891 Trades Union Congress, 'and directly benefits had been given to them they put their hands into their pockets saying "I am all right [*sic*], let other people fight for themselves." '[13]

Tillett was convinced that the shortcomings of his fellows were not inherent, but produced by their conditions of life. 'Of all the circumstances which mould the character', he told an audience at Hull, 'the most vital are the circumstances of environment.' Social Darwinism held no appeal for Tillett. As a witness called before the 1891-2 Royal Commission on Labour, he argued that wages should be based not merely upon a worker's strength, speed and skill, but also upon the size of his family — that is, upon need — and even upon such criteria as his generosity, courage and independence of mind. The fervour with which Tillett's public utterances were delivered, and his pamphlets written, stemmed from his rage against those who refused to acknowledge such considerations, and from his conviction that their failure to do so blighted the lives of a majority of his countrymen — morally as well as physically. The passionate excoriations of capitalism which now began to punctuate his speeches served to distinguish him from the Fabians who argued with dry logic that poverty was a problem whose solution would promote the interests of the state. Tillett was more concerned to calculate its human costs and to rouse his audiences to a sense of outrage.[14]

Thus, by late 1892, Tillett had become a leading figure in the British socialist movement. His position within it, however, was ambiguous. A member of the Fabian Society, he shared its outlook only to a limited extent. An impassioned and perhaps reckless orator, he did not advocate revolution, although many believed that he did. A popular preacher in the Labour churches, he subscribed only super-ficially to the 'religion of socialism', for he did not possess a complete alternative vision of society. Indeed, at this point, it is easier to say what Tillett was not than what he was. His decision to stand as a parlia-mentary candidate therefore assumes great significance, for it provided him with the perfect opportunity to articulate his goals and to define his attitudes towards the major questions of the day.

III

Tillett's parliamentary campaign in Bradford during the summer of 1892 highlights his great energy, oratorical ability, hatred of exploit-ation, and determination to help 'raise the standing of the life of the workers', as he put it in one speech. At the same time, it suggests the boundaries of his vision, and the personal characteristics which later were to weaken his militancy and lessen his effectiveness as a labour leader.

Sometime between May and September 1891 Tillett decided to make the fight at West Bradford. A variety of factors must have influenced him, not least that other well-known new unionists were standing elsewhere. Although there was not yet a national independent labour party, the candidacies of John Burns at Battersea, Keir Hardie at West Ham, Havelock Wilson at Middlesbrough, H.H. Champion at Aberdeen and Cunninghame Graham at Glasgow (Camlachie) strongly suggested that there was one in the making. Social Democrat candidates in London and Salford, and four members of the Scottish Labour Party standing in working-class constituencies north of the border likewise must have helped the dockers' leader to accept nomination. Moreover, if Tillett was successful in his contest, he would be able to work against the Shipping Federation from within the House of Commons. This course must also have commended itself to Havelock Wilson, the leader of the Sailors' and Firemen's Union. It is likely that he and Tillett consulted about it. The temptation to stand was reinforced when a thousand West Bradford electors signed a petition urging Tillett to do so. As W.H. Drew, of the Bradford Trades Council, optimistically reported to the 1891 annual delegate meeting of Tillett's union: 'They had canvassed the district as much as possible with the result that a unanimous opinion prevailed that Mr Tillett would win easily.'

When it began to appear likely that Tillett would enter the contest, he was approached by representatives of the Liberal Party, which had held West Bradford since 1880, and offered £100 towards expenses, plus a free fight against the Conservative in another constituency. This aroused Tillett's fighting spirit and may have been a further reason why he agreed to stand: 'People wanted him to be a good boy, a lick spittle, a kind of pampered young man at the feast', he declared in his opening campaign speech at the Princeville Board School in West Bradford. He was determined to be none of these. Finally, as a reason for making the campaign, Tillett had conceived a personal animosity towards the Liberal incumbent, Alfred Illingworth, whom he credited with every fault it was possible for a capitalist to possess.[15]

This was not surprising. Bradford had been the scene of a protracted and particularly violent strike during the winter and spring of 1891. Sparked by the attempt of the worsted manufacturer Samuel Cunliffe Lister (later Lord Masham) to reduce wages by some 15 to 33 per cent, the Manningham Mill strike lasted almost six months. Starvation finally drove the strikers back to work, but not before pitched battles in the Town Hall 'Dockers' Square raised tensions to an unprecedented level. Tillett had been one of numerous outside speakers called in to keep up morale among the strikers and had also attempted to raise money for them. He could not have failed to notice that Illingworth supported the forces of order.[16]

In the long run, the failure of Tillett's fund-raising efforts for the strike, and the defeat of the men, proved to be of greater consequence than victory would have been. These developments led to the formation of the Bradford and District Labour Union, whose objects were 'to promote the interests of the working class in whatever way it may from time to time be thought advisable, and to further the cause of direct labour representation on local bodies and in Parliament'. The bitter feeling in the aftermath of the strike ensured that the new organization would have a sizeable following. Its leading members were local socialist trade unionists who already exercised considerable influence in the community. Chief among them were Fred Jowett, the powerloom overlooker who later became a Labour Member of Parliament and Cabinet Minister; George Minty, a local leader of the Vehicle Workers' Union and a member of William Morris's Socialist League; W.H. Drew, a founder-member of the Weavers' Union; and James Bartley, a journalist. Less than one month after the defeat of the Manningham strike, they offered Tillett the West Bradford nomination, and promised that the Labour Union would cover his election expenses. In addition, they approached Robert Blatchford, who first agreed to stand for East Bradford, and then withdrew two months later when it became apparent that he could not conduct a parliamentary campaign and edit the *Clarion* simultaneously.[17] Blatchford was another of the great characters in the British labour movement. A recent convert to socialism, he had founded the *Clarion* to expound its principles when his employer at the *Sunday Chronicle* objected to his doing so there. A jovial, outgoing personality, he seems at first glance quite different from the moody, and then teetotal Tillett. In fact, the world view of both men was similar, though it took time before this became apparent. Despite occasional differences, they became lifelong political allies.

Traditionally Liberal trade unionists had dominated working-class politics in Bradford. In 1892 they still accounted for a majority on the executive of the Bradford branch of the Labour Electoral Association, and retained considerable (though not determining) power on the Bradford Trades Council. Local branches of the Machine Woolcombers' Society, the National Woolsorters' Society, the Stuffpressers' Society, the Overlookers' Society and the Boot and Shoemakers' Union were headed by 'Lib-Lab' voters who supported Illingworth during the election. Their chief spokesman was Samuel Shaftoe of the Woolcombers, a former secretary of the Trades Council, treasurer of the Bradford branch of the English Home Rule Union and a member of the executive council of the Eastern Division of the Bradford Liberal Association. Shaftoe and the 'Lib-Labs' were incensed by Tillett's candidacy, and particularly by his refusal to accept a straight fight against the Conservative in East Bradford. Suspicious of any politician who wanted to increase the powers of the state, they may also have hesitated to oppose Illingworth because he was the city's largest employer. Undoubtedly they resented Tillett's intervention in the Bradford scene, which threatened their own hard-won position in the Liberal Party. Therefore they opposed the dockers' leader during the campaign, and they actively encouraged working-class electors to cast their ballots for the Liberal factory owner.[18]

There were two ways to answer the 'Lib-Labs'. Though they were contradictory, Tillett and his supporters tried both. One way was to present Tillett as the candidate who most faithfully represented Liberal ideals. Outside speakers invited by the Tillett organization often took this line, even though their candidate had already proclaimed his independence from Liberalism. Tillett deserved Liberal support, according to Katharine St John Conway (later Mrs Bruce Glasier and a founding member of the Independent Labour Party), because he was 'a Liberal in fact though not in name'. This theme was also taken up by Sidney Webb, who listed his own Liberal credentials — membership in the National Liberal Club, the London Liberal and Radical Union, and the National Liberal Federation — presumably to demonstrate his qualifications for arguing that it was in the best interests 'not merely of Labour, but of Liberalism itself to back up Ben Tillett'. The corollary to this suggestion was that the official Liberal candidate did not, in fact, represent genuine Liberal ideals. Certain of Alfred Illingworth's statements were cited in support of this view. As a manufacturer, he held that the wages of his men were sufficient but wasted on drink; and that it would be 'the grossest cruelty' to deprive married mothers of the opportunity to work in his factory. But it was over the question of child labour that more progressive Gladstonian Liberals were most likely to oppose him. 'When Mr Tillett came to Bradford', Illingworth explained at one Liberal rally:

he took up the question of the age at which children should be allowed to go to work . . . He [Mr Illingworth] had representatives from the Chamber of Commerce, and from parents of Bradford, and neither was for raising the age of children from ten to any higher age. But . . . he saw there was a strong feeling in the House of Commons on the part of those who did not well understand the factory system, and twelve years of age was regarded as the minimum age which would be accepted. He went in for eleven, and he did that as a reasonable compromise . . . Let there be steady progress.[19]

Such views provided Tillett with an opportunity which he did not fail to exploit. On 13 February 1892, one month before his campaign began in earnest, he sounded the note which would become its basis. 'The tendency of the present age', he wrote in the *Weekly Star*:

is to supersede the old aristocracy of the land by the snobbery of capitalists and a class of landowners more unscrupulous, more evil in their machinations, more eager for wealth and greedy for fame and power, and ready to ride over their victims whose cry never reaches their ears or their hearts.

To a working-class audience, Tillett could add a significant twist to the argument that Liberals were as bad, or even worse, than Tories. 'Fifty years ago', he explained:

the land owning interest was opposed to the middle class capitalist. The former had either died out or gambled away their wealth . . . A new order was springing up . . . The rich capitalist was replacing the old landlord, and he generally took into possession of the land less conscience . . . There was then no Liberalism or Toryism, but there was capitalism (cheers).

This was the second method of winning over working-class Liberals to the Tillett camp. Recent events in Bradford had prepared many local workers for the advent of an independent labour party, despite their long-standing links with the Liberals and the continuing influence of some 'Lib-Labs'. The ambiguous remarks of such middle-class supporters as Katharine Conway and Sidney Webb notwithstanding, Tillett's statements on the failings of both established parties and the necessity for a new one composed of workers were consistent and uncompromising. His independence of the Liberal Party was less questionable than that of John Burns, who faced only a Conservative opponent in Battersea, and who had already displayed on the London County Council a strong desire to co-operate with the Liberals. Likewise it was more pronounced than that of Keir Hardie, who encountered only a Tory opponent at West Ham, and who promised electors that he 'would support the Liberal programme in its entirety'. Havelock Wilson was the only labour candidate to fight successfully a three-cornered race, and his immediate accommodation with the Liberal Party after the election was to throw his independence in doubt. With Tillett, however, there could be no question: he was independent of the Liberals, and as he exclaimed at an early campaign rally, 'he gloried in it'. Looking back to Tillett's campaign some twenty years later, Joseph Burgess, founder-member of the Independent Labour Party, believed that it 'laid down the lines on which Independent Labour candidates ought to act'.[20]

Tillett then entered the lists as an outspoken advocate of independent working-class representation. 'There was nothing to be hoped for from the present day politicians', he declared. Their sole purpose was to maintain privilege and place. Furthermore, as he put it:

> Mr Gladstone had snubbed the Labour Party, Mr [John] Morley had insulted it, Lord Salisbury had twitted it, and Balfour in his cynical fashion was trying to be philosophical about it. Churchill had got hysterical (laughter) and there was not a man in either of the great parties who was not opposed to the Labour programme and to the very spirit that impelled the Labour movement.

He catalogued the reforms which neither party would advance, and which, in his opinion, would transform society.

> He wanted factory legislation. He wanted machinery to be protected, proper sanitary arrangements to be made, the separation of the sexes, the appointment of women as inspectors, and an obligation on the part of the employer to supply an exact statement of work given out and the wages paid for it without being asked for it . . . He wanted the people to have the land and the money.

His formal programme was worked out in close consultation with the Bradford Union. It combined the old democratic Chartist goals with a series of wide-ranging social and economic reforms. Tillett's platform included adult suffrage and single voting qualification, equalization of electoral districts and abolition of university representation, payment of Members of Parliament, quadrennial Parliaments, abolition of the House of Lords, abolition of property qualifications for any public office, and finally a demand that was probably directed at the monarchy: 'The immediate abolition of ridiculous and useless offices of State . . . ' In addition Tillett called for a compulsory 8-hour day or a 48-hour work week, establishment of a Government Labour Bureau to transfer workers from overemployed to underemployed places, reorganization of the Poor Law administration so that all citizens unable to work, for whatever reason, would receive 'ordinary means of living', the establishment of state and municipal workshops, nationalization of the land, and 'Home Rule for England, Ireland, Scotland and Wales on a thoroughly democratic basis'.[21]

This last demand was designed to cut into Illingworth's considerable support among the Irish community in Bradford. In the general election of 1892, Gladstone again carried the Irish Home Rule standard. It had previously divided the Liberal Party; but in Bradford, the Gladstonians were victorious. Illingworth was regarded as a staunch Home Ruler, and received an endorsement early in the campaign from the Bradford branch of the Irish National League. Tillett attempted to distinguish between the 'namby pamby Bill' supported by his opponent, and the kind of Home Rule he would endorse: 'he would help to get the land for the Irish people . . . so that its wealth should be shared by those who helped to make it, and so that every man and woman should take a part in elective votes in the government of the country'. But Michael O'Flynn, chairman of the Bradford branch of the League, remained unconvinced: if Tillett sincerely wanted the emancipation of Irish and English workers 'he would be better able to accomplish that object by leaving the division than by letting in a Tory'. Tillett was back to square one. How could he convince Liberals that a vote cast for himself was not, indirectly, a vote cast for the Conservative candidate?[22]

In a letter of 25 April to the editor of the *Bradford Observer*, Tillett attempted to meet this question head on. 'The hitherto undisputed right of capitalists, manufacturers, landowners, brewers, to absorb the total political representation of the country is again being urged', he wrote:

> and a spirit of 'Don't poach on my preserves' is manifested by the mealy mouthed of both parties . . . To Liberalism my standing may mean the probable loss of one seat, if their aggressive attitude is still maintained toward Labour. My resignation would mean the breakup of the [labour and socialist] movement begun in real earnest in Yorkshire, and I should deserve the everlasting odium of my class . . . The selfishness of the party monopolists must be labour's text for a real, healthy, democratic State representation on independent lines.

He also hoped to overcome the resistance of working-class Liberals to his candidacy through sheer force of personality and momentum. He was fast developing into one of the labour movement's great orators. 'His hearers are carried away by Ben's talk', wrote one who heard him:

> and Ben himself, as he stands on tip-toe with his head held back, and his whole body swaying with the motion of his speech, seems carried away too, with some mysterious force.

Fenner Brockway, the future Labour MP and Lord Brockway, described Tillett during this campaign as a man who possessed a 'magnetic personality'.

> In appearance he might have been mistaken for a parson; he wore a broad brimmed black hat, a loose coat, and his features had the idealism of an evangelist. He had a wonderful gift for speech . . .

And Fred Jowett, who participated in the Bradford campaign, recorded that Tillett raised his voice, 'with great effect for sympathetic appeal, for exhortation, or for scathing, scorching denunciation'. Tillett's drive was conducted at a whirlwind pace, especially as polling day approached. On 1 July, he addressed four meetings between 7 p.m. and midnight: the first in Green Lane before 'upwards of 1,200 persons'; the second at 'the bottom of Thornecliffe Road where from four to five hundred people were collected'; the third in the yard of the Whitley Lane School where 'there must have been two thousand persons present'; and finally in Drummond Road where 'some 3000 people were waiting'.[23]

Despite Tillett's great energy and determination, his campaign occasionally struck an awkward note. An avowed socialist, Tillett did not once mention the word 'socialism' during the run up to the election, preferring to speak (but only once) of the ideal state to which he looked forward. He seems to have consciously refrained from envisioning the socialist millenium, remarking on at least three separate occasions that he would not do so (7 March, 14 May, 26 May). He also reprinted in his campaign literature the commendation he had received from the elders of the Congregational church: 'We have reason devoutly to thank God that our Leader of undisciplined labour is a man like Tillett, a good soldier of Jesus Christ, and not a Marat or a Ravachol.' As polling day approached, he became so incensed with the Liberals that he even suggested the possibility of an electoral alliance between Labour and the Conservatives, though he quickly backed off when greeted with an outburst of disapproval from his supporters.[24]

Tillett also displayed towards the electorate the same ambivalency which characterized his relationship with the rank and file of his union. Bradford's workers, he charged, had failed to do their duty or to appreciate him sufficiently.

> He had spent the best years of his life and the best energies he possessed for the benefit of his class . . . If he represented them they would have to do their share of the work or he would chuck it. He believed in a division of labour, and if his part were working, speaking and travelling, it was their part to contribute the means for his doing so. There had been a meanness shown which was despicable.

Perhaps such outbursts were more reflective of his personal insecurity than of his political outlook. Yet it seems unlikely that the one did not affect the other. Tillett's failure to articulate his socialist vision becomes relevant here: did he foresee a 'division of labour' in the presumably classless 'ideal state' to which as a socialist he was committed? Perhaps Tillett's trade union preoccupations led him to focus on the fore and middle ground. He viewed politics and hence the parliamentary campaign 'through trade union glasses', he told one Bradford audience. Indeed he only agreed to make the contest on the understanding that he could give up his seat, if parliamentary duties interfered with his work for the dockers. If, on the one hand, this may be taken as a virtuous gesture of self-abnegation, it may also be understood to reveal Tillett's lack of commitment to a wider goal. Keir Hardie, it may be recalled, abandoned his position as a trade union leader in order to devote himself to the labour and socialist movements. Thus, even at the height of his reputation for being a socialist new unionist, perhaps the seeds of Tillett's later apostasy were already perceptible.[25]

IV

Not surprisingly, the Bradford contest drew national attention. Tillett brought in Pete Curran of the Gasworkers' Union, Tom McCarthy and Tom Mann of the Dockers' Union, and the Fabians Hubert Bland, Katharine Conway and Sidney Webb to speak for him. Vaughan Nash, who helped to write a classic account of the 1889 dock strike, and H.W.

Massingham of the *Star* were prominent journalistic supporters. Local interest in the campaign was intense, and polling day, 'which was beautifully fine', saw the heaviest turn-out to date in Bradford's history. Out of 10,400 eligible voters, 9,108 cast their ballots.[26] The Liberal and Conservative candidates provided their supporters with transportation to the polls. Tillett had only one carriage for this purpose lent him by John Lister, an affluent friend. Bills and posters adorned Bradford walls, even on the day of election: 'the canvass for Mr Illingworth is satisfactory. His triumph is now certain. Steady work will ensure a large majority over both his opponents', read one Liberal effort; Labour responded with 'Hurry up! Ben Tillett is winning. Increase his majority'; and the Conservative candidate issued a poster with a Union Jack at the top, followed by the words: 'Play up, West Bradford, Flower wins'. But when the ballots were counted in the evening, and the results declared by the Mayor of Bradford at half past ten, Alfred Illingworth, the Liberal, emerged victorious with 3,306 votes; Ernest Flower, the Conservative, came second with 3,033 votes; and Tillett trailed, although making a strong showing with 2,749 votes.

'One must go back to the April riots of 1891 to find a parallel to the appearance of the centre of town last night', wrote a journalist for the *Bradford Observer* the day following the poll. The crowds jamming the streets were in high spirits, but whether in good or ill humour was difficult to tell. In Darley Street, where the road was being repaired, extra police were needed to disperse 'youths throwing stones about'. Elsewhere a band of 'fourteen or fifteen young men pushed through the crowds brandishing heavy knobbed walking sticks and singing music hall compositions'. Despite such overtones, however, the scene appears to have been more reminiscent of Dickens' Eatanswill than the Manningham mill strike. The crowds were intoxicated with alcohol, not Tillett's evangelical rhetoric. Amid the excitement of the evening, however, one portentous note was struck. 'One hundred members of the Girlington Labour Club' took possession of Dockers' Square, from which the Manningham strikers had been driven a year and a half before. Standing upon the shoulders of his comrades, Fred Jowett predicted that the initial set-back would not halt the march of the Bradford Labour Union. And in an emotional speech to his followers in the Vanmen's rooms, Sackville Street, Tillett elaborated upon the theme. 'I am not defeated', he cried to ringing cheers:

You are not defeated (loud cheers). Tonight you have had your first Baptism . . . You have come out of your thraldom [*sic*] and have

said you will have this old country of ours for us and our children
. . . The light will come . . . and we shall not be long before we shall
go to the poll and shout 'Glory Hallelujah' for the democracy . . . [27]

Notes

1. *Daily Chronicle*, 14 January 1891; *Hull News*, 7 December 1889.

2. For the battle in the London Trades Council and the new unionist view of
it, see the *Labour Elector*, 11 January and 18 January 1890; see also, Paul
Thompson, *Socialists, Liberals and Labour; The Struggle for London, 1885-1914*
(Routledge and Kegan Paul, London, 1967), pp. 41-61.

3. *Hull News*, 7 December 1889; *English Illustrated*, vol. 7 (1889), p. 101.

4. *Daily Chronicle*, 12 September 1890.

5. *TUC Annual Report, 1890*, p. 140; *Monmouth Times*, 9 January 1891;
Seafaring, 31 January 1891; Tillett's letter to W.H. Drew, who had offered him
the nomination,was printed in the *Workman's Times*, 22 May 1891; *Workman's
Times*, 28 August 1891. Tillett was selected as an alderman by the popularly
elected London County Councillors. At that point in its history, the LCC was
divided between 'Moderates' and 'Progressives', the latter, with whom Tillett
immediately allied, including Burns, Charles Freak, Will Crooks, Fred Henderson,
Sidney Webb and other new unionist sympathizers. Tillett never played a prominent role on the Council. It seems to have been important to him chiefly for
widening his rapidly expanding circle of contacts. As a result of his LCC membership he was able, later, to call upon Lord Rosebery, the former Liberal Prime
Minister and LCC chairman, for a character reference.

6. Fabian Society Papers, Nuffield College, 'Celebrities File'.

7. Tom Mann and Ben Tillett, *The New Trades Unionism: A Reply to Mr
George Shipton* (London, 1890), p. 15.

8. The three most important 'labourist' interpretations are Perry Anderson's
'Origins of the Present Crisis', *New Left Review*, vol. 23 (January-February
1964), pp. 26-63; Tom Nairn's 'The Nature of the Labour Party I and II', *New
Left Review*, vol. 27 (September-October 1964), pp. 38-65, and vol. 28
(November-December, 1964), pp. 33-62; and Gareth Stedman Jones's 'Working-
Class Culture and Working-Class Politics in London, 1870-1900, Notes on the
Remaking of a Working Class', *Journal of Social History*, vol. 7, no. 4 (Summer
1974), pp. 460-508. The counterblasts were written by E.P. Thompson, 'The
Peculiarities of the English', *Socialist Register* (1965), pp. 311-62, and Stephen
Yeo, 'A New Life: The Religion of Socialism in Britain 1883-1896', *History
Workshop Journal*, vol. 4 (Autumn 1977), pp. 5-56. See also Jonathan Schneer,
'Ben Tillett's Conversion to Independent Labour Politics', *Radical History
Review*, vol. 24 (Fall 1980), pp. 42-65, for a middle position.

9. *Seafaring*, 31 January 1890 and 14 February 1891; *Daily Chronicle*, 17 September 1890; *Bradford Observer*, 7 March 1892; *Workman's Times*, 16 October
1891.

10 Stephen Yeo's recent article, 'A New Life: The Religion of Socialism'
offers a penetrating analysis of this phenomenon.

11. *Workman's Times*, 17 July 1891; *Daily Chronicle*, 17 September 1890;
Monmouth Times, 9 January 1891.

12. *Trade Unionist*, 11 July 1891; Tillett, 'The Labour Platform: New Style',
New Review, vol. 6 (January-June 1892), p. 175; *Labour Prophet*, April 1892,
Tillett, 'Labour Platform', p. 175.

13. Fabian Society Papers, Box 2, Tillett to Pease, 3 April 1891; *Monmouth Times*, 9 January 1891; *TUC Annual Report, 1891*, pp. 45-6.

14. 'Man's Individual Responsibility', a lecture delivered by Ben Tillett at the Alhambra Music Hall, Hull, on 25 September 1891, and printed later in the year as a pamphlet; *Parliamentary Papers* (1892), vol. XXXV, p. 143.

15. E.P. Thompson, 'Homage to Tom Maguire' in Asa Briggs and John Saville (eds.), *Essays in Labour History* (Macmillan, vol. 1, p. 308; 1967); Dock, Wharf, Riverside and General Labourers' Union, *Minutes of Annual Delegate Meetings* (1891); *Bradford Observer*, 4 March 1892.

16. See Thompson, 'Homage to Tom Maguire'; and J. Reynolds and K. Laybourn, 'The Emergence of the Independent Labour Party in Bradford', *International Review of Social History*, vol. 20 (1975), pp. 313-46.

17. *Clarion*, 17 September 1891; the Fabian Society also contributed over £140 to Tillett's expenses; for more on Jowett in particular, and the early days of the Bradford Union, see Fenner Brockway, *Socialism over 60 years: The Life of Jowett of Bradford* (Allen and Unwin, London, 1946).

18. For development of the argument that workers were suspicious of politicians who wished to increase the powers of the state, see Henry Pelling, *Popular Politics and Society in Late Victorian Britain* (Macmillan, London, 1968), ch. 1.

19. *Clarion*, 17 September 1891; *Bradford Observer*, 27 June 1892 and 24 June 1892.

20. *Bradford Observer*, 4 April 1892 and 4 March 1892, Kenneth O. Morgan, *Keir Hardie, Radical and Socialist* (Weidenfeld and Nicolson, London, 1975), p. 151.

21. *Bradford Observer*, 14 May 1892 and 7 March 1892.

22. *Labour Union Journal*, 23 June 1892, *Bradford Observer*, 25 April 1892.

23. *Bradford Observer*, 8 March 1892; Brockway, *Socialism over 60 years*, p. 40; *Bradford Observer*, 2 July 1892.

24. *Labour Union Journal*, 2 June 1892; the Congregationalist quote appeared also in the *Labour Union Journal* of the same date. It was taken from the *Independent*, no date was cited.

25. *Workman's Times*, 28 August 1891.

26. At the general election of 1886, out of 9,500 voters, 6,598 cast ballots; in 1885 the figure had been 8,046 out of 9,500; *Bradford Observer*, 6 July 1892.

27. *Bradford Observer*, 5 July 1892.

5 THE EMPLOYERS' COUNTER-OFFENSIVE: BRISTOL AND HULL, 1892-3

In retrospect the summer of 1892 seems to mark the crest of the new unionist wave. It had swept Hardie, Burns and Havelock Wilson into Parliament; it had borne the emerging leaders of unskilled casual labour into battle with employers and frequently to victory along a flood tide of labour militancy. Now, however, the tide began to turn. Triumphs there still would be, most notable among them the formal establishment of an Independent Labour Party in January 1893. Defeat, however, predominated from this point forward for the new unionist movement. In Lancashire, the textile workers suffered a grave set-back, despite a strike of five months' duration; in the coalfields, the Miners' Federation of Great Britain brought out 400,000 men in its first industrial dispute — and lost. Two miners were shot dead in Featherstone during this dispute.

For Ben Tillett, too, the summer of 1892 marked an apogee, despite his electoral defeat in Bradford. After all, that had been something of a symbolic victory. And the victory in the London docks in 1889, as well as the successful organizing tour he had undertaken immediately thereafter, remained fresh in the public memory. Tillett now enjoyed a national reputation as a socialist new unionist leader. The organization which he headed was generally regarded as the quintessential new union. With the developing employers' counter-attack, however, both it and its leader were in for stormy, difficult times.

The parliamentary campaign in Bradford had been, in one sense, a desperate attempt to break the circle drawn by the Shipping Federation around the Dockers' Union. Dedicated to the extirpation of waterside unionism, the employers' organization maintained pressure by provoking a series of disputes directed now not against the outposts but the strongholds of union strength. For their part, the dockers' leaders hoped to avoid a confrontation. Given the renewed trade depression, they feared that the union could not match the employers' resources. They proved unable, however, to fend off two hammer-like blows which the Shipping Federation struck first in Bristol and then in Hull.

I

The Bristol dock strike is a revealing episode in Tillett's career. In keeping with the union's cautious policy, he initially opposed the action of the men; after they struck, he persisted in counselling prudence and moderation. As the strike developed and grew more bitter, however, his own rhetoric became sharper. 'If there is a "row" on', the dock director, Sidney Holland, once wrote to Tillett, 'you are the man to keep the men up to fighting'. This may or may not have been correct. Given time for reflection, Tillett's advice was almost always moderate. In the heat of battle, however, his pugnacious instincts were likely to lead to rhetorical flourishes which he came to regret. The Bristol affair illuminates this peculiar pattern. Before it was over, Tillett had been charged by the legal authorities with sedition.[1]

The dispute opened on 5 November 1892, when Bristol timber merchants hired non-union labourers to work alongside Dockers' Union members. This was viewed by the men as the thin end of a wedge; if the employers could open the closed shop, as for example in Cardiff, then the union's power would be broken, since there was always a surplus of labour. Consequently, they walked off the job, submitting their grievances to the local industrial arbitration board. The employers, however, refused to discuss the matter. Instead, they contracted with a representative of the Shipping Federation, Graham Hunter, to procure black-leg labour, declared a lock-out, and would not allow the men to return to work without the Shipping Federation ticket. The bulk of Bristol's dockers responded by downing tools. At this point, the local union officials realized they were out of their depth and wired to London. On 17 November, Tom McCarthy arrived in Bristol to assume command of the strike. Six days later the first blacklegs appeared. Feeling ran high: the following evening, when Graham Hunter's train came in, he was met at the railway station by an angry crowd armed with sticks. Truncheon-wielding police were needed to rescue him and to disperse the men. Tillett arrived the next day.

His first move was to attempt to calm the troubled waters. If antagonism did not reach a crisis point, a settlement still might be arranged. Addressing a crowd from the Narrow Quay in the Bristol Dock, he reminded his audience that he 'had had something to do with over 200 strikes and had learned never to lose his head' — a curious boast in the light of subsequent events. He added that the men must:

be well ordered and obey implicitly what their officials said, and look at the man who would set their authority at defiance as an enemy of the movement . . . Dockers in other parts of the country would promise to give their fellow workers in Bristol assistance if required (cheers). He wanted them, therefore, to show themselves worthy of that sympathy by simple, sober and prudent conduct.[2]

In addition to the national deterioration of economic conditions, which seemed to make a pacific policy necessary, Tillett may have had personal reasons for wishing to avoid a strike. As he confided in a letter to Burns, 'I don't feel equal to it from a physical standpoint.'[3] Moreover, Tom Mann had just given up his post as president of the union in order to devote himself to full-time socialist agitation on a wider front. Perhaps Tillett feared to engage the enemy without the assistance of his old friend. Having delivered his conciliatory speech he returned to London, no doubt hoping that it would not be necessary to intervene at Bristol again. McCarthy, however, stayed behind.

Despite Tillett's efforts, tensions did not abate but continued to rise. The strike spread beyond the docks to Sanders' Confectionery Works and the alum workers at Pochin's Factory; this suggested that the original impulse behind the new unionism had still not run its course, and indeed that a militant policy, if followed from the start, would probably have been more popular with the men, and possibly more effective than the cautious one Tillett pursued. Taking a leaf from the London strike of 1889, McCarthy organized processions through the Bristol streets, and weekly demonstrations at the Horsefair Grounds. Like Tillett, he feared the big battalions of the Shipping Federation, but concluded that he had no alternative. From the outset the employers demonstrated their intent to crush the union rather than to negotiate a compromise. Behind them lay the reservoir of black-leg labour supplied by the Federation through Graham Hunter, between 50 and 150 Bristol constables to protect them, and (after 22 union pickets were found guilty of assaulting strike-breakers) troops and cavalry as well.

With the dispute growing daily more bitter, the union executive in London voted to provide the Bristol men with strike pay. In addition, Tillett felt obliged to make periodic appearances in the city. He utilized the weekly demonstrations, however, to attempt to calm rather than inflame the men. 'Instead of holding a demonstration next Sunday', Tillett advised them on 11 December that they should attend:

the churches and chapels and pray that God might strike the

employers with a human touch, that he might strike sympathy and
nobleness into their hearts, to banish the selfishness, the blindness
and the greed that could not see the labourers' suffering.

He also attempted to defuse the explosive situation by asserting long-
range goals. The men should form a labour party 'for the purpose of
securing direct labour representation upon all public bodies which are
now systematically used in the interests of the employers against that of
the workers'.[4]

Such sober utterances, however, did not correspond at this point
with the general mood. For the men on strike, no work meant little or
no food, despite strike pay. 'The families were getting hungry and very
hungry at that', one participant recalled many years later. As would
soon become evident, they were becoming angry as well.'Yesterday
7,000 met in a place called "The Horsefair" and exhibited a great disposition to even greater violence than has been usual of late', W.R.
Barker, mayor of the town, wrote to H.H. Asquith at the Home Office.
On 12 December, sensing that trouble was imminent, he banned not
only the weekly gathering in the Horsefair Grounds, but McCarthy's
processions as well. But there were still men and women in Bristol who
remembered the Reform riots of 1831. On 18 December at an illegal
meeting in the Horsefair Grounds, local leaders referred to them, promising to 'teach the timber merchants that there should be a second or
third revolution if necessary'. McCarthy then called for a 'peaceable'
torchlight procession on the evening of 23 December. Tillett, who was
present as well, delivered perhaps the most provocative speech of his
career to date. He was 'very excited' according to a police spy, who
also attended the gathering. Tillett still wanted the men to follow their
leaders — but into battle if necessary. 'If it came to a fight', he cried,
'they could fight too, with fists or clubs, and if it came to guns they
could pick them up also.' Then came a remarkable outburst: 'I will if
necessary, defend my home and wages by any means, violent or
pacific', he vowed, and demanded that his audience take the oath with
him. It must have been a remarkable spectacle. Thousands of striking
dockers grimly repeating these words: 'if the necessity demands, I will
protect my home, my interests, my wages, by means of violent or
pacific measures'.[5]

Years later, Tillett was disposed to make light of the affair. The
speech at the Horsefair Grounds 'was a call for order and discipline', he
insisted in his autobiography. This will not do. A close reading of his
own version of the speech shows him arguing against individual acts of

terrorism, but in favour of mass action planned and directed by responsible leadership. 'For single individuals to create disturbance brought the movement into disrespect', he had warned.

> If the worst came to the worst, and violent action were necessary, let the leaders participate . . . and all act together . . . if intimidation were imperative then they should intimidate by the crowd . . . the leaders should organise it . . .

It is therefore hardly possible to agree with the *Bristol Mercury*'s startlingly sympathetic assessment of Tillett's speech on 19 December, as 'implying nothing outside the law'.[6]

Several factors probably prompted Tillett's outburst. For one, there could be no compromise with the Shipping Federation which was plainly bent on the union's destruction, a conclusion Tillett seems alternatively to have accepted and rejected. If ever there was a time in his career, however, when class warfare would have appeared inevitable to him, this was it. Equally important, Tillett, an emotional man, was deeply moved by the suffering of the men on strike and their families. 'Help me for the kiddies' sake', he had written to Burns as the strike entered its second month.

> I know that you have plenty of friends. I want the children fed, they are not to be punished. Some of the cases are really awful, and I shall not be able to eat my Christmas dinner unless I see that some of the youngsters are given some food.

Moreover, Bristol was Tillett's birthplace and early home. Is it possible that the scenes of hardship he witnessed during the strike reminded him of his own unhappy childhood? As Tillett surveyed his audience of desperate, hungry dockers, some of whom perhaps he had known as children, he may simply have been carried away by the drama of the moment. Throughout his career, friends and opponents alike remarked that his speeches often took their tone from the mood of the crowd he addressed. In Bristol, this had serious consequences.[7]

Immediately after the speech, Tillett returned to London, perhaps already doubting the wisdom of his words, and fearful of their effect. McCarthy, however, remained in Bristol and applied for permission to hold a torchlight procession on the night of 23 December. After some hesitation, the mayor agreed to allow the march, but along a different and less central route than had been demanded, and without torches.

McCarthy's response was predictable: 'We are sincerely desirous of keep-ing the peace of the city', he wrote to the chief superintendent of police in a letter printed on 19 December in the *Bristol Mercury*:

> but cannot consent to have our line of route marked out for us, and with all due respect will only give way when a stronger force than our own is pitted against us, and then only under strong protest.

What then transpired may best be described by the chief superinten-dent himself, James Cann, who, on the night in question, stationed fifty police (the 'stronger force') across the Bristol Bridge to halt the proces-sion. 'After arriving at the bridge', Cann recounted in a description of events forwarded to the Home Office:

> I heard a noise . . . and saw a large concourse of people coming up the Welsh Back at a running pace. There was no semblance of a pro-cession; it was all disorder . . . the crowd came on, hooting and making very great noise; . . . I judge there were not less than 5,000 people . . . They occupied the whole of the road . . . and foot passengers ran to get out of their way. I and other Police officers there held up our hands and shouted and endeavoured to stop them. But they broke through the rank of Police . . . I turned my head to the left to give instructions . . . and received a heavy blow on my chest which knocked me down . . . As I fell, eight or a dozen fell on top of me. I was underneath a number of men. I struggled and extri-cated myself as quick as I could, and I saw four constables lying on the ground by the side of me.
>
> During this time a large number of men, which I estimate at 400 or 500 had gone over us and up through Bridge Street. Some Police officers were carried up about fifteen yards into Bridge Street. I rallied the Policemen . . . The demeanour of the men was very threatening, standing in front of the Police with their fists clenched saying 'we will go through'.[8]

The street fighting which followed, and which lasted until midnight, was ended by the intervention of a force of Dragoons.

The authorities were determined to prevent further disruptions. All meetings of more than four persons were proscribed. The mayor even demanded − unsuccessfully − that a force of cavalry be permanently stationed in the town. In addition, he charged three local leaders and Tillett, who had not even been present on the evening in question, with sedition.

Tillett was accorded a hero's welcome when he returned to Bristol on 7 January for the preliminary hearing. He was met at the railway station by a brass band, and his carriage was unhitched and drawn through the streets by enthusiastic well-wishers. Strangely, his speech, before a crowd estimated at seven thousand, was brief, lasting only three minutes. Nevertheless, Tillett found time to vow that the labour movement would triumph 'come weal, come woe — were he to be hung, drawn and quartered'. He continued: 'There was a duty stern and relentless before them — a duty to organise, a duty to demand the full rights of a full life that God had given them. They must . . . make . . . the workers of Bristol the controllers of Bristol's destiny.' And the next day, despite a storm of snow and sleet, an estimated five thousand turned out to hear him promise again that:

> come what might, they would go through with the fight. The fight was not for a day, and not for a year, but for eternity . . . when their present strike had finished, their work would have just begun (hear, hear). It must not finish at trades unionism — it must not finish until the workers of all grades and degrees commanded absolutely the whole machinery of the state, the whole machinery of government, of production, control and distribution.[9]

Here was the revolutionary language and the socialist vision of an alternatively organized society so conspicuously absent during the Bradford campaign. Significantly Edward Aveling, Eleanor Marx's common-law husband, stood by Tillett's side on the platform, and addressed the crowd when the dockers' leader had finished. Yet Tillett's conversion to Marxist principles, if it may be classified as such, was shortlived.

He had no sooner left Bristol than he began to play down both his militancy and his socialism. He had participated in 'just over one thousand strikes', he informed the crowd at one rally, 'yet he had never to his knowledge incited man or woman to injure any other man or woman or child, or to damage property or anything of value'. Faced with a trial for sedition, he did not take advantage of the forum thus presented him to speak for socialist or trade unionist principles as had, for example, his friend, John Burns, in the famous 'History will absolve me' speech delivered from the dock after 'Bloody Sunday'. Rather he was successful in moving that the trial be transferred from Bristol to London, where the judge commended him for looking more innocent than anyone else in court. Bail, which had been set at £1,000, was paid by Sir John Hutton, a member of the London County Council; his lawyer, Lord Coleridge, was, according to Tillett, 'a gentle person of gentle voice, whose quiet tones and forensic ability were a great asset in my favour'. It was the defendant himself who won the case, however, by demonstrating that he could speak faster than any reporter or police shorthand expert could record. Tillett thus cast doubt upon the accuracy of the transcription of his speech and the jury acquitted him. Meanwhile, the strike in Bristol dragged on until the spring of 1893, when the men finally conceded defeat.[10]

II

While Tillett's trial was pending in London, trouble brewed in Hull. As it was a stronghold of the new unionism and of the Dockers' Union, it was a natural target for the Shipping Federation. Until 1893, however, the Federation could make little headway there, largely because the port's largest firm of shipowners, Thomas Wilson, Sons and Company, remained on excellent terms with the union. Indeed, on 21 November 1891, the dockers had gone so far as to honour their employer, C.H. Wilson, with a special dinner, at which he pledged 'to do all in his power to be of service in assisting the labour movement'. Tillett, who was present, responded in an excess of good fellowship, exclaiming that 'he sometimes wondered that out of such a system [capitalism] there could be developed such a Wilson with such a heart'. Two years later, Wilson's heart presumably had hardened; early in 1893 his firm had joined the Shipping Federation. This opened the way for an attack upon the Hull waterside unions which that organization was quick to exploit.[11]

On 20 March 1893 the Shipping Federation opened a 'Free Labour' Bureau in the Hull docks, promising preference of employment to all who registered with it. Strike talk began immediately. Tillett opposed it. Still dreading a confrontation, and perhaps fearing that a strike would jeopardize his case currently being tried in London, he hurried north to calm the men. The bureau 'would die of itself', he said, if only they took care to avoid it. By this time his message was predictable: 'they must not get angry and take any action unless they had definite instructions from their leaders'. Throughout the next two weeks, with a strike declaration hanging in the balance, his position remained the same. Hoping to avoid a contest, he issued a four-point programme for

the men:
1. Do not get excited.
2. Do nothing to provoke a conflict.
3. Go quietly to work . . . and do not allow the employers to place you at a disadvantage with the public.
4. Take no action without the consent of your leaders.

Such appeals for peace, however, were in vain. Although he was prepared to accept the 'free labour' bureaux in the hopes that the men would boycott them, and because a strike would be both costly and dangerous, Havelock Wilson, whose National Amalgamated Sailors' and Firemen's Union was also under attack, seemed anxious for a confrontation. On 3 April, Wilson called upon all Hull dockers to strike, for Hull gasworkers to declare a sympathetic walk-out, and for all other unskilled labourers in the city to down tools as well. The dock companies, however, moved before the men could act: on 5 April they imported 400 'free labourers' to unload ships owned by Messrs Wilson, Bailey and Leetham. Hostilities had commenced.[12]

The first day set the tone for the remainder of the strike. One of the 'free labourers', a Mr Dennis, had obtained a revolver which he fired at several pickets. Police rescued him from the barrage of stones which followed this rash act, and placed him in a shed for his own protection. When a Federation official later came to remove him, Dennis assumed that the man was an angry docker, and shot at him too, though again missing his target. The episode did not bode well, and not surprisingly Hull magistrates were soon calling for reinforcements. On 6 April, 160 Royal Scots, 90 Dragoons, two gunboats and numerous extra police were despatched to the city.

In the face of these measures the union rank and file responded with nearly unanimous support for the strike. Tillett, who was 'deeply sorry that a fortnight's undeviating and exhausting effort to avert this calamity' had failed, now reiterated that there could be no regular strike pay. Yet a secret ballot taken the day of the troops' arrival showed 3,500 dockers in favour and five opposed to downing tools. Still, Tillett was prepared to concede the main issue – the closed shop – rather than bring matters to a head. Almost one year before, he had supported the Cardiff strike to maintain a union monopoly of labour at the docks. Now, in a port where the union was much stronger and determined to fight, he would not countenance one. He suggested that the dispute be submitted to a government arbiter, but the employers refused. On 8 April he proposed to C.H. Wilson that union and 'free labourers' work together, provided that the latter received no special privileges. Wilson rejected this overture as well, thereby clarifying the nature of the conflict. The employers would not compromise; they intended not merely to establish 'free labour' bureaux, but to destroy the union. As in Bristol, the men were locked out. There was no alternative but to fight.

The question now became where to locate the scene of battle. For a moment it appeared that the strike would spread to other ports. In Cardiff, ship repairers downed tools in sympathy with the men of Hull; in Middlesbrough dockers threatened to do likewise; in Hartlepool, the Seamen's and Firemen's Union promised action; among the Tyne ports and in Swansea, dockers were willing to strike; and in London, Will Thorne predicted mass walk-outs. Tillett too threatened national action. 'They were on the eve of a very important move', he informed a Hull audience. 'It only required a little agitation to block every port in the kingdom.'[13]

Writing to his old comrade, John Burns, now seated in the House of Commons, Tillett took a militant line. 'The position here is damnable, damnable', he wrote. 'It is a case of sheer brute force against our common right to combine.' The intervention of the military was particularly galling. He wanted Burns to raise the matter in Parliamet, but on 12 April it was Keir Hardie who rose to move for the question to be put. Only seven members supported him. Tillett rushed back to London to meet with all the sympathetic members in the House, and to discuss with Burns whether the strike should be extended to other ports. Together they attended a meeting in Toynbee Hall of officials from Tillett's union and from the Seamen's and Firemen's Union which favoured 'a fight all along the line'. Havelock Wilson had recently promised to 'light the torch at London, Glasgow, Liverpool and Cardiff in order to give the Federation something to do and prevent them from collecting men to send to Hull'. Yet Wilson was prevailed upon to wait. The meeting was closed to journalists; but from Burns's diary we know that he succeeded in postponing a general strike by suggesting a national conference of the unions involved 'to discuss the whole situation'.[14]

That was on Tuesday, 12 April. During the rest of the week speculation mounted that a general strike was imminent. Certainly the Seamen's and Firemen's Union seemed to want one. It was already blocking ships in Cardiff and Newport. By 17 April it had sent telegrams to thirty-three other ports demanding sympathetic walk-outs. In London, 'seventy-six branches of the shipping trade' promised to strike if the 'free labourers' were not withdrawn from Hull, and a meeting of 2,000 dockers resolved, with only four dissentient votes, 'That we, the workers of the Victoria and Albert Docks in conjunction with the Seamen's and Firemen's and Coal Porters' Unions are in favour of a national strike'. Tillett, who had remained in London only long enough to win an acquittal from the Bristol charges of the previous winter, raced back to Hull on the 18th, in time to deliver an impassioned exhortation:

> that day, right up and down the length and breadth of England, the dockers were preparing for what would be one of the greatest strikes in history. The strike of the London dockers would sink into insignificance by comparison . . . when constitutional methods were useless, they must resort to the fierce arbitrament of a strike that should be widespread . . . that should shake even the government . . . There was no other way.[15]

Or was there? On the evening of the 18th, John Burns and J.H. Wilson met with their chief antagonist, C.H. Wilson and several government officials in the House of Commons. This represented a significant gesture for C.H. Wilson, who was supposed to abide by a statement of 11 April issued jointly by the Shipping Federation and Hull shipowners: 'No further communications should be held with the union leaders.' It seemed to indicate that a negotiated settlement was possible after all. As a result, Tillett's strategy shifted once again. The shipowners might be forced to relent − if only the men could hold out.

Consolidating the position in Hull, rather than extending the strike, was now imperative. National action must be postponed. Fund-raising for the Hull dockers took priority. 'Fellow workers', ran one appeal signed by Burns, Mann, Havelock Wilson, George Shipton, Clem Edwards, Michael Davitt and Tillett, 'Prompt, continuous and liberal help is required for the men in Hull.' The response was generous. The Railway Servants, Amalgamated Society of Engineers, Yorkshire Miners, Lancashire Miners and Sheffield Stove Grate Workers among others sent contributions. Funds were raised at public meetings in Leicestershire, Lincolnshire and Nottingham. The *Clarion* solicited £180 8s 3d from its readers. Tillett himself asked for money at meetings in Barnsley and Bradford. To the men of Hull he promised never to yield so long as supplies continued to come in. At a May Day rally he repeated the message of an American Civil War officer to General Sherman: 'Hold the fort, for I am coming.'[16]

Meanwhile, Hull was in an uproar. The strike had been extended to include all ships in the docks, not merely those affected by the original dispute. One thousand blacklegs performed the labour which the men now refused. They were protected by both police and military. Two divisions of cavalry daily paraded the city streets, and two gunboats were drawn up in the Humber. Opportunities for provocations were plentiful: 'stone throwing by the unionists and baton charges by the police were to be a normal feature of Hull life'. Local gunsmiths did a brisk business in revolvers, knuckle-dusters and 'life-preservers'. As W.H. Laren, a major in the Royal Dragoons reported to his superiors in London: 'The situation is acute.' The city was a tinder box, and on the evening of 24 April it literally burst into flame. Fire raged through the docks, destroying the Citadel Hostel and Wade's Timber Yards. When the fire brigade arrived, they discovered their hoses had been cut. 'Vast crowds collected on all sides', Captain A.H. Arlington, the gunboat commander, wrote in a despatch to the Admiralty, 'but their sympathy was certainly not in favour of those who were trying to put the fire out, and not one amongst them came to our assistance.' Arson by the men was suspected, though Tillett promptly claimed that blacklegs had set the blaze either purposely or carelessly with cigarettes. To himself he admitted that the situation was 'a serious one'. 'Grave position owing to fire. Grave misapprehensions as to cause of fire', he confided to his diary.[17] Other entries referred to arson, battles between pickets and police, rail lifting and attempted train wrecking. These incidents, the presence of the military, Hardie's questions in the House of Commons, and the employers' uncompromising stance all helped to rivet national attention upon the Hull dispute.

Inevitably talk of a national strike began once more. Wilson and W. Sprow of the Seamen's and Firemen's Union had not ceased to demand one. Burns's diary reveals that Clem Edwards, a member of the Dockers' Union executive was not entirely unsympathetic to the proposal, and that Tom Mann was only persuaded to oppose it at the last minute. Burns cleverly urged everyone with whom he discussed the issue to act as though a national stoppage was imminent, so that the Shipping Federation could not send all its blacklegs to Hull, but to vote against the motion at the national conference which was to meet on 22 April. On that date the opponents of the resolution scored a decisive victory, defeating the proposals by 45 to 27.[18]

No record of the debate survives, though it was reported to have lasted 8½ hours. Aside from Burns's references to Mann, Tillett, Edwards, Wilson and Will Thorne, we do not even know who were its participants. Yet it must have been the occasion for a fierce, but unsuccessful, attack upon the moderate policy, which had so far governed the new unionist response to the employers' counter-offensive. Burns, as usual, spoke 'vigorously against the policy of attempting for so small an issue so great a risk'. As we have seen, this was the common argument employed by the moderates. In addition, he probably argued that the unions affected had no funds for strike pay, that national action would alienate the popular support upon which the Hull dockers depended, and that the high rate of unemployment made blacklegging virtually inevitable. Tillett now agreed. He held that, as the strike had to be fought, it should be a defensive war of attrition limited to one port. Financial and moral support from sympathetic outsiders would eventually force the employers to temper their attitudes.[19]

Probably the advocates of caution were correct. Yet one would like to know more. Who were the 27 delegates who favoured a national strike? Did they represent a single organization, the Sailors' and Firemen's Union, or pockets of support for national action in several unions? Were they more or less close to the rank and file than the 45 who voted against them? In the absence of such knowledge there can be no final verdict on the feasibility of a national strike.

That there was significant support for the militant approach is evident. At a Victoria Park rally attended by 60,000, and intended to support the conference decision of the preceding day, 'a large minority . . . threatened to move an amendment in favour of a national strike'. Four days later, a meeting of 2,000 London dockers demanded 'a national strike from one end of the country to the other', and during the following week more protest rallies were held. In London's Victoria Dock, labourers working on the *Massachusetts* actually downed tools, hoping by their example to spark national action. Tillett hurried to the scene, determined to bring the men back to work. They had struck, he asserted, 'well knowing that there would be no funds to support them, and that it was necessary if the men at Hull were to be kept organized that they should have the services of every available person'. Against a rising chorus of dissent he attempted to continue:

He was not going to tell them in London whether he was in favour of a national and universal strike ('Oh, oh' and a voice, 'You are afraid of it'). He had his own convictions about such a course being pursued. (Renewed cries of 'You are afraid of it' and uproar.) Those who said he was afraid of it spoke very correctly. ('Oh, oh'.) He was afraid of a national strike (groans) because there would be no national strike, as the men were not ready and the trade was not ready (cries of 'we are ready' followed by cheers) — and if one section of the workers demanded a national strike it would be a fizzle ('Oh, oh' and uproar). The Hull strikers had charged him to say that the dockers of London could help them best by sticking to their work. (Groans.) No level headed or responsible man who knew the facts of the case would recommend a strike. (Disorder and cries of 'Get down'.) By striking, they would be injuring their union . . . how many of them would come out? (Cries of 'All'.) Not a bit of it. (Groans, and a voice: 'You are playing the Masters' game.') No; it was the men who endeavoured to force a panic strike who were doing that. (A voice: 'A strike made you, and if you don't fetch us out the union will be smashed up.')

'At this point', recorded one observer, 'the disorder became too great for Mr Tillett to make himself heard and he had to cease speaking.'[20]

There is another point to consider here. It is hard to imagine how the consequences of a national strike could have been more dangerous for the Dockers' Union than what eventually transpired. Faced with the grim determination of Hull's dockers not to yield, the employers modified their tactics — but not their goal, which was still to destroy waterside unionism in England's third largest port. On 15 May, Burns recorded laconically in his diary that he had 'prevailed upon C.H. Wilson to negotiate direct with Strike Committee and thus terminate strike'. In fact, it would appear that the employers played a deeper game. They were prepared to end hostilities for the moment, since the 'free labour' bureaux could be utilized to undermine the unions once work had resumed. The limits of the union's defensive posture were thereby revealed. Tillett had been prepared to accept the bureaux from the outset — so long as the employers would hire organized and 'free labour' without 'preference or prejudice'. After almost six weeks of deprivation and hardship, the men had gained nothing. Tillett's formulation did not represent the softening of Shipping Federation attitudes that he and other advocates of caution had expected. Yet wishful thinking on the part of the Dockers' Union executive transformed it into a major concession, and the basis for a settlement. At first Tillett demurred: did he resent the interference of Burns and Tom Mann who also seemed instrumental in arranging the 'new' situation? If so, a sharp note from Burns brought him around. 'Let there be no fooling about the strike and its termination', wrote the man once famous for waving a red flag, 'and don't allow personal feelings to stand in the way of settlement . . . Settle at once ere [?] disaster awaits you and your men secede.'[21]

But what could have been more disastrous than the 'compromise' signed by Tillett and three local leaders on 18 May? By its provisions, the 'free labour' bureaux were established on the docks, though its members would not receive preferential treatment: union officials would not be allowed to visit the workplace while the men were labouring; foremen and shipping clerks would not be allowed to join the union; and a whole series of other workers 'being relatively in the same position', would likewise 'sever their connection with the Dockers' Union'. Despite the guarantee, dockers holding the 'free labour' ticket were immediately accorded preferential treatment. The union men could not face the prospect of another fight, and a rush to register with the 'free labour' bureaux ensued. Trade unionism 'in our strongest citadel', as Tillett had referred to Hull only eight days before signing the agreement, was broken. Or, as Blatchford put it in the *Clarion* on 22 May, 'The result of the Hull dock strike, is virtually a defeat for the men.' Its effects were to be long lasting. The closed shop would not reappear in the Hull docks until 1966.[22]

III

The Bristol and Hull disputes are significant for showing that the tide had begun to turn against the dockers as it had against other new unionists during late 1892 and early 1893. The strikes are significant too for what they reveal about the dockers' leader, Ben Tillett, at the height of his reputation as a socialist labour militant.

During the first three years of the 1890s, Tillett fought the dockers' battle to the best of his ability, often at considerable personal risk, and almost always against great odds. By 1893, Tillett had become convinced that the labour and socialist movements were inseparable and had done his best to convert all trade unionists to this view. It is also true, however, that by 1893 Tillett had demonstrated idiosyncracies which could not but call his commitments, loyalties and judgement into question. This is particularly true of his conduct during the strikes in Bristol and Hull.

There was, for example, Tillett's unedifying tendency to utterly reverse himself — not once, but several times. He had begun the Bristol strike by counselling prudence, but during its intermediate stage had demanded of his willing followers that they swear an insurrectionary oath. And he had concluded by disclaiming in court, against all the evidence, any revolutionary intent. During the Hull strike, too, he had waxed militant and moderate in turns, first opposing any strike at all, later broaching the possibility of a national strike 'which should shake even the government', only to become finally one of its foremost opponents. Such contradictory behaviour, disturbing in itself, also could not help but bring into question Tillett's honesty and intentions. For example, could one accept his professions of militancy after his performance in court when he was being tried for sedition?

Tillett was a complex man, faced with complex problems. There is no single, simple explanation of his disconcerting predilection for changing course — a tendency which was to confound both friends and enemies, not only during the new unionist period, but throughout his career. No doubt, Tillett's pugnacious instincts often prompted his most blood-curdling pronouncements, which in calmer moments he preferred to forget or play down. No doubt, he was moved by the intransigence and cruelty of his foes, and by the hardships born by the rank and file and their families, to transports of fury and thence to dire threats of retribution which he had not the power to fulfil. Yet Tillett's peculiar temperament affords only a partial explanation of his inconsistent behaviour.

The fact is that the new unionists faced an insoluble problem in 1892-3. The dockers simply did not have the resources to meet the employers' counter-offensive head on, especially given the preferential treatment which the Shipping Federation usually received from the government. This was a calculation which Tillett had already made, though on occasion he seemed to ignore it. It helps to explain the emphasis upon 'solidification rather than extension', as Mann had put it even in 1890, and the cautious policy favoured by Tillett, Burns, Clem Edwards and the rest when J.H. Wilson raised the possibility of a national strike in support of the Hull port-workers in 1893. Tillett might threaten a national strike or other militant actions; usually, however, such statements were bluffs, designed to intimidate the masters. Except for those not infrequent moments when Tillett lost his head and allowed his combative instincts to take over, they were not intended to be carried out.

Most labour leaders attempt to bluff their enemies at one time or another. And all such bluffs depend upon the real strength which labour leaders in fact command. Thus labour leaders tend to develop ambivalent attitudes towards the rank and file. Whatever their commitment to rank-and-file democracy, union officials cannot help but wish for the men to perform on cue; to demonstrate solidarity and militancy

when necessary; to remain acquiescent otherwise and not jeopardize
delicate negotiations or agreements which the leaders have painfully
hammered out with the management. This common problem for trade
union leaders also helps to explain Tillett's conduct during the Hull
and Bristol strikes.

Tillett never resolved his contradictory relationship with the docker
rank and file. On the one hand, he knew it, understood it and sympathized with it as few other labour leaders did. Neither Mann, nor Burns,
nor even McCarthy had ever laboured as a casual docker; Tillett had.
Throughout his life, and especially during the new unionist era, he
proved capable of speaking for such men. He, better than anyone,
could translate the dockers' aspirations and resentments into inspirational oratory. Tillett was one of British labour history's great agitators
and organizers. On the other hand, Tillett developed towards the rank
and file a condescending attitude, which at times verged upon contempt.
During the Hull and Bristol disputes this peculiar dialectic seems particularly apparent.

Tillett leaves the overwhelming impression during those two battles
of being concerned above all with controlling the union rank and file.
Nearly all his speeches refer to the necessity of obedience to the union
executive. Even the oration which was judged seditious contained a
plea for maintaining the authority of the leadership. Tillett was arguing
there in favour of violence – but violence directed by the leaders of
the union. At that moment he seems to have conceived of the union
as an army engaged in a war between classes, and of himself as an
officer directing his troops. It is worth recalling, perhaps, that one of
Tillett's heroes was Napoleon. If Tillett seems to have oscillated
between militancy and moderation, here is the thread linking both
attitudes. His most ferocious declarations reveal the desire for control;
so, obviously, do those exhorting the dockers to remain calm.

IV

The impact of the débâcle in Hull could not be limited to a single port.
Whether Tillett's attempts to avoid engaging the Shipping Federation
had been correct, his fears about the implications of a major defeat at
their hands proved justified. Membership dropped: 'Since the big strike
a number of men had run away from the Union', Tillett reported at a
meeting in Wapping. 'There were chaps who were desirous of throwing
mud on the organisation and grumbling because more was not done by

the leaders.' Local officials neglected their duties: 'The whole responsibility had devolved upon the Central Office and Executive Council', Tillett complained at the 1893 annual delegate meeting. Dissension among the leadership surfaced as well. Burns had already begun to drift away; in November, after he had refused to participate in a Hull recruiting drive, the Dockers' Union executive council voted to suspend his parliamentary subsidy. Perhaps more significantly, Tom McCarthy, Tillett's close friend, protested that the general secretary had instituted 'one man rule' over the union.[23] The continuing trade depression intensified the dockers' miseries. By 29 December 1894 Tillett was writing to *The Times*:

> In the London docks particularly the labourers are losing all the slight gains they won during the dock strike. Wages are being reduced, the four hours minimum ignored, and a systematic fleecing of the wages for actual time worked takes place.

The Bristol and Hull dock strikes spelled the end of an era. The employers' counter-offensive, spearheaded by the Shipping Federation, had successfully turned aside the challenge of the new unionism. Minor disputes might still flare up, but the dockers would not take part in another major strike for nearly twenty years. A chapter in Tillett's life had ended as well. With the exception of the Bradford campaign, and his duties as an alderman on the London County Council, his attention since 1887 had been focused almost exclusively upon the flash points in the 'Labour War'. Now, as the socialist and labour movements entered a new, less dramatic phase, Tillett followed suit. He spoke less frequently in the open air to striking dockers, but appeared more often in committee rooms, at official meetings and, unfortunately for him, in court. He became embroiled in the factional disputes which beset the political and industrial wings of the labour movement.

Notes

1. Tillett Collection, MSS 74/3/1/32, Holland to Tillett, 5 January 1895.
2. *Bristol Mercury*, 26 November 1892.
3. John Burns Papers, Add. MS 46285, Tillett to Burns, 6 December 1892.
4. *Bristol Mercury*, 12 September 1892.
5. Tillett Collection, MSS 74/6/2/84/1-4, W. Pearce to Ian Mackay, 26 January 1951; Public Record Office (PRO), HO 144/A50898A, W.R. Barker to H.H. Asquith, 12 December 1892; *The Times*, 10 January 1893; Public Record Office, HO 144/A50898A, 'Deposition of John Short, Detective Inspector'.

6. Tillett, *Memories and Reflections* (J. Long, London, 1931), p. 163; *Prosecution of Ben Tillett, Speech delivered in Horsefair, Bristol, 18 December 1892* (Bristol, 1893). This was Tillett's version of the speech, printed as a pamphlet by the Dockers' Union during his trial.

7. Burns Papers Add. MS 46285, Tillett to Burns, 6 December 1892.

8. Public Record Office, HO 144/A50898A, 'Deposition of James Cann, Chief Superintendent'.

9. *The Times*, 9 January 1893; *Bristol Mercury*, 9 January 1893.

10. *Bristol Mercury*, 9 January 1893; Tillett, *Memories and Reflections*, p. 165; at any rate, this is how Tillett's daughter, Mrs Jeanette Davis, explained her father's acquittal to me.

11. *Eastern Morning News*, 21 November 1891; Clem Edwards, in 'The Hull Shipping Dispute', *Economic Journal*, vol. III (1893), argued that Wilson only joined the Federation after being pressurized by marine insurance companies and other shipowners. See also Raymond Brown, *Waterfront Organisation in Hull, 1870-1900* (University of Hull Press, Hull, 1972), pp. 66-87, upon which I base much of my narrative.

12. *Hull Daily News*, 23 March 1893; *Eastern Morning News*, 3 April 1893; Brown, *Waterfront Organisation in Hull*, pp. 70-1.

13. *Eastern Morning News*, 10 April 1893 and 11 April 1893.

14. Burns Papers, Add. MS 46285, Tillett to Burns, 11 April 1893; *The Times*, 8 April 1893.

15. *Eastern Morning News*, 18 April 1893.

16. *The Times*, 6 May 1893; Dock, Wharf, Riverside and General Labourers' Union, *Minutes of Annual Delegate Meetings* 1893; *Clarion*, 27 May 1893; Tillett Collection, MSS 74/7/2/1, diary entries 26 April, 29 April, 1 May 1893.

17. Brown, *Waterfront Organisation in Hull*, pp. 74-5; Public Record Office, HO 144/X41472, Laren to Adjutant General, 17 April 1893, Arlington to Secretary of the Admiralty, 24 April 1893; Tillett Collection, MSS 74/7/2/1. This is a scrapbook of clippings concerning the Hull strike, and occasional notes in Tillett's hand.

18. Burns Papers, Add. MS 46313, see diary entries for 15, 16 and 22 April 1893.

19. Burns Papers, Add MS 46313, diary entry for 22 April 1893; these were the general arguments against a strike advanced on 6 May 1893 by the editors of the *Workman's Times*, who had close connections with the Dockers' Union.

20. *Workman's Times*, 29 April 1893; *Eastern Morning News*, 28 April 1893; *Western Gazette*, 2 May 1893.

21. Tillett Collection, MSS 74/3/1/5, Burns to Tillett, 15 May 1893.

22. Brown, *Waterfront Organisation in Hull*, pp. 87-8.

23. *Weekly Star*, 29 July 1893; Dock, Wharf, Riverside and General Labourers' Union, *Minutes of Annual Delegate Meetings* (1894).

6 DISCORD IN THE LABOUR MOVEMENT, 1893-9

I

Tillett's experiences as a new unionist had made him into a labour militant. A temperament so restless and combative as his generally wanted to meet fire with fire. Hence his nearly insurrectionary appeals in Bristol, his calls for a national strike during the Hull dispute, and his whirlwind parliamentary campaign in Bradford. These battles showed Tillett at the height of his powers as a labour agitator and spokesman of the socialist movement. At the same time, however, they revealed his tendencies towards authoritarianism and emotionalism. Tillett was too mercurial ever to be predictable, even during a period when he had carved out a prominent role in the socialist new unionist crusade. During the next six years the pressure of events was to alter his outlook drastically, inducing him to abandon this hard-won position. In 1893 he was about to enter perhaps the most personally trying period of his career.

The background to Tillett's parliamentary bid, and likewise to his role in the bitter conflict with the Shipping Federation, had been his participation in the continual manoeuvring and political struggle within the labour movement as a whole. There the battle was primarily against the representatives of the older and more pacific craft unions whose political links were usually with the Liberals, or it was against those new unionists who, for whatever reasons, accepted 'Lib-Lab' arguments. At the annual meetings of the Trades Union Congress, Tillett played an increasingly important role as one who favoured cutting all ties with the Liberals and establishing an independent labour party with a socialist programme. By 1892, he was sufficiently well known and respected by the TUC delegates to win election to the standing orders committee, and to the influential parliamentary committee. The latter was the formal political arm of the trade union movement. Hitherto, and especially under the influence of Henry Broadhurst, it had devoted itself to strengthening labour's connection with the Liberals. It was, however, the body which could best advance the programme of the new unionist militants, if only they could capture it. And, in 1892, with Burns, Will Thorne, J.H. Wilson and Tillett on the committee, they obviously intended just that.

The great aim of the new unionists was to swing the TUC behind the demand for an independent labour party. This might be achieved, if the parliamentary committee could be induced to recommend it. Accordingly, Tillett, who attended his first parliamentary committee meeting on 9 November 1892 at the City Hall in Glasgow — this was some months after his Bradford campaign, and shortly before the strike in Bristol — chose to serve on a subcommittee whose purpose was to prepare a scheme for assisting independent labour candidates.[1]

Simultaneously, plans for the formation of an Independent Labour Party were carried forward outside the committee. A central figure in these planning stages, and the Independent Labour Party's guiding force once the plans had come to fruition, was Keir Hardie, the Scottish miners' leader. He resembled Tillett, in that he had come to socialism gradually and by way of the Liberal Party; but he was unlike him in most other respects. A sturdy man, with a full beard, he appears in his photographs to resemble a biblical prophet: and for him, socialism was always a creed best expressed in the language of the Sermon on the Mount. He was also a canny politician who in 1892, when Tillett was unsuccessfully contesting West Bradford, won the parliamentary representation of West Ham. In the past his path and Tillett's had crossed; in the future they would cross swords. In January 1893, however, they met in Bradford to congratulate each other and other socialist and labour leaders present at the founding conference of the national Independent Labour Party.

In view of the attention paid to the words and actions of the later Independent Labour Party stalwarts and Fabians at the conference, it is worth recording that Tillett was an equally central figure there. The location of the meeting was itself testimony to the strength of the local working-class movement for which Tillett had been standard bearer only six months previously. His position as general secretary of the Dockers' Union, and above all his membership on the TUC parliamentary committee, and its subcommittee dealing with independent labour representation, enabled him to push the trade union movement toward the Independent Labour Party from within. Consequently, the views Tillett expressed at the Bradford convention were of particular importance.

Tillett is famous for having declared at the founding conference of the Independent Labour Party that:

he wished to capture the Trade Unionists of this country, a body of men well organised who paid their money and were Socialists at their work every day and not merely on the platform, who did not shout for blood red revolution and when it came to revolution sneaked under the nearest bed.

Later in the proceedings, Tillett went further, deriding the socialists in contrast with Conservative-led English workers.

Not far from this place was a body of Lancashire operatives who were ruled by Tory leaders, but for real, vital, effective work there was not a Socialist Party in the whole world who could show such effective organisation as those men could (cheers). Therefore he did not want the men who were more advanced to deride and insult such a body . . . If the Labour Party was to be called the Socialist Labour Party he would repudiate it.

These statements were interpreted both at the time and later as simple chauvinistic attacks upon the continental socialists, whom at one point in the conference Tillett was to term mere 'harebrained chatterers and magpies'. Although he made enemies by these declarations, Tillett had chosen his ground carefully. His motives were more complex than might have been supposed.[2]

It must not be forgotten that as the Independent Labour Party was meeting in Bradford, Bristol's dockers were on strike. Tillett wanted, and obtained, from the conference a resolution supporting the strike; but he wanted also hard cash for the strike fund. The fledgeling party was in no position to make such a donation, but the trade union delegates in attendance were. This is a partial explanation for Tillett's appeal to the Tory-led coal miners and textile workers. He hoped they would come to the financial aid of the Bristol dockers.

There is another explanation. Tillett understood the necessity of trade union support for the Independent Labour Party, if it was to fulfil its political aspirations. As a member of the TUC parliamentary committee he was strategically placed to work for it. His attack upon continental socialism must be seen in this context. He wanted to underline the British origins and orientation of the Independent Labour Party in order to attract the support of trade unionists who distrusted the Social Democratic Federation and other socialist organizations in Britain for their foreign-born membership and links with continental socialism. He was trying to make easier his own work in the TUC parliamentary committee, trying perhaps to overcome his reputation as a firebrand with its older members.[3]

Whatever his intentions, however, Tillett's Bradford performance did permanent damage to his reputation among certain socialists, who were disturbed not only by its chauvinism but also by its opportunism. This was a charge which was to dog Tillett throughout his career. Here it may be said in partial mitigation that personal advancement, at least, does not seem to have been his primary goal in 1893. Tillett's interjections in the conference were poorly conceived and, no doubt, revealing; but they had been made on behalf of striking dockers and primarily in order to strengthen links between the trade unions and the movement for independent labour representation. Of course, they did not bode well. Tillett's opportunism became increasingly blatant in later years, and increasingly selfish. At the 1893 Independent Labour Party foundation conference, Tillett revealed tendencies which finally came to overshadow, in many minds, his achievements and constructive efforts. Perhaps this is one reason why historians have paid so little attention to his activities there.

In the immediate aftermath of the conference, however, Tillett's efforts to strengthen the movement among the trade unions for independent working-class representation in the House of Commons continued unabated. Two weeks after leaving Bradford, he presented the subcommittee of the TUC parliamentary committee with a draft proposal for assisting independent labour candidates. Two months later it was submitted to the entire parliamentary committee which 'after amending the suggestions in several points the secretary was instructed to issue to the trades'; and some six months after that, in September 1894, Tillett was sufficiently satisfied with the final product to introduce it on behalf of the parliamentary committee before the assembled TUC.

The basis for his proposal was a political fund to be administered to independent labour candidates by elected representatives of the unions that contributed to it. The Congress passed not merely this proposal, but an amendment to it, moved by James MacDonald of the Social Democratic Federation (who is not to be confused with the future Prime Minister, James Ramsay MacDonald), stipulating that 'Candidates receiving financial assistance must pledge themselves to support the principle of collective ownership and control of all the means of production and distribution . . . ' In addition, a 'socialist resolution' was carried committing the Congress to work for the 'nationalisation of the land, mines, minerals, royalty rents and the whole means of production, distribution and exchange'. In celebration:

the victors leaped to their feet, and led by Ben Tillett, who waved his sombrero aloft, gave out such rousing cheers for the 'social Revolution' as never shook those ancient walls since Cromwell's day.

It seemed as though the goal of the Independent Labour Party, to link the trade union and socialist movements, had been realized.[4]

In fact, the socialist foothold in the TUC was tenuous, and John Burns for one was determined to dislodge it. His motives remain obscure. He voted for the socialist amendment to Tillett's motion at the 1894 TUC, but had refused earlier to attend the Independent Labour Party conference at Bradford. It would appear that he regarded the leaders of the Independent Labour Party, including his old associates Mann and Tillett, not as comrades, but as rivals to be discredited. As the Member for Battersea, in which working-class Liberalism remained strong, and to which he had accommodated, he may have regarded the strengthening of an Independent Labour Party with TUC support to be dangerous to his own political standing. He may have shared the resentment of certain old-style craft unionists for the middle-class socialists who now could influence TUC policy through new unionist members of the Independent Labour Party like Tillett, Mann, Hardie and others. He took the 1893 TUC as an occasion to attack them for forming a 'bogus' independent party and for accepting 'Tory Gold' from Maltman Barry, an acquaintance of H.H. Champion with ties to the Conservative Party; (the intention here was to remind his audience of an earlier occasion, in 1886, when Barry, then a Conservative agent, had helped to fund two Social Democrat candidates in London, hoping thereby to split the anti-Tory vote. When the terms of this transaction, which had been sanctioned by Hyndman and Champion, became public, many socialists thought that their leaders had been the catpaws of the Conservative Party.)

Now, however, Tillett was quick to defend the Independent Labour Party from Burns's charges. 'First of all, it was a poor reward', he wrote to Burns from Belfast where the TUC was meeting:

> that after the severe fight at last Glasgow Congress, after a very anxious time in getting the resolution into form and adopted by the Parliamentary Committee in the hour of victory for our cause you should (or you appeared to me and to others) attack the very men who had been instrumental in inducing the Congress to accept the principle of Independent Labourism.

He went on to disclaim any connection with Barry or Champion, and

to promise that 'every prominent man in the Socialist Labour Movement' would echo Burns in repudiating them. Finally, he warned that:
'our common enemies and the reactionaries within our movement will
sneer at our incompatibilities of temper, or our incapacity to experi-
ment in the elementary forms of brotherliness'. Tillett's letter, however, was of no avail. Burns had already embarked upon the course
which eventually led him to take office in the Liberal governments of
Campbell-Bannerman and Asquith. He was determined to rid the TUC
of its most important members in the Independent Labour Party.[5]

Burns's opportunity arose immediately after the 1894 Congress. At
an October meeting of the parliamentary committee, he successfully
moved that a subcommittee (upon which he would sit) should be
appointed to revise the standing orders of the TUC. The three recommendations which resulted from its deliberations were clearly intended
to weaken the socialist voice in the Congress. They were to end the
representation of trades councils — which were socialist strongholds —
in the Congress; to establish proportional representation — which would
permit the conservative coal and cotton unions to dominate the
Congress; and to exclude as a delegate to the TUC anyone who was not
either working at his trade or employed as a permanent salaried official
of his society. This last proposal was obviously aimed at Keir Hardie
and Tom Mann (president and secretary, respectively, of the Independent Labour Party), as Hardie himself explained in the *Labour Leader*
on 29 December.

> The only change such a rule would make would be the exclusion
> from future Congresses of the following: Henry Broadhurst, John
> Burns, Thomas Burt, Keir Hardie and Tom Mann . . . the Amalga-
> mated Society of Engineers . . . pays Mr Burns £100 a year for repre-
> senting their interests in Parliament. He would, therefore . . . be still
> eligible to go to Congress. Mr Burt is still an official of the North-
> umberland Miners Union. The new rule, therefore has been formed
> for the express purpose of excluding Broadhurst, Mann and myself.

Burns shrewdly realized that Broadhurst, who did not belong to the
Independent Labour Party, was too anti-socialist to fight the subcommittee with any effectiveness. When the time came to vote, the parliamentary committee divided evenly. After three days of struggle,
however, the chairman, David Holmes, secretary of the Cotton Weavers
Union, cast a deciding ballot in favour of Burns's proposals, despite an
unwritten rule that the parliamentary committee chairman should never

tip the scales when rules were being voted upon. 'There were as many shortcomings, as much wire pulling and as much cant in the Socialist movement as anywhere else', Tillett lamented afterwards.[6]

He had, of course, worked assiduously on the anti-Burns side. Congress's instructions to the parliamentary committee had been only to reorganize the method by which matters were to be brought forward for discussion. His article for the *Labour Leader* on 22 December concentrated on this issue: 'If any Philadelphia lawyer can read into the new instructions any direct connection between them and the Congress instructions . . . I am mistaken.' With regard to Burns's charge that the present system allowed ambitious middle-class socialists and professional agitators to dominate the TUC via the trades councils, Tillett was contemptuous: 'Trades unionism is in danger', he agreed, but 'the dangerous persons are [those] posing as the tin gods of liberty'.[7]

When the 1895 Congress met in Cardiff, Tillett launched an intensely personal attack: 'No more abolition of the House of Lords,' he cried, glaring at Burns:

> no more statements in Trafalgar Square against the propertied classes and their domination; no more opposition to autocratic government . . . The Trafalgar Square methods had given way to Brummagem methods. The House of Lords denouncing had given way to the adoption of House of Lords methods. Here the opposition to the old Trade Unionists, so called, when the old Trade Unionist was a lick spittle of a party, a mere puppet, had given way, and the very progressive persons had adopted the most reactionary methods . . . The men whose hands had been in this would have an opportunity of knowing that their old friends were not dead yet. It was the politician, the voice and the hand of the party politician, that had been at the bottom of this.

When it was time for Congress to vote upon the resolution, the president, Councillor Jenkins of Cardiff, ruled that voting would proceed according to the new standing orders. Pandemonium ensued. But when it subsided and the ballots were cast, Burns's subcommittee emerged victorious. One historian of the TUC estimates that even if the voting had been by the traditional method, the committee would probably have received a majority, having engaged in extensive pre-convention lobbying.[8]

II

Engaged in a fruitless battle to defend the position of the Independent Labour Party within the TUC, Tillett was simultaneously losing ground within the party itself. At first all seemed to go smoothly with Tillett and the new organization. His articles often appeared in the Independent Labour Party journal, the *Labour Leader*, and intermittently during 1893-4 he wrote a regular column for it. He undertook organizing tours for the party, and at its second annual conference, in Manchester in early February 1894, was elected to its national administrative council, joining his friend Tom Mann, who had become the secretary of the Independent Labour Party. Tillett also campaigned for its candidates in the by-elections, putting in appearances at Attercliffe, Mid-Lanark, where the miners' leader Robert Smillie was standing, and Southampton, where a young journalist, J. Ramsay MacDonald, had embarked upon his quest for a parliamentary career. The Independent Labour Party, Tillett said, was in the best tradition of the English working-class movement which, due to 'the common sense of its leaders and the law abiding instincts of the masses', almost always followed 'the true and constitutional line of progress'. The extension of the franchise to almost all men would soon result in an Independent Labour Party majority within the House of Commons, with 'the reorganization of society on a more systematic and equal basis', as the inevitable result.[9]

If such moderate and sober pronouncements were designed to assure his position within the new party, they failed. Tillett's name does not appear as a delegate to the third annual conference of the Independent Labour Party in April 1895, or at any of the succeeding party conventions. After the summer of 1895 he played no major role in the organization.

Unfortunately, the points of contention between Tillett and the Independent Labour Party hierarchy remain obscure. Of course, one point must have been Tillett's chauvinism and opportunism most blatantly manifested at the founding conference in 1893. Chisholm Robertson of Stirlingshire, the speaker immediately to follow Tillett, had demanded to know 'whether Mr Tillett meant to say that Karl Marx . . . was a chatterer and a blatherer?' In the *Workman's Times* Edward Aveling and Shaw Maxwell, the first general secretary of the Independent Labour Party, condemned Tillett's speech and insisted that the 'vast majority' of delegates had likewise opposed it. Even the non-doctrinaire Blatchford publicly chastised Tillett in the pages of the

Clarion. 'The most regrettable incident of the conference', he wrote:

> was the speech of Ben Tillett against the Continental Socialists. This
> speech was universally deplored by the delegates . . . The Labour
> cause is the Labour cause in Germany as in England. Justice is not a
> geographical idea. We cannot quarrel with our Continental comrades.
> Socialism is only half won until it has made brothers of us all.

Blatchford was no more prepared than Tillett to stand by these sentiments some twenty years later; but, on the whole, the Independent
Labour Party was. At Bradford in 1893, we may discern portents of
the split between nationalists and internationalists which in 1914
shattered the European socialist movement.[10]

Despite these criticisms, Tillett's flirtation with labour's right wing
continued. His opposition to Burns's attack on the Independent Labour
Party notwithstanding, he sided with opponents of that party, Burns
among them, in London politics. This must have further exacerbated
the party's distrust of him.

It will be recalled that Tillett had been appointed as an alderman
to the London County Council during the summer of 1891. Although
he never played a prominent role on the LCC, he appears to have been
favourably impressed by the efforts of its Fabian members (among
them Sidney Webb) to form in the metropolis a compromise party of
labourites (like Burns) and left-wing Liberals. Late in 1894, in another
example of the sort of inconsistency which seemed increasingly to char-
acterize his conduct, Tillett, a founding member of the Independent
Labour Party, despatched a letter to the press urging trade unionists
to vote for the Progressive candidates of the Fabian Liberal alliance,
and thus against the socialists, in London's imminent school-board
elections. The Independent Labour Party was understandably disturbed.
On New Year's Day a paragraph appeared in the *Labour Leader*: 'At
the London meeting of the [ILP] General Council some very strong
opinions were expressed anent Ben Tillett's letter . . . and a resolution
disapproving his action was passed.' Tillett responded in a letter of the
same date to *The Times*, urging 'economic revolution' but refusing to
repudiate entirely the London Progressives. This can hardly have satisfied the aspiring party builders in the Independent Labour Party.[11]

Yet another source of friction between Tillett and the Independent
Labour Party leaders was not political but temperamental. Originally
something of a puritan, the dockers' leader had begun to develop a taste
for good living which, later in his career, was to undermine many of his

earlier values. Even now, Tillett could not rest content with half measures, and the man who had once voted on the London County Council to prohibit dance music in public parks on Sundays chose to celebrate his new worldliness in the pages of the *Clarion*. 'British prudery', he asserted, 'is a fraud, a delusion and a sham, blacklegging sex, invincible in its stupidity.' Many of the Independent Labour Party members with tender Nonconformist consciences would have found Tillett's defence of women who worked in night clubs particularly offensive: 'At least they earn by hard and artistic work their livelihood, which is more than can be said by a great number of prudes.' This kind of thing cannot have pleased dour and earnest Keir Hardie, let alone the sentimentalists like David Glasier who were grouped around him in the Independent Labour Party.[12]

If Hardie and the leadership of the Independent Labour Party had legitimate grounds for complaint against Tillett, however, the dockers' leader himself had certain grievances against them. That Tillett believed the workers unjustly envied successful labour agitators was well known, but he can hardly have expected the *Labour Leader* to deride his views in verse. Yet on 28 April 1894, Hardie printed the following stanza:

I am Alderman Ben Tillett and I've got a first class billet
But I wish the hobnailed people wouldn't tread upon my corns
If anyone supposes that my bed is made of roses
In stern reality it's like a mattress stuffed with thorns.

Nor can Tillett have been satisfied with the attitude of the *Labour Leader* towards certain difficulties he was having with the rank and file. Accusations of financial extravagance had dogged Tillett for years, and during the summer of 1894 they became public.[13] If he thought to find an ally among the leaders of the Independent Labour Party or the editor of its newspaper, however, he was greatly mistaken. 'Much capital is being made out of the fact that a meeting of dockers which was held to hear an address from Ben Tillett . . . broke up in disorder', Hardie began unobjectionably enough in a *Labour Leader* article of 4 August devoted to Tillett's tribulations.

One man reproached him for receiving his salary of £300 a year and riding on his bicycle while the dockers were starving. Even if this is true, there are a few hundred thousand doing the same thing whom the dockers never think of attacking. Tillett is not to blame for their condition; he has certainly done something to try and better it.

Tillett, whose salary was £150 must have thought he deserved better than this. His regular column for the journal (appropriately enough entitled 'Cycle Notes') was allowed to lapse. This, it may be added, was no great loss to anyone. Tillett's prose, which was convoluted at the best of times, achieved in the pages of the *Labour Leader* some truly spectacular formations. Nor was his advice to readers (he recommended purchasing wooden bicycles, for example) much better. Yet the breach which now existed between Tillett and the Independent Labour Party leadership (Tom Mann excepted) was nearly unbridgeable. In the future, circumstances and common enemies would occasionally bring them together. More commonly, however, they kept their distance from each other.

Tillett was the main loser as a result of the falling out, although arguably the labour movement as a whole lost the most. It took the dockers' leader twenty years to reach the centre of the political labour movement again. For two decades, from 1894 to 1914, he remained on the periphery — sometimes to the right, sometimes to the left of the Independent Labour Party and Labour Party stalwarts. This was something akin to purgatory for a labour leader who had been prominent in attacking 'Lib-Labism'. With the leadership of Britain's main working-class party deeply suspicious of him, how could he fulfil his parliamentary aspirations?

The dispute with Hardie and his followers had immediate political repercussions as well. Tillett, who intended to contest West Bradford again, was dependent for victory upon the local Independent Labour Party in which, one supporter observed, 'at present chaos appears to reign'. This was the only reference to his candidacy which the *Labour Leader* would make during the entire campaign. It was left to Blatchford to announce on 29 June in the *Clarion* that 'Ben Tillett stands exactly where he was, the duly chosen champion of the ILP in the Western Division [of Bradford] to meet all comers at the coming election'.[14]

Tillett had not ceased to snipe at Liberals and Tories since 1892. Nor had he neglected his constituency, helping to establish a Bradford Labour Club, and delivering an occasional sermon at the local Labour church, including the Christmas sermon itself on 25 December 1894. His campaign, once it was formally launched in July, however, seems curiously anti-climactic compared to the furious pace he had set three years before. Its lack of fervour contrasted too with the general eagerness of the national Independent Labour Party to enter the lists. In its first general election, the national office confidently sponsored twenty-eight candidates.[15]

Tillett's early speeches dealt, rather dully, with the failures of the legislative machinery in the House of Commons. What was needed, he contended, was a system of committees and subcommittees such as the London County Council employed. His appeal to the Roman Catholic electorate was unimaginative and, perhaps, too transparent. In 1892 he had bearded the lion in its den, proclaiming before the Bradford branch of the Irish National League that he would support democratic Home Rule, but not Gladstone's 'namby pamby' Bill. Now he promised, if elected, to favour state aid to Catholic schools, thus side-stepping the issue of Home Rule altogether. As a result, some local Catholic clergy instructed their parishioners to vote either for him or the Conservative candidate, but against the Liberal who opposed state subsidies for parochial education. Nevertheless the Irish National League backed the Liberal 'Home Rule' candidate.[16]

There were still occasional flashes of Tillett's early style. At a campaign rally on 9 July addressed first by Fred Jowett, and entertained by Miss Harker of London who sang 'Three fishers went sailing into the West', Tillett, stripped to his shirt sleeves, delivered a speech:

> in an impassioned style [which] had frequently an electrical effect in exciting the enthusiasm of his hearers. The issue, said the speaker, was a question of poverty against riches, of slavery — the remainder of the antithesis was lost in cheering, at the close of which Tillett continued, 'of want against luxury, of sadness against great joy'.

The retirement from the district of Alfred Illingworth, the Liberal incumbent, also provided him with an opportunity to speak effectively. Tillett was pitted against Charles Horsfall, a businessman, whom he denounced as an interloper. 'Here he had been in the field some four or five years', Tillett described himself:

> He had already stood as a candidate . . . and yet after all this work on the part of his supporters and in spite of his longstanding engagement in the constituency here was a full pursed Liberal manufacturer dumped into the field against him . . . Why should this man come between him and the Tory?

This was a clever twist. In the previous election Tillett had borne the onus for dividing the working-class vote. This time, Horsfall's belated appearance provided Tillett with the opportunity to label the Liberal candidate as a 'wrecker'. 'I have not said this without weighing my words', Tillett averred, and:

> I tell every Liberal who votes for a Liberal candidate and does not vote Labour, that he might just as well vote Tory. Every vote lost to Labour will strengthen the hand of the Tory, and if I do not get in, Mr Flower will, and the Liberals will be responsible for returning to Parliament the hereditary enemy of the working class.[17]

According to Blatchford, Tillett's strategy was to win 'more votes than those of every Socialist in the division'. Tillett hoped to attract 'a good proportion of the weak kneed, the almost persuaded, the waverers and partly persuaded'. In the light of this ambition, the results were deeply disappointing. When the ballots were counted, Flower (the Conservative) led with 3,936; Horsfall followed with 3,418; and Tillett trailed with 2,364, almost 400 votes less than he had received in 1892. The defeated candidate, however, chose to interpret the figures in a favourable light. 'He did not think that any of them had anticipated their efforts would have been attended with so much success', he announced rather surprisingly.

> They set out upon the task of soundly thrashing one of their enemies. They could not take them both on at once . . . They had not been spreading their forces for nothing, and if the Liberals did not come to their side, and fight side by side with them, they would keep them out.

What the Independent Labour Party leadership thought of this invitation to their chief enemy went unrecorded.[18]

III

Whatever Tillett might say in public, the parliamentary campaign had gone badly. So had his attempt as a member of the TUC parliamentary committee to foster the Independent Labour Party and to secure a leading place within the new party's ranks. Coupled with the series of parallel defeats suffered at the hands of the Shipping Federation, the psychological impact upon Tillett was considerable. At one point during the second Bradford campaign, and perhaps because he foresaw its out-

come, his tone became self-pitying. Confessing that he grew weary of
'the hardships of a labour agitator's life', he:

> said that he would rather be following some simple calling than be
> an Ishmael amongst respectable people . . . The press, he said, gave
> him no encouragement, but misrepresented him and made
> calumnious statements about him.

It was left to the courts, however, to administer the *coup de grâce* to
Tillett's faltering self-esteem, militancy and enthusiasm.[19]

During the spring of 1895, Tillett brought to court the *Morning*, a
journal which had accused him of buying a bicycle with union funds.
Unhappily, the judge, in his summing up, seemed to suggest that the
general secretary of the Dockers' Union had only received some of his
own back again. This was in fact the position taken by the defence. Its
lawyer, Sir Edward Carson, Conservative MP for Dublin University,
former Solicitor-General for Ireland, and an inveterate opponent of
Irish Home Rule, had a field day listing the occasions when Tillett had
accused his enemies of much worse than embezzlement. 'You are not
on Tower Hill', Carson admonished Tillett as the latter attempted to
respond. 'Nor you in Ireland', was the snappy reply. The members of
the jury, however, remained unmoved: the *Morning*'s attacks upon
Tillett had been exaggerated, they conceded, but they did not constitute libel. Tillett, who had hoped to win £500 in damages, found
himself unable to pay his lawyers and was forced to apply to his union
for a loan.

The effect of having to make such an application upon a nature so
quick to imagine slights and insults may be imagined. Tillett's relations
with Burns, a trustee of the union and therefore in partial control of
its purse strings, had never been easy; now they reached rock bottom.
Even his friendship with Mann was threatened. Mistakenly believing the
latter to have opposed his request for funds, Tillett sent Mann a letter
accusing him of conduct that had been 'faithless, cowardly, selfish and
mean', and declaring their relationship at an end. Mann's conciliatory
response goes some way to explain why, in fact, their friendship
survived greater disturbances than this. 'Ben, old man', the former
Dockers' Union president wrote, 'if I am guilty of the things you
allege against me I think you would be acting wisely in giving me the
cold shoulder once and for all'. But he had not acted as Tillett
supposed, and went on to prove it. He then concluded:

You declare all friendship off now, well let it be so but not with my endorsement. I plead no virtue, I lay nothing against you, and I shall be only too glad to meet and fraternise, and whether you will or no, I shall continue to love and admire you.

Here was a quarrel which Tillett could not continue.[20]

He did, however, continue to quarrel with the judge and prosecuting attorney, whom he held responsible for the negative verdict reached at his trial. 'I had neither law nor fair play', he complained in an article which can only have strengthened the scepticism among the general public with which his claims were already regarded. Carson was:

the most outrageously insolent of the Irish barristers now practising in England . . . His style is one of badgering bullying insinuation, foul innuendo . . . neither law nor morality actuating his abuse.

The judge, Tillett proclaimed on another occasion, 'absolutely refused me protection when in the witness box, but practically became the leader against me'. That there was one law for the rich and another for the poor had been a standard dictum among working men for many years. One would have thought that now Tillett would accept it, and take care to avoid the courts. In fact, his troubles with lawyers and the law were far from over. The suit for libel was merely a prelude to a more important case which not only strengthened his sense of persecution and isolation from respectable society, but also weakened his commitments to independent labour and socialist politics.[21]

After the 1889 strike in London, Tillett had hoped to extend the newly organized Dockers' Union to the European ports. Contact had been made with the Amsterdam dockers, though no official or permanent links had been established. During the winter of 1895-6, however, the idea was revived. Tillett became the secretary of an International Federation of Ship, Dock and River Workers, and soon was despatching invitations to the organization's first conference. It was held in London on 27 July 1896 at the Cranborne Hotel, with Tom Mann presiding. 'We intend', Tillett promised hopefully but unrealistically, 'to take action simultaneously all over the world.' Next, Havelock Wilson and Mann travelled to Antwerp where they attempted to conduct recruiting drives in concert with local labour leaders. The Belgian authorities acted quickly; the agitators were escorted to a ship bound for England and informed that they would be arrested if they dared to return. On 24 August 1896, therefore, Tillett arrived in their stead and, as he disingenuously explained in his autobiography, 'somehow . . . found myself involved in a procession at its head'. On the banner carried by the marchers he led were the words 'Bread or Blood'. He had been told by the Belgian authorities as he disembarked that he would not be permitted to address open meetings; later he claimed that since only dock workers had been present at both the procession and a rally held later that evening the restriction had been observed. The police, however, thought otherwise. Tillett was arrested and held incommunicado in an appallingly filthy cell for 26½ hours, during which he managed to punch one of his jailers and to sing every labour song he could remember. Then, without warning, he was bundled into a cab, brought to the dock and placed aboard a cross-channel steamer. Immediately upon reaching home he despatched an angry letter to *The Times* complaining revealingly that he had been subjected 'to the indignities of a felon'. In fact, it was not the loss of dignity which was most significant; Tillett's health, always precarious, broke entirely as a result of his brief but harsh incarceration.[22]

He had returned to London prepared to turn the affair into a *cause célèbre*. His letter to *The Times* had been intended merely as an opening salvo. The Belgian socialist, Vandervelde, raised the matter in his country's parliament. Simultaneously, Lord Salisbury, the British Prime Minister and Foreign Secretary, was deluged with letters protesting about Tillett's treatment. The victim himself demanded an apology from the Belgian government. He was unable to press the point, however, having become too ill. 'The reaction after all the excitement', he swore in a deposition two years later, the:

> loss of sleep and pain from non-urination, the bad smells and the chill caused a severe nervous prostration accompanied by vomiting and inability to take food . . .

Two months later he was out of bed, only to discover that he could not resume his activities. 'I found myself so weak that I became giddy and felt quite ill on the slightest exertion', he explained to Burns after failing to attend a meeting of the London County Council. His doctors judged that he required complete rest and sunshine. On 3 January 1897, he sailed for New Zealand.[23]

Ill health plagued Tillett throughout his career. Since 1887 he had already collapsed three times: after the Tilbury strike when, apparently, he nearly died; during the first annual delegate meeting of the Dockers' Union in 1890; and after the Cardiff defeat in 1891. A year later he confided in a letter to Burns that he did not feel physically able to lead the Bristol strike. Yet if the dockers' leader was small and frail, he possessed a combative and egotistical personality. This disjuncture between his physical condition and his temperament proved significant. Over the course of his career, a pattern emerged. When healthy, Tillett would work at a feverish, indeed manic, pace. Letters, pamphlets, proclamations and articles would flow from his pen; he would embark upon ambitious speaking and organizing tours, he would take up with great energy the cause of the moment, all the while carrying on the multitude of administrative tasks which fell to him as general secretary of a major union. His activities would reach their climax: a strike would be won or lost, a political manoeuvre succeed or fail. Immediately afterwards Tillett's health would break. He would be out of commission for months at a time, his illnesses real but accompanied by psychosomatic symptoms and depression amounting on more than one occasion to complete nervous breakdown. Self-pity and a propensity to dwell upon the insurmountable difficulties ahead characterized these periods. At such times his public utterances were often personal, deeply pessimistic and rancorous.[24]

The series of defeats and humiliations during the latter part of the new unionist era, capped by the Belgian fiasco, produced just such a physical and mental reaction. By 1896 Tillett had demonstrated already that he was in the mood to seek relief from the hardships of an agitator's life. Now his illness strengthened his desire for sympthy from his friends, recognition of his achievements and acceptance by the respectable society from which he was excluded. He was disposed also to seek compromise, where before he had seemed almost to relish confrontation. In short, he was about to perform a great about face.

Always critical of the rank and file, his attitude towards them during late 1896 assumed a carping, hectoring tone. 'Your own culpable neglect has encouraged the sordid employers to cheat and rob you', he charged in a manifesto issued to the London dockers soon after the Belgian adventure and printed on 29 August in *The Times*. The reverse side of this coin was his need for them to recognize his efforts on their behalf. 'For ten years I have fought in the ranks for my class, for my mates', he wrote in a message to the union on the eve of his departure for New Zealand.

All the agitation, worry without rest, has told upon me and now I am exhausted; without the greatest care and scientific aid I should have died half a dozen times during my illness. I am now informed that I must have complete rest.

In Bradford, to which he travelled in order to confer his blessing upon Fred Jowett, his successor as the Western Division's socialist parliamentary candidate, Tillett reversed his 1892 position, calling explicitly for an alliance with the Liberals. 'A socialist', he declared, 'could play the game of politician without any detriment to his socialism.'[25]

In New Zealand Tillett continued to be ill. According to his doctor he suffered from:

> profound nervous breakdown and depression. He has marked diminution of muscular power and some amount of insomnia with a strong tendency towards coma of a nervous and asthenic type. His circulation is enfeebled with a proneness towards limited congestion of the skin and internal organs.

When he was able to rise from his sick-bed and address an audience, Tillett's descriptions of England were always grim; his references to the labour movement pessimistic. 'In the old country', he told a gathering in Christchurch, 'they hardly knew what victory was; they knew what failure and defeat was.' He confessed at one rally held in his honour that he missed his wife and children. Yet the country's scenery and climate appealed to him, and for a while he toyed with the idea of settling there. These plans were abandoned, however, when it became apparent that there would be no funds for the position of national organizer which the New Zealand trade union movement had intended to create for him.[26]

During the summer of 1897, Tillett moved on to Australia. There, presumably, his condition improved, for no sooner had he arrived than he created a sensation by reluctantly agreeing to toast Queen Victoria's health. 'It might as well be her as any other old lady', Tillett said. With the American trade unionist, Samuel Gompers, whom he had met before the 1895 TUC, Tillett arranged a tour of the United States, but found himself too weak to undertake strenuous travel. The journey was postponed from September 1897 until February 1898, and then again until June, during which time Tillett recuperated again in New Zealand. He did not return to England until October 1898.[27]

Tillett's sojourn in the Antipodes and America had been undertaken for reasons of health. His observation of the labour scene in Australia, however, permanently influenced his political outlook. Already in a mood to question the efficacy of militant trade unionism, Tillett now embraced wholeheartedly the process of binding industrial arbitration which an Australian Labour government had initiated. Since the Tilbury strike, except for a brief period during the immediate aftermath of the great victory of 1889 in London, Tillett had looked to the state to maintain a balance between labour and capital. This was the key to his understanding of socialism: a democratically elected government would inevitably uphold the interests of the working class and therefore could be trusted to regulate the economy and other aspects of daily life. His experiences in Australia reinforced this view. The state, he now believed, could reconcile all class antagonism, acting through officially appointed boards of industrial arbitration on which both labour and employers would be represented.

Yet Tillett's own experiences would seem to have contradicted the lessons he learned in Australia. The state, at least as it was presently constituted, was hardly likely to fulfil the role which Tillett envisioned for it. The response of the British government to his lawsuit against the Belgians after the contretemps in Antwerp taught this opposite lesson — but Tillett was disposed to ignore it.

His demands for some form of restitution from the Belgians and for aid from his own government were unsuccessful. Before his trip, Tillett had written to F.H. Villiers of the Foreign Office, insisting that the incident had not been a mishap as he had originally supposed, but a deliberately planned

degradation to myself . . . I therefore consider myself justified in withdrawing my request for an apology and explanation of my treatment, to demand reparation for the unwarrantable incarceration and illness caused by the same.

The British Consul seemed sympathetic: 'I am strongly disposed to think that . . . the Belgian authorities did exceed their legal powers', he admitted to Salisbury. Although the Foreign Office agreed to argue Tillett's case before a distinguished French jurist, Arthur Desjardins, in an International Court of Arbitration, British ministers were hardly anxious to help a labour agitator sue the Belgian government. The case was not tried until 26 December 1898, more than two years after Tillett's incarceration. His lawyers do not appear to have taken great pains preparing his brief: 'otherwise', wrote one friendly minister, 'the Commercial Department would not have shown so much indifference to the case'. Not surprisingly, when it was finally brought to arbitration, Tillett lost. The British and Belgian governments however, pre-

sented Desjardins with a 'piece of plate of the Louis XVI epoch con-
sisting of a centre piece and pair of candelabra', out of gratitude for his
efforts. The gift cost £200, a figure substantially higher than the plain-
tiff's annual salary.[28]

Only five years earlier, Tillett's response to such treatment would
have been outrage. He would have been confirmed, probably, in his
opinion that the government was in league with the employers, and
would have redoubled his efforts to fight both through militant industrial action. Now he wrote instead: 'The union's most efficient work is
the prevention of strikes.'[29]

For Tillett an era had ended. Not coincidentally, the same was true
for the working-class movement in general. The high hopes of the new
unionist era had been dashed on both the political and the industrial
fronts. Everywhere employers' combinations were reversing the early
new unionist successes; everywhere the Independent Labour Party was
on the defensive (even Hardie lost his seat in the 1895 election); everywhere the courts were finding against the advocates of labour. Tillett
was not unique among working-class leaders in suffering a series of
defeats. But he reacted to them differently than most, perhaps partially
because of his idiosyncratic temperament. He was on bad terms with
the leaders of the Independent Labour Party and with Lib-Labism
alike. His personal fortunes and friendships were at a low ebb. He
seriously contemplated leaving England altogether.

Defeat in battle can be a double-edged sword. Defeat at Tilbury and
in the early stages of the struggle with the Shipping Federation had
broadened Tillett's outlook and strengthened his resolve. A steady diet
of defeat, however, proved debilitating to his militancy. Tillett was not
so much tenacious (though he could be stubborn) as he was mercurial.
He had become convinced that his early assessment of working-class
strength had been vastly inflated. Workers were more likely to lose in a
conflict with their employers than to win. This did not lead him to give
up his aspirations for the working class, but to a reconsideration of
tactics, which amounted nearly to their reversal. He now held that
labour would be wise to abandon strikes for the conference table, as, in
his opinion, the Australian working class had done in accepting binding
industrial arbitration overseen by the government.

Tillett was now nearly 40 years old. During the past decade he had
greatly altered his political and industrial views. With so volatile a
personality, however, it would have been rash to predict that the youth-
ful militant had settled into a comfortable and politically moderate
middle age.

Notes

1. TUC Parliamentary Committee Minutes, p. 151, British Museum micro-film. The committee was carrying out the instructions of the Congress, which had accepted Hardie's proposal that such a scheme be prepared.

2. Independent Labour Party, *Report of the First Annual Conference*, 1893, p. 5; see p. 3 for his earlier statement.

3. See below, pp. 105-6 for socialist reactions to Tillett's speeches.

4. TUC Parliamentary Committee Minutes, 30 January and 9 March 1893; B.C. Roberts, *The Trade Union Congress, 1868-1921* (Harvard University Press, Cambridge, Mass., 1958), pp. 139 and 142; *Clarion*, 15 September 1894.

5. Burns Papers, Add. MS 46285/150, Tillett to Burns, 6 September 1893.

6. *Labour Leader*, 2 March 1895.

7. The exact instructions of Congress were: 'That on account of the great increase in the number of matters placed on the agenda paper for consideration of the Congress and the limited time available for their proper discussion, the Congress is of the opinion that the various subjects should be grouped and remitted to Grand Committees of the House of Commons or sections as in the British Association. Such committees having arrived at a decision on the questions remitted to them shall report to Congress for confirmation. The Parliamentary Committee being instructed to carry out the terms of this resolution which shall come into operation at the next Congress.'

8. The vote was 604,000 to 357,000. Tillett's speech is printed on p. 98 of the *TUC Annual Report*, 1895; Roberts, *The Trade Union Congress*, p. 51.

9. Ben Tillett, 'The Need of Labour Representation', written in 1894, printed in Frank W. Galton (ed.), *Workers on their Industries* (Sonnenschein, London, 1896).

10. *Workman's Times*, 21 January 1893; *Clarion*, 21 January 1893.

11. For more on the London Progressives, see Paul Thompson, *Socialists, Liberals and Labour: The Struggle for London, 1885-1914* (Routledge and Kegan Paul, London, 1967).

12. *Clarion*, 2 November 1895.

13. In July, 1891, Burns wrote to Mann complaining of extravagance and bad accounting by Tillett in claiming minor expenses from union funds. See Dona Torr's pamphlet, *Tom Mann* (Lawrence and Wishart, London, 1944), p. 34.

14. *Labour Leader*, 6 July 1895.

15. For some of Tillett's political speeches see, for example, the *Barnsley Independent*, 20 October and 29 December 1894; for more on the Independent Labour Party during the 1895 elections, see Henry Pelling, *The Origins of the Labour Party* (Macmillan, London, 1954), pp. 163-8.

16. *Bradford Observer*, 8 July and 11 July 1895; *Labour Echo*, 3 July 1895; *Bradford Daily Argus*, 15 July 1895.

17. *Bradford Observer*, 9 July and 11 July 1895.

18. *Clarion*, 13 July and 20 July 1895; Tillett Collection, 'Ben Tillett at Kensington Hall, Girlington', a clipping in a scrapbook with no date or title to indicate which newspaper it came from.

19. *Bradford Observer*, 11 July 1895.

20. *Evening News*, 27 March 1895; see also the *Morning*, 29 March 1895, which printed the judge's summation; Dock, Wharf, Riverside and General Labourers' Union, *Minutes of Annual Delegate Meetings*, 1895. The loan was £350 'to clear off expenses incurred in the libel action against the *Morning* newspaper'. He never managed to pay it back. The following year he still owed £335. In 1899 the union agreed to forgo the rest.

21. *West Ham Herald*, 6 April 1895; Dock, Wharf, Riverside and General

Labourers' Union, *Sixth Annual Report*, 1895.

22. International Transport Workers' Federation Papers, Modern Records Centre, Warwick University, no. 87, Tillett to Charles Lindley, leader of the Swedish dockers, 7 July 1896; see Tillett's account of the episode in his autobiography, *Memories and Reflections* (J. Long, London, 1931), pp. 176-81; *The Times*, 28 August 1896.

23. Public Record Office, FO 10/771, Tillett to Salisbury, 28 August 1896. 'Ben Tillett's Sworn Deposition', 3 October 1896; Burns Papers, Add. MS 46285, Tillett to Burns 3 November 1896.

24. Burns Papers, Add. MS 46285, Tillett to Burns, 6 December 1896.

25. *The Times*, 25 December 1896; Brockway, *Socialism over 60 years: The Life of Jowett of Bradford* (Allen and Unwin, London, 1946), p. 66.

26. Public Record Office, FO 10/771, G.E. Deamer, BSC, LRCP, LM, etc. to Foreign Office, 11 May, 1897; *New Zealand Times*, 25 March 1897; *Lyttleton Times*, 7 June 1897; I would like to thank Mr H.O. Roth, deputy librarian at the University of Auckland, for sending me xerox copies of his collection of newspaper clippings concerning Tillett's trip to New Zealand.

27. Tillett Collection, MSS 7416/1/60, 'Ben Tillett in Australia', a paper delivered to the Melbourne University Historical Society Conference by K.S. Inglis, August 1951; Sam Gompers Collection, Boston Public Library, microfilm, vol. 30, no. 296.

28. Public Record Office, FO 10/77, Tillett to F.H. Villiers, 5 October 1896; FO 10/771/166, Edmund Morris to Curzon, 5 August 1898; FO 1034/68.

29. Dock, Wharf, Riverside and General Labourers' Union, *Annual Report*, 1900.

'COOING DOVE/STORMY PETREL', 1899-1910

The first decade of the twentieth century saw the British working class further develop its political muscle with the formation of the Labour Representation Committee in 1900 and its emergence as the Labour Party with 29 representatives in the House of Commons six years later. At the same time, the decade witnessed an extension of the employers' counter-offensive in the industrial sphere, eventually bringing into question the right to strike itself. In this ebb and flow of labour's fortunes, Tillett was an active participant. He had returned to England determined to reassert himself in both the political and industrial arms of the movement. He had begun the previous decade on their left wing and then moved toward the right; however, he reversed this process during 1900-10, when, approximately midway through the decade, he shifted dramatically to the left. Increasingly his gyrations were influenced by personal ambition.

Until late in 1906, Tillett could usually be found far to the right of where he had been in his new unionist heyday. No sooner had he returned to England than he launched a land promotion campaign for the Queensland government in Australia. 'I would be failing in my duty to the working classes of Great Britain if I did not inform them [that] . . . there are countless acres of the finest land in the world lying idle at this moment', he explained. This was hardly calculated to endear him to socialists and labour militants, who believed in improving conditions at home. Hardie was outraged that Tillett should 'lay himself under contracts with capitalistic administrations'. Blatchford, an old friend, thought that 'even the . . . sometime lean and hungry Agitator grows fat and sluggish and forgets to Agitate'. From the United States, Samuel Gompers warned that Tillett was popularly supposed to owe favours to the Queensland authorities for financial assistance received during his recuperation, and that his advertisement for them was in the nature of a quid pro quo.[1]

In fact, Tillett's new outlook stemmed from the negative lessons administered by the Shipping Federation during the new unionist era, and from the inspiration provided by Australia's method for avoiding industrial conflict through binding arbitration. The rank and file of the dockers however, did not necessarily share his unwonted moderation.

With unemployment at the docks shrinking as a result of the trade boom caused by the Boer War, and the possibility of a successful strike thereby enhanced, conflict within the union between leader and led was likely.

In the event, Tillett's pessimism was vindicated. When, in June 1900, militant London dockers declared a wildcat strike, and Thames-side workers throughout the port began coming out in sympathy, they faced a Shipping Federation more than able to deal with them. An article in *The Times* admiringly described how the employers' combination 'has now reduced to a science the overcoming of labour disputes such as the present' London strike:

> Not only do they keep at the docks a depot ship and sheds ready for the newcomers introduced to take the place of strikers, but they have always on hand complete sets of bedsteads, bedding, blankets, plates, basins, knives and forks, towels and other such things for no fewer than 5000 men.

Tillett, drinking whisky mixed with raw eggs as a supposed tonic to preserve his voice for public speaking, could do little more than appeal unavailingly to Australian unions for funds. On 10 July the strike collapsed amid bitter recriminations, the men voting three to one to end it unconditionally.[2]

For Tillett, this latest set-back confirmed his worst fears: about the prospects of trade union militancy, even during a period of relative prosperity; about the failings of the men he led; and about the strength of the employers' organization. No sooner were the men back at work, than he issued a stinging rebuke to the militants who had set the strike in motion:

> Those very members who were directly the cause of the dispute ratted in a most disgraceful manner, blaming those who had tried to reason the position out with such foulness of method and manner as to be brutish.

As for the membership at large, it too was culpable for failing to appreciate his efforts on its behalf:

> After all the years of training and worry, all the educational work, the reductions in labour's task, the increase in wages and general improvement, ingratitude curses those of us who have toiled with

singleness of heart . . . To give heart work, to live on one's nerves and soul, to have the fear of disloyalty eating one's life away, is what kills the servant of the workers.

If he had feared to engage the Shipping Federation while it was in its infancy, how much more so when the 'free labour' movement was well established? He now believed that it was the duty of the union executive to overrule such 'harebrained' activities as sympathetic walk-outs like the London dispute. Strikes meant 'loss of wage, sometimes loss of work, as well as causing a bitterness quite unnecessary if diplomacy and goodwill had ruled'. They drained the union treasury and could jeopardize the entire organization. Therefore, he wrote, 'dockers' rights must be obtained by strategy, and by what was better, by tact, and by what was the essence of tact, by common sense'.[3]

Increasingly in Tillett's mind, government-regulated binding arbitration represented labour's only chance of gaining parity with the employers. He wanted union representatives and management representatives to argue their opposing cases before an arbiter appointed by the state, or to advocate their claims before a board composed of equal numbers of workers and employers. He could point not merely to Australia as a positive example of what this might achieve, but to his own country as well. Boards of arbitration had been established in Britain since the 1850s, and had proved particularly successful in the building, iron and steel, hosiery, and shipbuilding trades.

It seems, however, that Tillett began advocating this practice for dockers just as it was falling into general disuse. Tillett could plausibly argue to his own rank and file, for whom trade unionism was a comparatively recent development, that it was a great advance for their representatives merely to appear before an arbiter on equal footing with the employer. The novelty of this sort of equality, however, had long since worn off among craft unionists, whose societies had been established for more than half a century, and who had been appearing before arbiters for decades. They were looking for new methods of advancing their claims just as Tillett was discovering an old one. Thus craft unionists could legitimately accuse the general secretary of the Dockers' Union of attempting to reinvent the wheel. This was one of the reactions to Tillett's efforts to move the class struggle into the arbiter's chambers.[4]

A second response to Tillett's new position was more overtly antagonistic. 'He could not quite understand the logic and consistency of Mr Tillett', W. Brace of the Miners' Union argued after the general secretary of the Dockers' Union had spoken in favour of industrial arbitration at the 1901 annual meeting of the TUC. 'He says the capitalist system is wrong. Then why is he creating an Arbitration Court to perpetuate it?'[5]

In fact, Tillett no longer seemed interested in replacing capitalism with socialism. Rather, his thinking was dominated by a loathing of strikes and a determination to maintain intact the union he had helped to build. Probably he was correct in thinking that the Shipping Federation had become too strong for the union. It did not necessarily follow, however, that compulsory arbitration would protect the working class.

A verbatim transcript of arguments presented to an arbiter appointed by the government to resolve a dispute in the tinplate industry suggests the drawbacks to industrial arbitration from labour's standpoint, and also affords revealing glimpses of Tillett in his new role.[6] In August 1903, certain Swansea factory owners attempted to halve wages and then locked out those who objected. Some 18,000 workers belonging to Dockers', Gasworkers', Steelsmelters' and Tin and Sheet Millmen's Unions were eventually affected. On 7 January 1904, Tillett, Will Thorne, John Hodge (of the Steelsmelters' Union) and several lesser lights journeyed to Swansea to put the men's position before Sir Kenelm Digby, the government-appointed arbiter. Tillett was the main spokesman for the men, displaying a forensic skill that recalled his early ambition to become a barrister. The basis of the dispute was one employer's attempt to reduce wages at his factory, despite old-fashioned machinery, to the rates paid by a competitor whose modern equipment doubled worker productivity. The owner of the older plant maintained that even with the reduction his employees earned a comfortable living: one, John Murphy, had made six boxes a minute for ten and a half hours, earning £3 8s. In his cross-examination of the plant foreman, Tillett attacked this contention from two angles. First, he asked, was John Murphy a typical worker?

> Q You know this labour of so little skill that a man is able to make six cases a minute?
> A Yes and I have a witness that was with me.
> Q Can you make six a minute?
> A Not without practice.
> Q But you are a skilled man?
> A Oh yes . . .

Then Tillett attempted to show that even if a worker could earn three pounds in a day, the opportunity to do so was rare. He skilfully led the foreman into a corner:

> Q How often could he earn it?
> A If employed regularly he could do it every week.
> Q Could you give the Arbiter any estimate taking your own works of the number of weeks he could earn it? Twenty out of the fifty two?
> A I have not my books at hand.
> Q Can you say from any actual experience?
> A I have not prepared records. Having so many figures I could not recollect them all.

As Tillett had explained to the rank and file of his union, he hoped by such negotiations to reduce 'the brutal savagery' that marred 'the relations of workers and capitalists'. At the close of the session he moved a vote of thanks to Digby, the arbiter: 'I can only reiterate our appreciation of the courtesy and dignity you have displayed. We have both looked after our interests, and the good temper that has been manifested today has been largely due to your conduct of the whole matter.' His peroration was an explicit denunciation of the class war:

> I can only assure you of our confidence in your judgment and your sense of justice . . . feeling that men filling your very useful function in the state . . . will help materially in the near future to bring about that industrial peace that ought to reign where there are brains and common sense and practical men able and willing to work together not only for their particular class but for their trade and country.

This appeal notwithstanding, Digby — whose refrain throughout the proceedings had been a plaintive: 'You are so much more familiar with these points than I am' — refused every demand put forward by the men, and awarded all but one of the employers' claims.[7] Not until the government had strong incentive to favour the working class would industrial arbitration protect the docker rank and file. Tillett's advocacy of the process remained unpopular in dockland until the First World War.

Tillett, however, was rarely intimidated by opposition to his views. During the first fifteen years of the twentieth century, he introduced or sponsored at nearly every Trades Union Congress a motion favouring industrial arbitration. He may even have welcomed the 1901 House of

Lords' judgement on Taff Vale (which held unions and their leaders liable for company losses during strikes) in the mistaken expectation that once striking had become impossible, trade unionists would support courts of arbitration instead. Where practically every trade unionist agreed that the decision was a devastating blow to labour, Tillett deprecated the 'condition of alarm and panic' into which the TUC had fallen. 'He did not believe that the voice of these legal functionaries was going to reduce trade unions to the state that had been described', Tillett asserted in 1900, before the House of Lords had finally decided the case:

> he only wished to goodness that they would try it. It would do a world of good and stir up those who had got an easy belief in things. He did not believe, however, that the judges would be so silly.

To the 1903 TUC he delivered a speech on Taff Vale that revealed the contradictions and inconsistencies inherent in his position and character. 'Fifty years ago,' he declared, 'the employers fought them individually; now they attacked their funds in an endeavour to sap their life blood.' Having acknowledged that the Taff Vale judgement was a threat to labour, however, he still would not advocate its reversal. 'They should stand by the laws of their country and not try to shield themselves behind their societies.' Surprisingly, his pugnacious instincts were directed against those trade union leaders who opposed Taff Vale and yet paid the court-imposed financial penalties for striking. 'Mr Bell's society [the Amalgamated Society of Railway Servants] had tamely paid £40,000 or so. If Mr Bell and his colleague, James Holmes, had done six months in prison it would have been better for them all.' Before his own union, Tillett indicated his willingness 'to go to the stake, the gallows or jail . . . I am not afraid to face the soldiers, policemen, judge and law'. When — or even why — such sacrifices might be necessary, was not clear.[8]

In fact, the controversy proved to be a decisive event for both Tillett and the labour movement as a whole. The culminating triumph of the employers' counter-offensive, which had begun in response to the new unionism, the Taff Vale judgement, by threatening the right to strike and thus the very life blood of trade unionism, galvanized the pre-new unionist trade union leaders into action. They had remained aloof from the Independent Labour Party for a variety of reasons, among them its socialist platform, its close association with the new unionism, and its intransigent opposition to Liberalism with which many of them identified. Now, even though Liberal Party leaders promised to reverse Taff Vale once they regained power, these old-style trade unionists had become convinced that labour needed its own independent voice in Parliament. Two years before the House of Lords had handed down its verdict on Taff Vale, a majority of delegates at the 1899 Trades Union Congress were already sufficiently worried by the employers' quickening attack upon trade unionism to accept Keir Hardie's resolution empowering Congress's parliamentary committee to convene a special meeting of labour and socialist bodies 'to devise ways and means for securing the return of an increased number of labour members to the next Parliament'. The meeting, which duly convened in the Memorial Hall, Farringdon Street, London, on 27 February 1900, carried out its mandate, establishing the British Labour Party once and for all, though calling it the Labour Representation Committee until its first general election in 1906.[9]

As the leader of a mass union, Tillett naturally attended the inaugural conference. He successfully moved the motion which established the new organization's independence from the TUC. Yet he had not been one of the inner circle which had arranged the meeting. Here is an index to the decline of Tillett's reputation, for only seven years earlier, in 1893, he had been one of the prime movers behind the formation of the Independent Labour Party.[10]

Tillett's attitude towards the Labour Representation Committee was ambivalent. Ambitious as he was, and perhaps wishing to assert himself in the embryonic Labour Party, he managed to gain election to its executive committee in 1901. Ill health and a six-month visit to the United States, however, all but precluded his active participation in its affairs. Or was he blocked from playing a more influential role? The old Independent Labour Party hierarchy, with whom Tillett had clashed in the past, was a dominant force now on the Labour Representation Committee. Hardie, after all, had taken the chair at the founding conference, and it had been his formula ('Let us have done with every 'ism that is not labourism') which had brought the socialists and trade unionists together. Perhaps renewed conflict between Tillett and Hardie was inevitable.

A major disruption of Tillett's relations with the Labour Representation Committee leaders occurred in 1903. At some point since his return from Australia, Tillett had become acquainted with Horatio Bottomley, the successful, if highly disreputable, businessman and newspaper proprietor, and the prospective Liberal candidate for South Hackney. He and Tillett were such good friends that the latter sent his daughter, Jeanette, to live with Bottomley when she wanted to leave home; and Bottomley appointed Tillett to edit the 1903 May Day edition of his newspaper, the *Sun*. [11]

During the late summer of that year, Tillett spoke at a rally with Bottomley. He later insisted that it was 'a peace meeting in Hackney under the auspices of the workmen's clubs and a Liberal Council', although his critics claimed that it was a Bottomley campaign rally. In any case, Tillett's action was misguided to say the least; the Labour Representation Committee had not yet established its viability as a third force in British politics. For one of its most prominent members to speak from the platform of a Liberal candidate, who had a Labour Representation Committee opponent, was a clear breach of party discipline and common sense. These were matters pointed out to Tillett by Charles Horne, secretary of the Hackney Trades Council, in a letter which went on to indict Bottomley as a 'company promoter'. Tillett tactlessly showed this letter to Bottomley, who took the remarkable step of suing its author. Tillett, for his part, did not remove his name from the list of Bottomley's supporters, although he declined to speak again from his friend's platform. Nevertheless, the leaders of the Labour Representation Committee were aghast. Hardie thought: 'it would do others of the wavering brotherhood a world of good' if 'an example could be made of . . . Tillett'. The latter responded by charging that the editor of the *Labour Leader* was attempting to intimidate him: 'My contention against Hardie is that his roundabout attack upon myself is a combination of menace and whine.' [12]

Tillett had aspired to be the parliamentary candidate of the Labour Representation Committee for the Eccles division. Now his adoption was far from certain. Will Hughes, the Eccles division secretary, pressed for clarification of Tillett's standing within the organization. 'Is Ben Tillett still an adopted candidate of the LRC?' he asked. 'Is there any difference of principle between the LRC and Ben Tillett?' Ramsay Mac-Donald, general secretary of the fledgeling party, sent Hughes a list of alternative candidates, but acknowledged that the Dockers' Union leader was still a member of the Labour Representation Committee. Hughes then called a meeting to clear the air. Tillett, who was nothing if not persuasive, thereupon succeeded in convincing the local chapter to support his candidacy. He was, then, the standard bearer for the Labour Representation Committee at Eccles. During the 1906 general election, however, some of his campaign literature identified him as 'the Liberal and Labour candidate'. Such ambiguity, coupled with the antagonism he had already generated, did not bode well for his electoral chances.[13]

Had Tillett's health remained strong, he none the less might have won the seat. The general election, when it finally took place early in 1906, proved an overwhelming success for the Liberal Party and, on a more modest scale, for Labour as well. Twenty-nine Labour Representation Committee candidates were swept into the House of Commons on a tide of anti-Conservative sentiment. They benefited, too, from a mutually convenient electoral arrangement with the Liberals which gave one or the other party a straight fight against the Conservatives in selected constituencies. Tillett, unfortunately, was in Jamaica recuperating from his latest bout with asthma and dermatitis. Informed that the election had been called, he was too ill to travel home. His wife campaigned in his stead. Significantly the Liberals had not withdrawn from the constituency; it is distinctly probable that the Labour Representation Committee did not press them for such a concession on Tillett's behalf during the secret negotiations. The hierarchy no doubt preferred to keep the difficult leader of the dockers at arms' length. His behaviour in the House might prove even more embarrassing than outside. Nevertheless when the ballots were counted, Tillett achieved a creditable poll. G.H. Pollard, the Liberal, won the seat with 5,841 votes. He was trailed by the Conservative, T. Stottard, who received 5,246 votes, and by Tillett, with 3,985. Hardly content with these figures, Tillett, when finally he did return to England, complained that the Labour Party had supported his candidacy only half-heartedly. Perhaps it had. It would be many years before he and the party's leaders would come to terms.[14]

II

So far, Tillett's critique of the Labour Representation Committee had come from the right. This accorded well with his advocacy of trade union moderation and of government-regulated boards of industrial arbitration, neither of which were stated policy of the Labour Representation Committee. One senses, however, that Tillett's personal differences with Hardie and other leaders of the Independent Labour Party, now strong on the Labour Representation Committee, were also responsible for his estrangement from it. At this stage, Tillett appears to have cared less about the content of his attacks upon the Labour Representation Committee than that the attacks should continue.

The general secretary of the Labour Representation Committee,

Ramsay MacDonald, was a close associate of Hardie's who had joined the Independent Labour Party in 1894. He shared with the former miners' leader an extremely flexible and pragmatic political approach, having been, with Hardie, the moving force behind the secret electoral negotiations with the Liberals. He did not, however, share Hardie's unswerving commitment to socialist principles, and he was less quick than Hardie to sympathize with the rebellious spirit which animated many in the labour movement. Handsome, possessed of a mellifluous voice, a persuasive manner and the financial means (acquired through journalism and marriage) to devote himself full time to organizing for the Labour Representation Committee, his imprint upon it was soon evident. Under his leadership the organization was cautious, moderate and pragmatic. It was increasingly difficult, in short, to attack it from the right — unless the attacker was outside the party altogether.

Critical of the leadership of the Labour Representation Committee as he was, Tillett did not wish to abandon the organization entirely, perhaps because he had been so closely associated with the founding of its direct ancestor, the Independent Labour Party, perhaps because he still genuinely believed that the working class needed an independent political voice. At any rate, despite his disavowal of militant trade unionism and loose associations with the Liberal Party, he did not follow the example of other disgruntled labour leaders, like his former comrade John Burns, for example, into the Liberal fold. Yet if his criticism of the cautious, pragmatic Labour Representation Committee was to continue (and there had been no reconciliation with Hardie), then it must come from the left. This seems the most likely explanation for the political transformation Tillett was about to launch.

After his defeat at Eccles, one finds Tillett less often identified with the Liberals, and more closely associated with the Social Democratic Federation, the very body he had derided in 1893 at the founding conference of the Independent Labour Party. It is impossible to say whether it was Tillett who first courted the Social Democratic Federation, or whether it was the socialists who, anxious to attract the dockers' leader, made the first move. Two months after the general election, on 8 September 1906, a Social Democrat reporter for *Justice* attending the TUC found it 'difficult in cold print to convey an adequate idea of the impassioned poetry of [Tillett's] utterances'. Later that autumn, Hyndman journeyed to Eccles to place upon Tillett the imprimatur of his party's approval. Those local electors who had plumped for Tillett in the candidate's absence 'had voted for principles without the charm of personality', Hyndman asserted, while the subject of these remarks announced another political conversion. 'Marx was more ripe than he considered him in his callow youth', Tillett declared.[15]

Tillett could not, however, move from the right to the left wing of the labour movement in one jump. The first annual Labour Party conference in 1907 shows him uncomfortably attempting to straddle both positions. On the one hand, he appeared as the party's outspoken critic, the gadfly at what was otherwise essentially an exercise in self-congratulation. His first move was to attack Hardie for supporting an executive motion which, in Tillett's view, would free party MPs from delegate control. This was a manoeuvre which seemed to ally him with the democratic rank and file. On the other hand, Tillett placed himself at the head of a faction of conservative trade unionists who resented the Independent Labour Party dominance of the party. Rising to speak for the second time at the conference, Tillett moved that 'Every Labour Party Member of Parliament, candidate and delegate, shall be a member of a bona-fide Trade Union, Professional or Trade Organization recognized by the executive.' In defence of this motion, he said:

> The trade union official who did something towards adding a shilling to the wage and to put some more food upon the table of the worker was doing a greater work than the sentimental men talking about theories.

As at the founding conference of the Independent Labour Party in 1893, Tillett was attempting to ingratiate himself with the 'old guard'. Delegates with long memories, however, were probably reminded of another instance in Tillett's career, in 1894, when he had risen to defend the socialists in the TUC from the 'old guard' who, led by Burns, were attempting to purge them.[16]

Unsuccessful in 1894, Tillett was again defeated — this time by 553,000 to 381,000 votes. Members of the Independent Labour Party who had agreed earlier in the day, out of deference to certain labour leaders, that one did not have to be a socialist to join the Labour Party were able to argue convincingly that neither should party members be forced to join a union. Tillett, in response, could only remark, sourly that 'the ILP members had shown their desire to stand by their middle-class friends'.[17]

Although the Social Democratic Federation had supported Tillett's attempt to exclude the middle class (and its socialist rivals in the Independent Labour Party) from the Labour Party, the motion cannot have gone down well with a majority of the socialist rank and file. One week after the conference, Tillett attempted to regain lost ground in the broad socialist movement, again by reversing an earlier position. It will be recalled that he had declared in 1893 that, if the Independent Labour Party was named the Socialist Labour Party, he would repudiate it. On 8 February, however, he informed the *Labour Leader*: 'I desire the Labour Party to be a National Socialist Party and shall work to that end.' In trying to purge the Independent Labour Party he seemed to have moved to the right; in the matter of party titles, he had moved to the left — in so far as those labels held significance for him. Bruce Glasier, however, had little doubt where Tillett stood, nor where the Independent Labour Party should stand in relation to Tillett. Presumably, both Hardie and MacDonald shared his views. The Dockers' Union general secretary, Glasier wrote, 'should be forever disqualified . . . from comradeship in the ranks of self-respecting members of the Party'.[18]

That Tillett still found it difficult to adopt an unambiguous position became apparent in another attack upon the Labour Party hierarchy. 'The statement of Mr Keir Hardie, that "Woman's Suffrage" will be the first of the proposals of the Party in the House', he protested in a letter to MacDonald:

is either unwarrantably authorised, or it is mendacious arrogance on the part of the leader of the Party. If it is not either of these, it is at least a grave blunder of leadership.

Here Tillett seemed to speak at once for the rank and file who wanted to establish democratic control over the leaders, and for the reactionaries who opposed votes for women. As a tactical manoeuvre, however, his intervention was a failure which served merely to increase his disrepute with the Independent Labour Party. In Eccles, the local branches threatened to withdraw official support, should Tillett again be adopted as the constituency's parliamentary candidate.[19]

This was a move Tillett found himself unprepared to counter. Ill health again interrupted his activities, and his doctors ordered complete rest and sunshine. Unable to afford another sea voyage, Tillett was rescued by Bottomley who recorded: 'I was instrumental in getting up a fund to enable him to take a holiday in Australia, and . . . a little farewell dinner which I gave to him at the House of Commons'. Bottomley was now the Liberal Member of Parliament for South Hackney. Nevertheless, Tillett, who sailed for Melbourne aboard the SS *Essex* on 30 March 1907, celebrated his arrival in Australia by announcing that he was a 'revolutionary socialist', a self-description pleasing to his old friend Tom Mann, who now lived in Melbourne, and who perhaps had not been following Tillett's career too closely.[20]

Mann had emigrated to Australia in 1901, where he had quickly assumed a prominent role in the labour and socialist movements. Unlike Tillett, he was not impressed by the state-regulated system of industrial arbitration, nor by the 'state' socialism which a Labour government claimed to have established there. Indeed, as a result of his experiences in Australia, Mann repudiated his old parliamentary socialism in favour of revolutionary syndicalism. In his opinion, nationalization merely replaced private owners with state bureaucrats whose interests were equally inimical to those of the working class. Better, then, a society organized by the trade unions in an industrial parliament which would supersede the traditional political parliament altogether.

Certain aspects of Mann's new outlook must have appealed to Tillett, whom we find at one New Zealand rally, exhorting the crowd with extracts from the syndicalist preamble to the constitution of the American Industrial Workers of the World. Subsequent events, however, were to show how limited Tillett's conversion to syndicalist principles really was. More likely, in 1907 Tillett was in a mood to appreciate the vigour and militancy of Mann's new philosophy, and his emphasis upon the importance of trade unions. These, after all, were precisely the attitudes which were missing in the British Labour Party under Hardie's and MacDonald's domination.

Tillett returned to England in the spring of 1908 and immediately assumed the posture he would maintain until the outbreak of the First World War. 'The wage system', he declaimed in his first public address since his arrival:

> was a damnable system. If they failed to teach their people that it robbed the child from the cradle to the grave, and that so long as it existed it must work for war, rapine and starvation, because it always made for poverty, they would have failed to do their duty.

'There is no solution but revolution', Tillett was to state later in the summer, 'no amelioration but comes from agitation or physical force'. Nine years earlier, Tillett had come back from Australia the apostle of industrial moderation. Now he returned as the uncompromising advocate of class war.[21]

Between 1906 and 1914 a growing and increasingly vocal minority within the labour movement came to feel that the Labour Party had betrayed socialism. This belief was based on its failure to formulate a programme, or to state publicly its acceptance of the socialist goals, including nationalizing the means of production, distribution and exchange. In addition, rumours abounded (which were confirmed fifty years later) of Labour's electoral arrangement with the Liberals. Finally, to many, the Labour Party leadership (Hardie always excepted) seemed tame. A new generation now shared responsibility with the former miners' leader and Ramsay MacDonald. Of these, the most significant were Arthur Henderson and Phillip Snowden.

Militants could find reason to be offended with both men. Henderson was a former Liberal Party agent, and the victor at a 1903 by-election at Barnard Castle, which he had contested as a candidate for the Labour Representation Committee. His platform, however, had not differed in its essentials from that of his Liberal opponent, and he carried into the Labour Party many of the attitudes associated with the old Liberal-inclined craft unionists. A large man, with a tendency to overweight, he seemed to embody the respectable, hard-working, self-improving, teetotal, religious working man. Snowden, on the other hand, was a slight figure, with a crippled leg. Formerly a clerk in the civil service, he had joined the Independent Labour Party in 1895. A quick wit and ready tongue had established his reputation as one of the movement's most persuasive speakers. Yet Snowden seemed more interested in the spiritual regeneration of the working class than in its immediate material advancement. Tillett instinctively disliked them both: Henderson, perhaps, for his associations with traditional craft union values; Snowden, perhaps, for his middle-class origins and mannerisms. Now, in his second reincarnation as a labour militant, and as one of the chief spokesmen of the movement's left wing, he enlarged the scope of his invective to include these new leaders of the Labour Party.

His first move was to join the Social Democratic Party, as the old Social Democratic Federation was now restyled. Within a year he had become one of its most popular speakers. He was now a regular contributor to the party journal, *Justice*, in which he put the case for 'revolutionary socialism and internationalism' as he understood it. 'The worker is a wage slave', he wrote on 18 July; 'the wage slave must sell his labour or die, the employing class having taken the means of living from him'. 'Capitalism must be fought whether we will it or not', he wrote upon another occasion; 'there is no peace because industrial war is permanent under capitalism. The capitalist must fight us, for his interests are antagonistic to ours as a class.'[22]

On 27 September 1908 he travelled to Hull, the scene of the bitter dock strike fifteen years previously. He was appalled, he told the Right-to-Work demonstration which he addressed there, by the:

> little pinched children, stockingless, bootless, clothesless and apparently by their wizened faces, foodless. Some of them were evidently homeless . . .

In contrast, Tillett cited the wives of wealthy men who:

> dress up poodles in thousand guinea collars with coats worth £1000 . . . They go in for hats ten feet round and they can't wear ordinary boots, but they wear carriage boots because they never walk . . . You have provided these damn scoundrels and ingrates with all their wealth; they look upon you with contempt . . . You say this is extreme, but hanging is better than starvation which the rich impose upon the poor . . . I don't care how you protest but don't go to the grave before you protest. You would not like to murder the rich, you are too kind, you would not take a mansion or a motor car from them. As for taking their lives, how wicked of you Ben Tillett to talk about it. I ask if it is not murder for them to starve you.

The multi-millionaire and philanthropist Andrew Carnegie, who had recently endowed some British libraries, was not exempt from Tillett's vengeance: 'I wish that some one of Carnegie's victims would make a hero of himself by cutting Carnegie's throat . . . ' Aghast, Richard Bower, a Hull town councillor, unsuccessfully urged the Home Secretary to prosecute the author of these remarks for sedition: 'Either Mr Tillett is a dangerous lunatic, or a criminal, and in either case ought not to be at large.' Probably ignorant of this correspondence, Tillett repeated his provocative suggestions in the pages of *Justice* two weeks later: 'Supposing one moment of sanity seized the poor', he wrote:

> Would it be any more murder to rise up and cut the throats of the rich, than that the rich should be legalised to torture the poor with the vilest agonising death of all, that of starvation? . . . There must come a day when the poor cut some throats.

Such sentiments were hardly calculated to enhance his authority within the Labour Party either. Tillett had chosen his ground; the rich aside, it was the Labour Party leadership and its moderate following whom he most frequently castigated.[23]

The former teetotaller was now, if not the champion of drink, at least the scourge of 'the Temperance bleating martyrs'. In October 1908, he demanded from 'the Secretary, Chairman and Executive of the Labour Party . . . explanations of Messrs Henderson, Shackleton, Richards, Crooks, Duncan, Snowden and others', who had campaigned on behalf of the government's licensing Bill. This was a measure dear to the hearts of many Nonconformists, an important element in the Edwardian Labour Party. Tillett had offended them before with his series of articles in the *Clarion* attacking 'British prudery'. Now in *Justice* he did not hesitate to provoke them a second time. 'If the Labour Party could select a King', Tillett wrote:

> he of course would have to be a Feminist, a Temperance crank, a Nonconformist Charlatan . . . an anti-sport, an anti-jollity advocate, a teetotaller, as well as a general wet blanket . . . Horse racing would vanish; the wines of Germany, France and the colonies would no more be at the service of the community; then some forms, if not all forms, of theatrical entertainment would have to be eliminated . . . as for music halls, they would be anathema! So long as the taint of Methodistic cant is on the leaders, so long as it is tolerated by the rank and file of the party, so long will the movement be more or less paralysed and its works futile.

A letter to MacDonald was less rhetorical, but almost equally provocative. 'In view of the urgency of the Unemployed question, and consequent distress among the poor,' Tillett asked, 'what authority or right has been given to the Temperance Section of your membership to give precedence to a [Liberal] party measure of Licensing . . . ?' This not unjustifiable query found its way into the press, which considerably irritated MacDonald. 'Nobody has given the Temperance question greater precedence than unemployment', he replied, but Tillett pressed the point. 'The time has come', he wrote on 30 October 1908, when:

> the Labour Party should assert its power and independence by refusing to involve itself with any question outside of direct economic and labour questions, and primarily that of unemployment.

All other matters, Tillett wrote in *Justice*, were 'red herrings'.[24]

Even as a member of the dissident left wing, Tillett proved more extreme than his associates. Ironically many of the Independent Labour

Party agreed with him that 'the Labour Party must make a straight out fight with capitalism', but they were not prepared to denounce their leaders as 'toadies', 'sheer hypocrites' and 'liars at five and ten guineas a time'. These were only some of the epithets which, late in 1908, Tillett affixed to the Labour Party leadership in a vitriolic pamphlet, *Is the Parliamentary Labour Party a Failure?* 'It appears deterioration sets in once men assume dignity and place', Tillett noted, setting the tone for the remainder of his text. 'Even at the risk of losing the empty vanity of Parliamentary honours, the Labour Party should be rebels in everlasting and open warfare against the powers that be.'[25]

This time, it seemed, Tillett had gone too far. At the 1909 annual conference of the Labour Party he attempted to backtrack: 'He wanted to say that he was a well wisher of the organization, that it was the inspiration of his early manhood that such an organization should exist.' Yet the motion he rose to second:

that no member or candidate run under the auspices of the Labour Party shall appear to support any measure upon the same platform as members of the capitalist parties

was a direct attack upon the party leaders for publicly supporting the Liberal licensing Bill. The motion was trounced by 788,000 to 113,000, probably a fair index of left-wing strength at the conference. In the course of the debate, Arthur Henderson, speaking for those whom Tillett had attacked in his pamphlet, threatened to quit the party 'if such a resolution was carried . . . because they [*sic*] would respect their manhood rather than be dictated to by men like Mr Tillett'. MacDonald warned the delegates not to 'cut off their nose to spite their face' by supporting the motion. Even Pete Curran, of the Gasworkers' Union, an old friend, opposed Tillett on this matter; another delegate reminded the dockers' leader that five years before Tillett himself had appeared on the same platform as Bottomley, a Liberal.[26]

Tillett, who again fell ill and could offer no rebuttal at the conference, used the pages of *Justice* in order to reply. 'The sooner the weeds are cast out the better for the movement', he wrote. 'Revolution and the propaganda of revolutionary ideals is the real work of the party.' Incredibly, Tillett chose to defend his conduct to Burns, now a Liberal Cabinet Minister: 'I am at war, John, with some of the poltroons abasing the movement we gave our youth and early manhood to.' He conducted the campaign from his regularly featured column for *Justice*, directing a steady stream of criticism at the Labour Party leadership.

'The rank and file . . . is ahead of the leaders; the Government is ahead of the Labour Party, taking the wind out of their sails and pinching their best goods . . . '[27]

Urging Labour to attack Liberalism from the left, Tillett found the famous Lloyd George 'People's Budget' of 1909, which intended to finance social reform through indirect taxation, the kind of fish which left only a bad smell behind. 'The workers already pay more than a fair share of the revenue out of a low standard of living', he maintained. 'They cannot afford to pay further burdens.' That the Labour Party as a whole supported the measure only moved Tillett to further denunciations. MacDonald, by indicating that he would vote for the budget, demonstrated 'spiteful ingratitude to the class who have given him position and honour'. Henderson and Snowden, prominent Labour members who also supported it, were similarly castigated.[28]

Having warned Prime Minister Asquith on 22 September in *The Times* that 'the workmen of this country are not so bovinely stupid' as to accept Lloyd George's additional taxes, Tillett was appalled to discover that the TUC enthusiastically approved of the finance Bill. 'The Congress has lost its old spirit of independence and freedom', Tillett lamented at the close of the annual gathering in 1909. 'The Budget fizzle was the most unblushing fraud.' He thought David Shackleton's presidential address represented 'flunkey mediocrity'. This stemmed not only from his objection to Shackleton's position on the budget, however, but also from an altercation between them early in the Congress over the Minister of Defence Haldane's promise not to use the territorials in labour disputes. 'Then Mr Haldane is a liar!' Tillett cried, interrupting Shackleton's advice to the delegates that the Secretary of War would honour his word.

> **Shackleton** I must ask Mr Tillett to withdraw that remark . . .
> **Tillett** I believe that all Cabinet Ministers are liars. They have proved it up to the hilt.
> **Shackleton** Order! Please take your seat Mr Tillett.

According to the record of the proceedings, Tillett sat down 'amid an emphatic expression of approval on the part of the delegates at the attitude of the President'.[29]

By this time Tillett had achieved a certain following in the labour movement which extended beyond his loyal supporters among the dockers. It consisted primarily, no doubt, of members of the Social Democratic Party who saw in Tillett a trade unionist who did not

mince words about capitalism or the failure of the Labour Party to effectively attack it; and of socialists who belonged to the Labour Party, but
who found the earthy attitudes of Blatchford's *Clarion* more to their
liking than the earnest sentimentality of the leaders of the Independent
Labour Party. Tillett's outspoken condemnations of the Labour Party's
moderation and parliamentary tactics must have appealed as well to
many members of the Independent Labour Party itself, but the abrasive
manner in which he expressed his opinions, and the fact that he had
reversed so many of them could not but discredit him among large
numbers of the rank and file. Tillett's fulminations were so wild that
occasionally it was difficult to tell whether he meant them to be taken
seriously. In one instance, for example, his opposition to the advocates of temperance led him to blame tea for causing indigestion, heart
disease, headaches, epilepsy, criminal vices, moral imbecility and
lunacy. On the occasion of the Tsar's state visit to England, Tillett
penned a public letter: 'Of all the crowned heads (and tails) you are
the most revolting brute and worst of the whole crew of evil despots
. . . Damn you, Nick . . . may your loathsome body sneak away from
our shores as you cowardly creep to a crapulous welcome.' The scepticism and distaste that his rhetorical excesses provoked was to prove a
distinct liability when he next stood for public office.[30]

III

At first it was not even certain that Tillett would find a constituency to
adopt him. In Eccles, surviving ill will proved to be insurmountable. 'I
feel it will be useless to spend too much time in the district', Tillett
wrote in the *Dockers' Record* in February 1909. He was already considering other constituencies, 'namely Lancashire and Coventry', but
eventually settled on East Northamptonshire. On 5 April 1909, he
formally withdrew from Eccles in order to free himself for the new area
of combat. His choice, however, proved a poor one. In December 1909,
when it became apparent that a general election was in the offing,
Tillett held several campaign rallies in the constituency. 'Though they
were good enough', wrote one observer, 'they did not give much
promise.' Moreover, the Labour Party did not approve of Tillett's intention to contest East Northamptonshire: in order to bar the Conservatives from office, the party executive had agreed to discourage three-
cornered fights and hopeless candidacies. Asquith's decision to appeal to
the country against the veto power of the House of Lords had put the

Labour Party on the defensive. The Liberal position was not one which labour leaders felt able to oppose. Party militants, Tillett among them, vainly protested that abolition of the second chamber was not even considered; but the Labour executive would not countenance contests in Liberal preserves – like East Northamptonshire.

Although Tillett was prepared to stand without endorsement and vowed on 9 December not to be driven from the division, an opening in Swansea Town proved too attractive to ignore. Because Swansea was a stronghold of the Dockers' Union, Tillett's chances there appeared better than in Eccles or East Northamptonshire. In the event, his parliamentary aspirations were again doomed to disappointment. From Labour's point of view, his 1910 campaign was only successful in generating antagonism.[31]

The Swansea election elicited the pugnacious and impolitic aspects of Tillett's character. Despite his invitation to contest the division, obstacles littered his path from the outset. It would appear that local militants – particularly Robert Williams, who later achieved prominence as an outspoken syndicalist and leader of the National Transport Workers' Federation – were instrumental in persuading Tillett to run. He was their third choice, however; two local leaders had bowed to a Labour directive that the anti-Conservative vote should be left entirely to the Liberals. Thus Tillett, who left East Northamptonshire partly because the Labour Party opposed his candidacy there, failed to receive endorsement in Swansea either. He stood, therefore, as an independent Labour candidate.[32]

The split between those who held that Labour should oppose both Liberals and Conservatives, and those who agreed with MacDonald and Henderson that the Tories must be kept from office at all costs, extended beyond Swansea's working-class electorate to the rank and file of Tillett's own union. On 17 December, the Number One Branch (Swansea) of the Dockers' Union unanimously approved Tillett's candidacy; but on the 28th, the Cwmbria and Cwmfelin branches appealed to him to withdraw. Reports that the Dockers' Union executive was likewise divided surfaced in the press on New Year's Day; and as late as 3 January 1910, the *South Wales Daily Post* hopefully predicted that Tillett would decline to enter the lists after all. Finally, and perhaps most difficult to overcome, Swansea, a Welsh town, gave every evidence of being devoted to Lloyd George. The Chancellor's budget – which Tillett opposed in no uncertain terms – was an extremely popular measure there, and the Liberal Party which intended to implement it was generally viewed with favour.[33]

Typically, Tillett attempted to meet these obstacles head on. Having failed to receive Labour's endorsement, and sensing that the party leaders had arrived at some understanding with the Liberals, he launched a vigorous counter-attack. 'As one of the founders of the present Parliamentary Labour Party', he wrote in a letter to *The Times* on 28 December:

> I can only express my sincere regrets and protest at the action of the Party leaders in making arrangements with the Liberal Party for electioneering purposes. The 'mutual agreement' is not only a surrender of principle, but is a betrayal of trust and authority.

In what must have been an oblique reference to his experience in East Northamptonshire, he continued:

> Seats have been thrown away, local organizations have been disrupted by the overweening anxiety of the politician Labour man to save his seat. In some cases it is poverty, but in the case of some that cannot count, ambition soaring to giddy heights and the Party principles to be abandoned for the Liberal 'Mess of Pottage'. [*sic*]. In every case where the Liberal is not standing there is an implied arrangement. In one short Parliament the Labour Party have surrendered the most precious principles of independence and have indeed sunk to the level of a wire pulling Tammany . . . With class antagonisms so definite it is pitiable that so called champions of Labour should 'arrange' with the enemy.

His contempt for the Lloyd George budget and for those workers who intended to support the Liberal candidate, Sir Alfred Mond, was equally forthright. 'There was neither reason nor excuse why any intelligent conscientious workingman should bolster up Liberal or Tory', he declared to an overflow crowd at the Star Theatre early in the campaign. And when members of the audience objected to his remarks concerning the budget, he exlaimed: 'You don't want to hear the truth. You are too cowardly to hear the truth . . . How dare you defend these capitalists?' He had set the mood for the rest of the campaign. In bitterness of tone and energy expended it would eclipse even the 1892 contest in Bradford.[34]

As in that earlier campaign, Tillett soon held his Liberal opponent to personify all the evils of capitalism. Like Alfred Illingworth at Bradford, Sir Alfred Mond was a Liberal industrialist with whom labour leaders had crossed swords before. Both Mond's father and his partner, Sir John Brunner, had been attacked by H.H. Champion and Tom Mann in the pages of the *Labour Elector* some twenty years earlier. Mann had managed to infiltrate the Brunner Mond Factory as a workman; his reports on conditions there formed the basis of the *Labour Elector*'s charges. Brunner, who enjoyed a reputation as a philanthropist (shared to a lesser extent by the Monds, father and son) threatened to sue his detractors. Although the matter had been settled to Brunner's satisfaction, Tillett resurrected it. 'The wealth that Mond inherits today', he charged:

> has been wrung out of the lives and sweat in the devilish employ-ment of the alkali works, where young men of twenty years of age, in the full flush of manhood, are destroyed within five years. In those trades there are the highest death rates, and when I started — I have a memory — Brunner Mond's were working their men 12 hours a day under the most unhealthy conditions where men were dropping off like flies . . . it was Tom Mann and myself that fought Brunner Mond and got the eight hours.[35]

A formidable Labour candidate had arrived upon the scene. Tillett's assertions were made in the Star Theatre 'so crowded that the doors had to be closed upon hundreds of people'. Mond reacted to the charges, as had Brunner when challenged by Mann and Champion: he instituted legal proceedings. If the intention was to intimidate Tillett, however, the suit failed its purpose. Served with a writ for libel, Tillett jauntily pinned it to his lapel where it remained throughout the campaign. With such a beginning it was unlikely that tempers would cool before polling day.[36]

Nor did they. The local Liberal newspaper, the *Cambria Daily Leader*, almost ignored the Conservative candidate, J.R. Wright, in order to concentrate on Tillett. His opposition to the budget, and unre-strained attacks upon the Labour leaders who supported it, were featured daily in its pages. Tillett was portrayed as a wild man, a wrecker, whom even the Labour Party could not abide. Mond himself was not above name-calling either:

> they had no Labour candidate in Swansea; he did not know what sort of candidate they had. The Duke's Docker, the Brewer's pet, the budget attacker in that Labour paper *The Times*! A man who was not recognized in this contest by the Labour Party, a man who had

attacked every labour leader . . . who had damaged the Labour cause irretrievably throughout the country . . . a man who called Phil Snowden — one of the most upright and best men he had ever known — 'the press flunky of Mr Asquith' . . . His candidature was a farce.

Tillett, of course, responded in kind — though his first riposte was below par: 'The worst thing he could call [the Liberal candidate] was Mond. That covered a multitude of sins.' Confronted with petitions from the Clydach Branch, and the Worcester Branch of his union, and from the men at the Crown Spelter Works and Port Tennant, to withdraw from the race so that the anti-Conservative poll would not be divided, he accused Mond of threatening to dismiss those workers who favoured his candidacy. Tillett's natural constituency was divided, and he knew it. 'It would not be his fault if he lost in his fight against capitalism', he warned an unruly audience in the Friendly Society Hall at Cwmbria, 'but the dishonour would rest with the workers'. Such statements were not likely to appeal to waverers. Attempting to leave the auditorium, Tillett's retinue was set upon by unfriendly members of the audience. Twenty men attempted to block his taxi, and then tried unsuccessfully to overturn it. James Wignall, a union official and one of Tillett's supppporters, went to hospital with bruised ribs. If anything, the episode served only to stiffen Tillett's intransigence.[37]

He had begun with statements critical of Lloyd George's budget and of the Labour Party leadership who made 'arrangements' with the Liberal enemy. He continued with attacks upon both his Swansea opponents for their anti-trade union activities. His programme included demands for the abolition of the House of Lords, free education up to and including university level, fair treatment for Roman Catholic teachers, and the extension of the Factory and Compensation Acts to every trade and calling. He opposed the government's plan to build Dreadnoughts, claiming that it ought to consider instead the 'bread noughts' of Britain. He advocated equal political rights for women, although three years earlier he had opposed the idea. As he explained in a letter to *Justice*, his candidacy was 'a fight for the clear economic issue of independence', by which he meant a fight for socialism and against the equivocal positions of the Labour Party. Pointedly endorsing the candidates of the Social Democratic Party — Hyndman, Quelch, Burrows, Gribble and Irving — he declared: 'We want the Socialist Party in Parliament.'[38]

Unfortunately, the passions generated by the campaign tended to obscure the fundamental issues. Never reluctant to indulge in personal attacks, Tillett tended to concentrate more and more upon Mond's alleged failures as an employer and human being. 'His was a poisonous and unhealthy trade', Tillett declared the Liberal candidate, 'and multi-millionaire as Mr Mond was, he was so inhuman and ungrateful that he attempted to deny to the victims even a small measure of compensation for the loss of health . . . ' This was a reference to Mond's vote against a workmen's compensation Bill. On 14 January, he accused Mond of attempting to bribe him to withdraw from the race. And, as the campaign drew to a close, he declared that 'he had never seen a more sordid, vicious and wicked fight than the Liberals were putting up. They had stooped to everything calumnious and dirty; there was nothing too mean and low for them.'[39]

Tillett's powers of invective, and his whirlwind pace seemed at first to bear fruit. Mond found it impossible to address at least one meeting of dockers and fuel workers. 'Someone called for three cheers for Mond: and the scene that followed baffles description; cheers mixed with groans and jeers . . . ' Tillett's drawing power, on the other hand, was immense. As one Conservative journalist observed:

a candidate who can attract and hold together 1,500 to 2,000 people at an open air meeting held in very unfavourable weather, and has to close one of the biggest buildings in town half an hour before the time announced for the beginning of proceedings, and to provide an overflow meeting for 500 people unable to secure admission, is not to be safely disregarded.

Conceivably the Conservatives publicized Tillett's candidacy in order to weaken Mond. The latter, whose strategy all along had been to depict Tillett as a man abhorred by responsible labour leaders, now attempted to counter Tillett's growing popularity by openly soliciting Labour Party support. J.R. Clynes, MP responded with testimony that he had 'never dealt with a firm which more readily recognizes Trade Unions'. It was left, however, to Ramsay MacDonald to administer the *coup de grâce* to Tillett's parliamentary aspirations in 1910.[40]

On 11 January, J.H. John, Secretary of the Welsh Artisans United Association and a long-time Liberal supporter, wrote to MacDonald explaining that he opposed Tillett's candidacy because it was hopeless, vituperative and likely to lead to the defeat of the 'progressive' Mond. 'I desire to know — and thousands of Swansea men would like to know — whether you and others of the National Labour Party approve of the

wrecking of Mr Tillett.' MacDonald's reply created such a sensation
that it deserves to be printed in full. 'Dear Sir,' it began:

> Mr Tillett is not supported by the Labour Party. I am sorry to say
> that it is quite true that Mr Tillett has lost no opportunity during
> the last few years to vilify and misrepresent the Labour Party. He
> has published a pamphlet [*Is the Parliamentary Labour Party a
> Failure?*] for the delectation of our enemies and (this to his credit)
> he has been wise enough to run away from it when challenged at
> Portsmouth to face the music.
>
> And since the Budget has been introduced, he has taken special
> delight and pains to show that he disagrees with the unanimous deci-
> sions and opinion of the Labour Party.
>
> Had I a vote in Swansea, it would therefore not be given to Mr
> Tillett unless I were assured that his policy in Parliament were not
> to follow the lines of his criticism outside.

John lost no time in delivering this letter to Mond who ensured that the
correspondence was printed in the local press. In addition, Swansea was
flooded with bills and posters delivering MacDonald's advice to the
local electors.[41]

Tillett was already beaten. In his desperation to overcome this new
challenge, his own rhetoric grew shrill and ugly. Mond, it was recalled,
was of German-Jewish descent. His portly figure and gutteral speech
lent themselves to satire. The Conservatives had appealed to the chauvinist sentiments of Swansea electors from the outset, reprinting from
the *Daily Mail* a series of articles by Blatchford (who supported the
construction of Dreadnoughts) on the 'German peril' in their newspaper, the *South Wales Daily Post*, and demanding tariff reform for protection against German-manufactured goods. In addition they lost no
opportunity to label Mond as 'the German Jew'. Tillett had refrained at
first from such tactics. On 8 January he explicitly repudiated them: 'He
believed in respecting every man's religion and religious scruples . . . It
was not a religious but a political election.' Faced with certain defeat,
however, Tillett actively courted the anti-Semitic vote. On the eve of
polling day, Tillett addressed 'at least 2,000 people' at an outdoor rally
where he facetiously noted that:

> the Free Churchmen and Nonconformists were calling a meeting for
> Mr Mond in Welsh; well the speaker was going to call one in German

or Hebrew . . . he wished to point out the illogical position of men supporting one opposed to their religion . . . Talk about the German invasion, Tut! Tut! You have it in Mond.

Before a crowd of 1,500 at the docks, Tillett drew a distinction between the Conservative Wright and Liberal Mond, both of whom he had previously denounced equally as capitalists.

Colonel Wright was a good old sort and a gentleman, though when it came to wages he was like the others. Mond was more careful and not so genial. The blood in his veins made him very careful; he was much more a skin-flint though he had more wealth.[42]

Tillett's position, however, was hopeless. His wife let slip to the press that this would probably be her husband's last parliamentary campaign. The results of the election cannot have encouraged Tillett to reconsider: Mond won easily with 6,020 votes. Wright, the Conservative, garnered 4,379 ballots. Tillett scraped in last with a mere 1,451 votes. It was a crushing defeat, and Tillett could only have been surprised at its magnitude. Asked to account for it, his first revealing response was that it stemmed from 'the incompetence of our class and the money of the other fellows'. Later, at another Star Theatre rally called to discuss the 'Lessons of the Election', Tillett waxed more absurd. He had been defeated by a combination of Calvinists and Jews, who were brought together by a shared belief in predestination. He retreated, however, from the anti-Semitism of the eve of the election. Jesus Christ and Karl Marx were 'two Jews who have put the whole world under debt to them'.[43]

To the readers of *Justice*, Tillett explained that his defeat had been caused by 'Perfidy and treachery of a particularly offensive character'. He was, of course, referring to MacDonald. At the Labour Party conference, which took place only a few weeks later, he complained of having been 'the victim of a clique', by which he meant his old enemies in the Independent Labour Party (Hardie, Glasier, MacDonald) and the new Parliamentary Labour Party leadership (Henderson and Snowden). Henderson, speaking in rebuttal, nearly completed Tillett's ostracism from the party.

He wondered when Mr Tillett would learn the difference between criticism . . . and the most malignant abuse . . . They had been endeavouring in the Conference for the last few years to have a standard of discipline . . . That standard could not be maintained if . . . [Tillett] made it his business to spend month after month writing . . . statements against the Executive and the Parliamentary Party . . . The Executive believed . . . that there had been no more weakening form of attack . . . than that for which Mr Tillett was responsible . . .

When the Dockers' Union leader attempted to answer 'Mr Henderson and his teetotal friends' he was shouted down. Had he continued to nurse any hopes of working within the party they must have flickered out then.[44]

Paradoxically, however, the Labour hierarchy's attack had enhanced Tillett's reputation with the left as a whole. To many he must have appeared as the sort of two-fisted, plain-speaking militant that the cautious party leadership so clearly lacked. In 1910, the labour movement was on the verge of a period of militancy beside which even the new unionist era paled in comparison. Tillett's exclusion from the official Labour Party placed him in a position to ride the militant wave to heights of popularity he had never reached before.

Notes

1. *Clarion*, 19 August 1899; *Labour Leader*, 9 September 1899; Samuel Gompers Collection, 'Outgoing Correspondence' letter book, Gompers to Tillett, 31 October 1893. It is impossible to ascertain the truth of these accusations. That Tillett felt defensive about them is apparent from his article in the *Labour Leader*. He wrote: 'The remuneration I get does not even afford me an honorarium, for it is practically swallowed up in liquidating the charges for halls, advertising, the hire of the lantern which I use, and the pay of the operator who works it.'

2. *The Times*, 14 June and 10 July 1900.

3. Dock, Wharf, Riverside and General Labourers' Union, *Eleventh Annual Report*, 1900; idem, *Minutes of Triennial Delegate Meetings*, 1905.

4. For more on arbitration, see E. Phelps Brown, *The Growth of British Industrial Relations* (Macmillan, London 1959), pp. 126-45.

5. TUC, *Annual Report*, 1901.

6. For the strike itself, see the *Western Mail*, 18 August 1903; the transcript of the arbitration is preserved at the Public Record Office, Lab 2/98 $\frac{CL + S}{L}$ 86/1904.

7. Dock, Wharf, Riverside and General Labourers' Union, *Annual Report* 1902; Public Record Office Lab 2/98.

8. TUC, *Annual Reports*, 1900, p. 79; 1903, p. 69; Dock, Wharf, Riverside and General Labourers' Union, *Minutes of the Triennial Delegate Meeting*, 1902.

9. Quoted in H. Pelling, *The Origin of the Labour Party* (Macmillan, London, 1954), p. 205.

10. Labour Party, *Annual Report*, 1900, p. 15.

11. See Julian Symons, *Horatio Bottomley* (Cresset Press, London, 1955); and Horatio Bottomley, *Bottomley's Book* (Odhams, London, 1909). Bottomley made and lost several fortunes and eventually was imprisoned for fraud; Tillett took that opportunity to attack Hardie indirectly, by praising to the skies his temporary successor as leader of the Independent Labour Party, 'Mr Phillip Snowden . . . a man of sterling integrity and ability, a born leader [possessing] . . . whole souled enthusiasm and charity of judgement'. Tillett seemed to imply that Hardie, whose name was made conspicuous by its absence, lacked these qualities. Of course, later, Tillett was equally vehement against Snowden.

12. *Justice*, 6 February 1919; this episode is described in the Transport House Labour Party Subjects File, LRC 11/362, 13/196-204, 461-9, 14/37-8; LRC 10/26, Lillie Hardie (for her husband who was ill) to J. Ramsay MacDonald, 27 October 1903; LRC 10/132, Tillett, to MacDonald, 5 October 1903.

13. Transport House, Labour Party Subjects File, LRC 6/164, 12/182, 11/173, Will Hughes to MacDonald, 11 October 1903.

14. *Eccles Advertiser*, 26 January 1906; Transport House, Labour Party General Correspondence File, 3/77-81, 4/114-17.

15. *Justice,* 6 October 1906.

16. Labour Party, *Annual Report*, 1907, p. 59.

17. *Labour Leader*, 8 February 1907.

18. *Labour Leader*, 1 February 1907.

19. Transport House, LP/PRO/13, Tillett to MacDonald, 27 January 1907; Labour Party General Correspondence Index, 11/179, Henry Derbyshire to Mac-Donald, 28 January 1907.

20. Bottomley, *Bottomley's Book*, p. 89; *Justice*, 13 June 1908.

21. *Dockers' Record*, June 1907.

22. Dock, Wharf, Riverside and General Labourers' Union, *Annual Report*, 1907.

23. Public Record Office, HO 170.408/4; *Justice*, 14 November 1908.

24. *Justice*, 6 February 1909; Tansport House, LP/TIL/08/9, Tillett to Mac-Donald, 19 October 1908; LP/TIL/08/10, MacDonald to Tillett, 20 October 1908; LP/TIL/08/15 Tillett to MacDonald, 30 October 1908; for the influence of the Nonconformists, see Stephen Koss, *Nonconformity in British Politics* (Batsford, London, 1975).

25. *Justice*, 12 December 1908; Tillett, *Is the Parliamentary Labour Party a Failure?* (London, 1908).

26. Labour Party, *Annual Report*, 1909, pp. 81, 83.

27. *Justice*, 23 January 1900; John Burns Papers, Add. MS 46285/192, Tillett to Burns, 13 January 1909; *Justice*, 29 May 1909.

28. *Justice*, 30 October 1909; *Clarion*, 28 May 1909.

29. *Justice*, 11 September 1909; TUC *Annual Report*, 1909, p. 128.

30. *Justice*, 18 September 1909; *Justice*, 19 June 1909.

31. *South Wales Daily Post*, 9 December and 23 December 1909.

32. Labour Party, *Annual Report*, 1910, p. 59.

33. *South Wales Daily Post*, 17 December and 28 December 1909; *South Wales Weekly Post*, 1 January 1910.

34. *South Wales Weekly Post*, 8 January 1910.

35. *South Wales Weekly Post*, 8 January 1910; Brunner Mond was the parent firm of the present day ICI.

36. *South Wales Daily Post*, 3 January 1910.

37. *Cambria Daily Leader*, 1 January 1910; *South Wales Daily Post*, 7 January, 10 January and 13 January 1910.

38. *South Wales Daily Post*, 7 January and 10 January 1910; *Cambria Daily Leader*, 10 January 1910; *Justice*, 15 January 1910.

39. *South Wales Daily Post*, 10 January and 15 January 1910.

40. *South Wales Daily Post*, 5 January and 13 January 1910.

41. *Cambria Daily Leader*, 14 January 1910.

42. *South Wales Daily Post*, 15 January 1910; *Cambria Daily Leader*, 8 January 1910; *South Wales Weekly Post*, 15 January 1910.

43. *South Wales Weekly Post*, 15 January and 22 January 1910; *Cambria Daily Leader*, 24 January 1910.

44. *Justice*, 22 January 1910; Labour Party, *Annual Report*, 1910, pp. 59-63.

8 THE AGITATOR REDUX, 1910-14

The period between 1910 and 1914 is known in British history as 'the years of great unrest'. During them the militant suffragettes, led by the redoubtable Pankhurst women, carried their agitation to lengths their adversaries had not dreamed possible; the Irish Unionists, with Conservative Party support, took the few remaining steps which made civil war with the Nationalists all but inevitable, and the Liberal government refused to intervene; and the labour movement adopted a policy of 'direct action' which seemed at times to threaten revolution.

Historians and contemporaries alike have failed to explain the causes of the upsurge in working-class militancy. Tillett was one of many who confessed that it took him completely by surprise. Today it is generally accepted that the low rate of unemployment made strikes practicable, and an overall decline in real wages, coupled with the contrast between upper and working-class life-styles, made them likely. It is still a matter of contention, as it was between 1910 and 1914, whether the failure of the Labour Party to pursue a more resolute course led to widespread working-class disenchantment with it and with parliamentary democracy in general; nor has it been established whether trade union leaders who opposed calls for 'direct action' won or lost rank-and-file support.[1]

The working class is often thought to have discovered the theoretical bases for its militancy during this period in syndicalism, a philosophy of revolutionary trade unionism associated with the French thinker George Sorel, and the American 'Wobblies' organized as the Industrial Workers of the World. Tom Mann, it is said, carried their message to British workers after learning about it in Australia, and checking with its leading French exponents on the way home. There were three essential points in his programme: first, the federation and amalgamation of existing British trade unions to reduce sectional jealousies and conflicts, and to strengthen them *vis-à-vis* the employers; second, a de-emphasis of political agitation as opposed to industrial agitation, which was aimed at finally provoking a general strike and revolutionary seizure of power by the workers through their unions; third, the organization of a socialist society based upon an industrial parliament in which all workers were represented through trade union membership.

In fact, Mann's strategy was not new to Britain. Syndicalist ideas had been circulating there since 1902, when British followers of the American socialist, Daniel De Leon, broke away from the Marxist Social Democratic Federation to establish their own newspaper, the *Socialist*, and one year later, their own political organization, the Socialist Labour Party. Despite the availability of syndicalist doctrine, however, it now seems unlikely that the British working class as a whole was converted to its principles. Rather, sections of the working class accepted specific syndicalist planks and a confrontational attitude that was syndicalist but also many other things.[2]

In his approach to syndicalism, as in so much else, Tillett expressed in exaggerated form the sentiments of a major portion of the working class. Probably he was already acquainted with its basic outlines, since he had visited Mann in Australia in 1907. Upon Mann's return to England, Tillett opened the pages of the *Dockers' Record*, the union journal, to his old friend's syndicalist preachings. Yet even at the height of the 'great unrest', Tillett only adopted those parts of Mann's programme that suited his own needs and temperament. 'Industrial and economic power was a much greater factor than Parliament', he asserted during the second general election of 1910, thereby articulating a fundamental syndicalist viewpoint – and, probably, a personal disinclination for parliamentary campaigns traceable to his experiences in Swansea rather than philosophical conversion. That the general strike would usher in socialist revolution was another syndicalist principle which Tillett advocated tirelessly during the period – all the while maintaining the necessity of compulsory arbitration! Yet despite these flaws, Tillett came in the public mind almost to personify the aggressive class consciousness of the syndicalist movement. He took pains to associate himself with the militant sections of the rank and file. He never hesitated to attack the moderate leaders of the Labour Party. He preached 'direct action' and the necessity of revolution at every opportunity. And he participated in the major industrial conflicts of the period.

One aspect of the syndicalist programme met with his sincere approval. Tillett had no doubts that unions should federate and eventually amalgamate into one giant organization – though his subsequent conduct suggests that he hoped 'one big union' would frighten the employers into granting concessions, and would never have to call a a strike. At any rate, Tillett had championed federation and amalgamation throughout his career. In 1891 he had advocated the formation of a comprehensive waterside federation. In 1895 he had tried to bring about an amalgamation between his own union, the Stevedores' Union,

Quelch's South Side Labour Protection League and the Liverpool dockers. In 1896 he had assisted in founding the International Federation of Ship, Dock and River Workers. And twelve years later, after his union had left that organization, Tillett persuaded the rank and file to affiliate with the International Transport Workers' Federation which replaced it. Thus, when Mann proposed in May 1910 that the time was ripe to bring British transport workers of all grades into one mammoth organization, Tillett was predisposed to agree. In July, he invited more than fifty unions involved in the transport industry to discuss this issue. Fifteen organizations sent delegates to the meeting which was held at Compositors' Hall in London on 22 and 23 September and at which Tillett delivered the keynote address. The result of its deliberations was not the amalgamation which Tillett and Mann had hoped for, but the formation of the National Transport Workers' Federation; as Tillett, with uncharacteristic modesty, explained in a letter to the German trade unionist Herman Jochade, this was at least 'a step in the right direction'.[3]

The launching of the National Transport Workers' Federation was a major event. It had been made possible not only through the agitation of Tillett and Mann, and the growing mood of insurgency among the workers, but as a result of support from the Stevedores' and Lightermen's Unions which previously had preferred complete independence. The shift in their thinking is partly attributable to the efforts of Harry Gosling, who headed the lightermen's society. Gosling had participated, in a small way, in the great strike of 1889, and he had taken up and attempted to impart to his fellow Thames labour aristocrats the broad perspective which Tom McCarthy had brought to the stevedores somewhat earlier. The descendant of a long line of lightermen, Gosling was a frail man, but tenacious with regard to principles. He was to play a major role, now, in the Federation.

The National Transport .Workers' Federation finally brought together in one organization Tillett's union with the other main body of British port-workers, the National Union of Dock Labourers. This had its headquarters in Liverpool, and was led by James Sexton, long one of Tillett's friends. Sexton had been a sailor (like Tillett) before finding work on the docks, where he suffered a disfiguring accident. An early member of the Independent Labour Party, his political opinions appear to have undergone an evolution not too dissimilar from Tillett's, with one important difference: his gradual shift to the right was uninterrupted, even during the 'great unrest'. As a strong trade unionist, however, Sexton could not but see the advantages posed by membership in a National Transport Workers' Federation. He brought to that body an organization which strengthened it considerably, and a cautious outlook which acted as a brake on some of its more militant members.

During the years of 'great unrest' the National Tranport Workers' Federation was to be involved in two of the major strikes which helped to give the period its name. In addition, it was to join with the Miners' Federation of Great Britain and the National Union of Railwaymen in the formidable Triple Alliance, which might indeed have commanded sufficient battalions to launch the general strike hoped for by syndicalists. The National Transport Workers' Federation was, in short, at the storm centre during those tumultuous years, and Tillett as a founding member and prominent leader of the organization, was in the midst of it.

The Federation's baptism by fire began on 3 June 1911. On that day, the coal bunkerers (the men who loaded coal into shipboard receptacles called bunkers) aboard the Southampton-docked liner, *Olympic*, demanded a wage rise. By 8 June, all coal trimmers (all men who worked inside the coal bunkers) were out on strike. The next day the *Olympic*'s entire crew walked off the job as well, and five days later three other shipping lines were struck. Simultaneously Havelock Wilson's National Sailors' and Firemen's Union called a national strike. This step had long been contemplated as a means of forcing the Shipping Federation to recognize the union. To everyone's surprise, dockers in ports throughout the country began to come out in sympathy. On 16 June, Goole, Glasgow, the rest of Southampton and Newcastle were affected; on the 19th, Hull; on the 20th, Liverpool and Manchester. The Sailors' and Firemen's Union was affiliated to the National Transport Workers' Federation, and hurriedly urged that a conference of the Federation should be called in London for 28 June. At this meeting, the Federation executive decided that another conference to consider 'drastic action' — by which it meant a London strike as well — would convene on 3 July, unless the shipowners agreed to recognize the Sailors' and Firemen's Union, and accede to their demands for higher pay.[4]

In the metropolis, Tillett was determined to turn the movement to the advantage of his own union. It was a desperate gamble. A year-long organizing drive had accomplished little. According to one historian of waterside unionism in the capital, Tillett's organization was practically 'extinct' there by 1906. The income of the single metropolitan branch lagged significantly behind provincial contributions to the union treasury. Even on the eve of the 1911 upheaval, about half of London's port-workers remained unaffiliated with any union. Moreover, Tillett's attitude toward the rank and file had not changed, despite his role in the labour movement as its champion. 'The people are conservative, stupidly so', he lamented in December 1910. Only one month before the strike began he had calculated 'that the Liberals have a hold on the majority of (a) Trade Union workers, (b) Labour Party organizations, and (c) radical workmen's associations'. Nevertheless, on 29 June, the day after the initial National Transport Workers' Federation meeting, he despatched an ultimatum to the Port of London Authority demanding wage increases to 8d per hour for all regular work and 1s for overtime. He must have hoped that provincial action, already in motion, would rebound to the benefit of London's dockers.[5]

He did not, however, intend to rely solely upon the National Transport Workers' Federation. Or, perhaps his dim view of the rank and file may help explain an extraordinary letter he wrote at this juncture to the man he held chiefly responsible for his Swansea defeat. Six months before, he had accused Ramsey MacDonald of 'delivering the Labour Party over to the Government'. In the not too distant future, he would deride him as 'the most pathetic figure in the Labour movement'. But now, as he explained:

> I noticed the tired look and the general weariness you exhibited at the last Conference, and can only feel you are working too hard. I don't agree with the policy and method of the Labour Party on vital points; but I do feel you conscientiously carry them out . . . besides bringing great ability and zealousness to the task. But I am second to none in valuing the work you put in, as most people ought to . . . I feel you will be on the right side (the Economic) when the time comes . . . I have quarrelled with you, but I wish you health and luck . . .

Written on 29 June, the same day that he despatched the ultimatum to the Port of London Authority, Tillett's letter casts a dubious glow over his continual professions of militancy and distrust of the Labour Party leadership. Did he foresee a long and dangerous strike and hope to win over the party as an ally? Perhaps this is the most creditable explanation of his conduct. Significantly, MacDonald, who wrote back to assure Tillett that he was not at all tired, remained aloof.[6]

Given the weakness of his union, and his reservations about the men, Tillett cannot have been disappointed when the London employers agreed to discuss his demands. Held on 10 July, under the auspices of the Port of London Authority, the process of negotiation alone signified a victory for the principle of federation. The employers represented at the conference were the Shipping Federation, the Short-Sea Traders (who later withdrew), the Wharfingers and Granary Keepers, the Master Lightermen, and the Port of London Authority itself. All had received strike notices from their workers, who were represented by the National Transport Workers' Federation. It was the first time in British history that such an inclusive bargaining session had taken place.

By 27 July, the provincial strikes had all been settled. In London, however, events hung fire. All of a sudden port-workers seemed to relish the prospect of battle. After nearly a decade of apathy and quiescence they were flocking to join the unions. This more than other considerations influenced the outcome of the negotiations Tillett had initiated. By the Devonport agreement (named after the chairman of the Port of London Authority) hourly wages were to rise from 6d for regular work and 8d for overtime, to 7d and 9d and men already earning that amount would now receive 8d and 1s. The employers had conceded a wage rise without a strike having occurred. Tillett recommended that these terms be accepted. At a mass meeting on the 28th, however, he, Thorne and Harry Gosling, president of the National Transport Workers' Federation, were shouted down. As Tillett remembered: 'Only respect for the Chair and platform prevented a violent antagonism.' Prepared though they were to return to the conference table, Tillett and the other Federation negotiators were brought up short by the refusal of the employers to alter any aspect of the settlement. On the evening of 2 August, therefore, another meeting of dockers demanded a general strike throughout the Port of London. Whatever qualms the leadership possessed were swept away before the nearly unanimous enthusiasm for militant action. The next morning, the second great London dock strike commenced.[7]

Unlike the dispute of 1889, the 1911 dock strike cannot be viewed as a single, coherent episode. Rather, it encompassed numerous disputes involving not only dock and wharf labourers of varying gradations (who often belonged to separate societies), but lightermen, tugmen, ship repairers, sailing bargemen, coal porters, carmen and stevedores as well. These men did not join the strike simultaneously but rather formulated demands and downed tools throughout the period in question. As has been observed, the movement gained in size and intensity with almost every passing day. This presented the leaders with a problem: they could not accurately gauge the militancy of the men because it continued to grow; therefore they were prepared to settle for terms which the rank and file found unacceptable.[8]

The 1911 dispute was singularly different from the earlier battle in another respect. Two of the principals of 1889 (Tillett and Burns) were again involved in a major Thames-side strike, only this time one was a Liberal Cabinet Minister. To Tillett, who was a deeply emotional and sentimental man, the symbolic irony of the situation must have been evident. 'The years have dealt more kindly with [Burns's] strength than his appearance', he observed rather snidely. Even in his compliments there was a suggestion of antagonism, perhaps tinged with jealousy: 'Burns must have his due', Tillett acknowledged. 'Although the dock agitator was now a Cabinet Minister he really forgot that at times.' For his part, Burns was inclined to patronise his former comrade. 'Tillett came to see me about Dock strike', he wrote in his diary after the Devonport agreement had been signed. 'Told him to bridle his tongue and settle before what had been secured had been frittered away. Gave him some tea . . . and tried to drill some good advice into him.' It is interesting to speculate about the emotions with which each man regarded the other. Unfortunately these are the only references to their interaction during the strike.[9]

Tillett faced a graver problem than determining his attitude towards Burns during the dispute. His opposition to the sympathetic walk-out and to the strike weapon itself was long-standing. On the other hand, as the inveterate foe of compromise within the Labour Party, and as the champion of trade union federation and amalgamation as preached by syndicalists like Tom Mann, he had identified himself with the most advanced elements in the labour movement. Over the past five years, however, no dock strike of major proportions had forced him to confront the contradiction between his earlier and later attitudes.

Tillett's behaviour during the strike reflects this dilemma. He was militant and conciliatory by turns. 'I am sure', he declaimed at one point, 'that in the future we shall have no other resort to protect ourselves but the use of arms.' Or, on another occasion, he threatened that the Transport Workers' Union would stop 'the whole supply of food throughout the country', if the army was called in to move cargo affected by the London dispute. A manifesto to 'the President of the Board of Trade, the Home Secretary and the Permanent Officials of both State Departments' was menacing:

You know the Transport workers have the Key to the Nation's industrial position, also we hold the power over the food supply, and if the Shipowners and Dock Companies still persist in their War against the Port Workers of the Country, then we shall bring about a state of war . . . Hunger and poverty has [*sic*] driven the Dock and Ship workers to this present resort, and neither your police, your soldiers, your murder and Cossack policy will avert the disaster coming to this Country . . .

On the other hand, a message 'to District Branch Officers and Members London Section' of his union advised caution:

You may be called upon to take drastic action, but you must at least allow us to exhaust every reasonable means of settling the issue without recourse to the arbitrament of force.

And to the 'Secretaries and Members of the Labour Party' he affirmed his commitment to 'using peaceful means to bring about improvements and increases in wages'.[10]

Luckily for Tillett, the conflict did not last long enough to force a choice between these contradictory attitudes. The strike was immediately effective, and each day that it continued resulted in increased participation. At its height it equalled in size the strike of 1889. Moreover, very hot weather meant that meat and other perishables the dockers had refused to touch were beginning to spoil. The country as a whole was threatened with a food shortage. This brought the government itself into the conflict. Within eight days of the strike's commencement, it had awarded, through binding arbitration, the men's claims. 'I do not want to keep you a moment in suspense', Gosling cried to the great crowd assembled in Trafalgar Square on 11 August. 'You have won the 8d and 1s.'[11]

For Tillett, the lesson of the strike was contradictory. That success was due primarily to the militant series of spontaneous walk-outs up and down the coast, and to the wildcat action of the London men seems obvious. Yet Tillett thought it 'quite possible that we should have made a better fight if there had been anything like discipline and uniformity'. At a victory celebration of 12 August, he declared to a crowd on Tower Hill that must have been considerably surprised at this revelation: 'For more than five weeks they [leaders of the National Transport Workers' Federation, himself included] kept the men back.' At the same time, Tillett was enthusiastic about the power which rank-and-file militancy had placed in his hands. During the strike the government had requested of the union that food and fuel for horses, trains and trucks be allowed out of the docks to keep the mail service in operation. 'But think of it', Tillett urged. 'The Government coming to us for permission!'[12]

The 1911 strike, therefore, is useful for revealing the ambiguities of Tillett's position during the 'great unrest'. He had understood the opportunities presented to the London branch of his union by the provincial militants and had been quick to take advantage of it. His efforts on behalf of the metropolitan membership were crowned with success. At the same time, however, his letter to MacDonald, the contradictory messages he despatched to the rank and file, government officials and union officers, and his critical response to the very rank-and-file militancy which had made victory possible, suggest an outlook at odds with the radical one he usually professed. As in the new unionist era, Tillett's frequent appeals for revolutionary action deserve cautious treatment; unfortunately, as in the earlier period, they were generally accepted uncritically. That they did not discredit him with the Dockers' Union membership, but rather confirmed his position as their leader, is a point that historians who wish to minimize the popular militancy of the 'great unrest' must dispute or ignore.[13]

II

Although Tillett could not know it, less than a year would pass before another major confrontation occurred in the London docks. He spent these months in a whirl of activity, the London victory putting his services in great demand. He spoke for striking miners in Wales, for the Social Democratic Party's organizing drives, for Mann who had been imprisoned after appealing to British soldiers to disobey, if commanded to fire upon striking workers. He had become friendly with George Lansbury, the former member of the Social Democratic Federation who had been driven from that organization by Hyndman's dogmatic Marxism, and who would temporarily leave the Labour Party when it failed to take up the cause of women's suffrage. Now Lansbury, Tillett and Robert Williams, whom Tillett had met during the 1910 Swansea electoral campaign, helped to found the *Daily Herald*, which soon became perhaps the liveliest left-wing journal in Britain since Cobbett's *Political Register*. Tillett wrote a regular column for it, switching from *Justice*, which could survive without his aid. This was a period in his life when, according to Lansbury, 'a breezy, cheery optimism flowed from' him. He travelled to the Continent to study German methods of trade unionism, in the process cementing his ties with the leaders of their transport unions. He did not anticipate the next battle in London and opposed it when it threatened to break out.[14]

The London transport strike of 1912 was perhaps the most bitter in the history of the port. It began on 19 May when the Society of Lightermen came out in protest of certain barge owners who refused to pay the new 8d and 1s rate, and because the Masters' Association as a whole refused to recognize the Lightermen's traditional closed shop. Two days later, both the Dockers' and Stevedores' Unions pledged not to perform any work normally performed by union lightermen; and on 23 May the executive of the National Transport Workers' Federation, meeting in London, called a port-wide stoppage. It immediately proved effective. Unlike the 1911 dispute, it appeared that the men came out in a body at the behest of their leaders, not individually and spontaneously. In fact, many had walked off the job prior to receiving instructions to do so; the Federation's call-out merely gave them official sanction. The government's response was prompt. The Clarke Inquiry was favourable to the claims of the men; but the employers, led by the flinty Lord Devonport, would accept nothing less than unconditional surrender. The National Transport Workers' Federation attempted to break the resulting deadlock on 10 June by calling a national strike, but the response was worse than disappointing. Only the provincial branches of the Dockers' Union heeded the call. Railway workers actually provided transportation for blocked goods and blacklegs. Grimly the London men settled in for a long siege. There could have been only one conclusion, however, and on 27 July the National Transport Workers' Federation declared the strike ended. The rank and file rejected this declaration; but starvation eventually drove them back to work. Not until mid-August did the port resume its normal activities.

As in 1911, Tillett played a leading role in the affair, and again his conduct was inconsistent. On the one hand, his public statements grew increasingly bitter and militant as the strike proceeded; on the other hand, much that he did was deliberately cautious. Nevertheless, Tillett's image as a revolutionary trade unionist was enhanced, not dimmed, by the dispute.

Tillett's opening address to the men, delivered from the upper windows of Maritime Hall on the day that the National Transport Workers' Federation voted to support the lightermen, reveals the ambivalence of his position: 'I want to emphasize that this dispute will, if necessary, not be confined to the Port of London alone, but will also become national', he thundered. He followed this militant threat, however, with a disclaimer: 'I did not want this sort of thing just now, but now it is started, though my heart is indifferent, I am going to do my best to fight for the workers again.'

Much may be deduced from these remarks. Tillett must have argued at the executive meeting of the National Transport Workers' Federation against enlarging the lightermen's strike to include the dockers and stevedores. Perhaps he still believed that strikes were a difficult, uncertain way to settle differences between masters and men; perhaps he feared to jeopardize the advances of 1911; most likely, he hesitated to commit the fortunes of the Dockers' Union in a struggle whose chief beneficiaries would be the lightermen, and this despite his much-vaunted advocacy of federation and amalgamation. It was on such grounds that Tillett was to oppose sympathetic action in support of Dublin's striking dockers in 1913 and the miners in 1921.[15]

No less likely, Tillett felt his hand to have been forced by the precipitate action of the rank and file, who 'refused to touch or handle any goods diverted' away from the striking lightermen. 'In this way', Tillett complained in September 1912:

> the strike became widespread, leaving the London committee of the NTWF and the Executive Council of the Transport Workers Federation with the option of acquiescing to the spontaneous action of the men or repudiating the same.

He had warned against precisely such a course the previous February: 'Action should not be taken without consulting your officials, or unless ordered by the Executive or by the Transport Workers' Federation.' In other words, despite his numerous professions of militancy, Tillett was as much opposed to direct action of the rank and file as were the trade union officials whom he so frequently castigated for conservatism.[16]

Tillett's rhetorical response to the steadily worsening position of the men was fierce. He introduced the possibility of a national strike on the first day of the London stoppage. By June 7 he was informing the Tilbury dockers that:

> the Shipping Federation were arming what they were pleased to call the civilian police with revolvers and truncheons, and which they carried in their hands ostentatiously. He had told Lord Haldane that if he permitted the capitalists to arm their blacklegs with revolvers and truncheons, they would arm their men with similar weapons.

The next day on Tower Hill, Tillett reiterated his warning that he intended the dockers to be armed, and continued: 'if only they valued themselves as they ought they would not allow so many millionaires to live — let alone die natural deaths'. By 10 June, at the regular Tower Hill meeting, Tillett was asking how many of his audience had received military training, and how many would volunteer to serve in the 'Transport Workers' Civilian Police'. 'Almost every man present held up his hand', the *Daily Herald* reported, whereupon Tillett 'advise[d] all of you volunteers to arm with the biggest cudgels you can get'. While the government pondered a request from employers that troops should be called into London, Tillett warned: 'Sedition or no sedition I want to say that if our men are to be murdered I am going to take a gun and I will shoot Lord Devonport'. The remainder of his sentence could not be heard for the thunderous cheering that resulted. Such statements, while perhaps useful for maintaining morale, may have proved counter-productive. Burns, hardly an unbiased observer, confided to his diary that evening that 'Tillett, it can be said, has prevented an early settlement by his personal attacks'.[17]

The threat of violence hung over the strike from first to last. From promising to arm the dockers with clubs, and to execute a single man, Tillett soon came to advocate more extreme and inclusive measures. Speaking in Hyde Park on Sunday, 7 July, he declared: 'if they could not win by peaceful methods . . . then they must take the power into their own hands. We must use other means', he added, 'and I openly state here that the only other means we have is violence and the use of every physical power we possess.' Goaded not only by this sort of encouragement, but by hunger, the presence of blacklegs and the spectre of defeat, many dockers attempted to fight with the police and strikebreakers. Riots and arrests were frequent throughout July, especially as the possibility of victory receded. On 1 August the *Daily Herald* reported 'serious rioting' at the London docks between strikers and blacklegs, 'in the course of which revolvers were freely fired and about twenty men were wounded'. Tillett, for his part, capped off his own verbal fireworks with an appeal for God to strike Lord Devonport dead. He asked those in favour to raise their right hand, and nearly everybody on Tower Hill complied. 'That's fine', Tillett remarked surveying his audience, and perhaps remembering the 1893 Bristol strike when he had also encouraged audience participation; 'now repeat after me. Oh God, strike Lord Devonport dead'. To this, the crowd added a chant of its own: 'He shall die, he shall die.'[18]

Dramatically superb, this spectacular appeal testifies more to Tillett's abilities as a demagogue than as a revolutionary leader. There is no evidence that the Dockers' 'Civilian Police Force' actually prepared for combat with the military, or that Tillett, whose entire career demonstrates his belief in the dictum that God helps those who help themselves, ever contemplated murder. His oratory represents a sympathetic emotional response to the hardships undergone by the striking workers and their families, not a serious call to revolutionary action. 'Egad! Ye bloated parasites, ye lords, ye wantons, ye inepts! Can you not see the work of your crazy hands and brains?' Here is Tillett's most genuine reaction to the strike. The hardships endured by the men drove him to frenzy. There existed another resolution to the debilitating deadlock in London, however, more realistic than Tillett's appeal for divine intervention. This was the national strike. He demanded that too; but the steps that might have led to its triumphant implementation were not taken.[19]

On 10 June the executive committee of the National Transport Workers' Federation voted by an 8 to 1 margin for national action, and Tillett himself moved that it begin at once. There was some opposition to his motion. Although James Sexton, of the National Union of Dock Labourers, voted with the majority, he warned that his society could only afford minimal strike pay, and therefore would prefer not to down tools; and Edmund Catheray, speaking for Havelock Wilson's Seamen's and Firemen's Union, which had benefited from sympathetic action during the 1911 dispute, flatly refused to be bound by the motion. In the event neither society came out. The nationwide stoppage, when the National Transport Workers' Federation called for it, proved a fiasco.[20]

The generally accepted explanation for its failure has been that the leaders overestimated their power to call a national strike, because they misread the lessons of the previous year. In 1911, with effective strikes in nearly every major port, it had seemed that they could turn national action on and off like a tap. Events in 1912 were to prove this assumption false, it is held, because no one among the leadership believed that agitation in the provinces to ensure concerted action would be necessary. That over-confidence played a role in the miscalculation seems evident, yet there were other causes for the failure as well.[21]

One such cause was lack of solidarity among the societies which composed the federation. As the discussion prior to the strike vote had indicated, two of its most important member unions had serious reservations about acting. Given this, Tillett, who had known the leaders of both societies for two decades, might have predicted the outcome. 'I do not trust either his wisdom or experience', he had written of Havelock Wilson in response to a query from Herman Jochade; 'the difficulty with [him] is . . . the failure to respect authority or discipline'. James Sexton too had been the subject of Jochade's curiosity, and Tillett had described him in similar terms: the National Dockers' Union had failed to pay dues to the International Transport Workers' Federation because of Sexton's 'laxity' and 'lack of democratic spirit'.[22]

Still another cause of the national strike's failure must have been the mixed feelings it inspired even among some of those who favoured it most strongly in public. That Tillett, and Gosling at least, preferred to limit the scope of the 1912 strike had been revealed nearly at the outset, in an extraordinary interview with the Home Secretary, Reginald McKenna. The meeting, which took place on 28 May, had the purpose of protesting government intervention in the docks to move essential foodstuffs. As Gosling, the president of the National Transport Workers' Federation, complained: 'If the Home Office wants some work done to preserve the people, we will consider it at once. But you are really taking sides . . . You did not come to us and say, "There is some food to be got out; will you move it?" ' Worse yet, as a result of the introduction of troops the strikers now believed 'that the government intends to help the employers knock us out . . . We are trying to keep the men in order . . . if we let them go they will go in most of the other ports and you will have to shoot a lot of them.' Tillett, who spoke after Gosling, then lectured the Home Secretary on the conservative function which the leaders of the National Transport Workers' Federation in fact performed:

> We have to summon up a considerable amount of personal courage, and use personal force at times, to control excited, hysterical, garrulous and perhaps foolish men who think they are injured. We have got all our work cut out to handle the crowd . . . and I want to say that where we fail, you will never succeed.

He went on to warn, as Gosling had, that national action was imminent, and then concluded: 'I did not want this at all.'[23]

The 1912 strike did as much as any dispute in which Tillett participated to confirm his reputation with the left wing, yet one is left wondering whether his attitude towards industrial conflict had changed since the first trip to Australia at the turn of the century. With hope for victory diminishing every day, his former self began to re-emerge. 'There was no man', he wrote in the *Daily Herald*:

who had tried harder throughout his life to prevent strikes than he had. Whenever he had been engaged in a strike, he had been forced to fight by the employers. The employers had forced this fight upon them . . .

He admired the men who were resolved that 'the dread struggle will go on, no matter what'. But he added:

there ought to be a more sane way possible than dislocation of trade, with its accompanying misery, hunger, madness and hunger cries . . . and the silent death struggle with capitalism. Surely there ought to be better ways.[24]

'Humanity's fortitude should not be allowed to accept its own destruction', Tillett told an interviewer from the *Daily Herald* on the day that the strike was proclaimed ended. There is no reason to doubt the sincerity of his sentiments. Enraged by the employers who relied upon starvation as their ally, he was above all appalled by the consequences of the struggle. His appeal for divine intervention was symbolic of his real impotence. 'Ben Tillett pictures queerly vague, irrelevantly attractive, but no business application in an emergency', Burns had written in his diary during the second week of the dispute. Demogoguery and empathy were not enough to win the dock strike. In the final analysis, Tillett did not know what to do, except to end it.[25]

III

Despite the defeat of the 1912 dock strike, Tillett remained in the limelight. During the two remaining years before the outbreak of the First World War, he continued to deliver the dramatic and violent orations which had re-established him as one of the handful of labour leaders with a national reputation. At the same time, the contradictions inherent in his position were becoming increasingly apparent.

At times he appeared to be backing away from the syndicalist position. Even after a successful strike, he wrote soon after the 1912 failure, in the 7 August *Daily Herald*:

the owners and masters of distribution and production soon balance to an equation the purchasing value of wages. And so the worker commences again the fight against the economic powers robbing him

surely of all the advantages of his enhanced wages in enhanced prices
of necessaries and rent and other things.

In fact, he alternated between syndicalist and Marxist interpretations of
the class struggle.

'The revolutionary organisation must mean One Union for all Transport Workers, at the very least', he wrote on 5 August in the *Daily
Herald*, 'with the objective of One Union for all labour'. This was, no
doubt, a lesson of the 1912 strike, when the railway workers had been
used to move goods which the dockers had blocked, and when members
of the National Transport Workers' Federation itself failed to honour
the strike. It was also fundamental syndicalist dogma. So was anti-
parliamentarianism, which Tillett espoused as well. 'Parliament is a
farce and a sham', he wrote in his 1912 annual message to the Dockers'
Union, 'the rich man's Duma, the employer's Tammany, the "Thieves'
Kitchen", and the poor man's despot.'

Simultaneously, he vitiated these assertions. In articles for the
Daily Herald and *Justice* he enumerated the difficulties of amalgamation. Although the early labour pioneers had theoretically opposed distinctions among workers, in fact their organizations had paralleled the
evolution of the separate branches of capitalist industry. These were
now so firmly established that it might prove impossible to overcome
the sectional differences that divided the working class. The differences
which had to be overcome were legion:

> There are no two unions alike in benefits, contributions, methods of
> dealing with recalcitrant members, rules for handling arrears, fines,
> probations, initiation fees, out-of-work and strike pay, sick and
> funeral monies and a hundred other details of administration . . .
> Then there are not many unions which have anything like a
> standardised relationship with the various national and interna-
> tional federations. Unions vary in their attitude and outlook on
> social and political matters. Even so far as trades councils, trade
> congresses and the international movement are concerned there is
> a great divergence.

For all these reasons, Tillett came reluctantly to 'admit that after more
than thirty years of Trade Union work, I find the theory of One Union
almost Utopian'. And since he had written 'we need all the help we can
get', as the 1912 dispute entered its tragic last stage, he was prepared
again to consider a Labour Party in the House of Commons. 'If

politicians can utilise their position by explaining the [need for] revolution,' he subsequently observed, 'then indeed they are earning their bread honestly as workers' representatives.' On 20 August he issued a manifesto to working-class electors of Midlothian and of East Carmarthen, where by-elections were about to be held: 'vote straight for Labour'.[26]

Yet, as before, he was hardly an uncritical supporter of the party. MacDonald and Snowden were:

> quick change artists like Jekyll and Hyde. They will roar like any bull for Free Trade on Liberal platforms; they will act the sucking dove in the pulpit and will snivel like Uriah Heep of their own humility and goodness . . . On top of these displays they will (as four hundred pounders in Parliament) vie with the dullest minister of state in demands for 'Loranorder'.

And when both the Labour Party and the Independent Labour Party refused to sponsor a candidate in the June by-election at Leicester, he took great delight in the candidacy of a local militant.

> The Labour Party is a fraud; political exigencies tie it to distasteful partnerships, unwritten and unsigned agreements . . . The real menace to the movement, the real reactionary body thwarting progress is the present Labour Party . . . There must be a new development . . . The Labour Party to live must die.

Before the 1911 strike, Tillett had assured MacDonald that he 'would always remain faithful to the concept of a working class political party'. He had not specified the party's name, however; now it became clear that he felt most at home within the British Socialist Party, the latest reincarnation of the old Social Democratic Federation, and 'the only party', according to Tillett, 'that taught revolution and told the worker he had either to fight or go down to the grave'. By the end of the year he had been adopted by the British Socialist Party to stand at Northampton.[27]

He could be relied upon to support almost any dissident movement. Within a few months of the defeated 1912 strike, he was campaigning for Lansbury, who had resigned the Labour whip, to stand for Parliament as a suffragist independent. With Lansbury under indictment for 'inciting women to crime', Tillett issued a 'Call to Arms' in his defence. 'There must be a revolt', he proclaimed. 'Every branch of every Trade

Union, Socialist and Labour organisation must raise a protest.' Almost by default he had become a strong supporter of the women's movement, though five years earlier he had termed Hardie's association with it an example of 'mendacious arrogance'. Now he reminded his readers that 'these women fed a million meals to the children during the dock strike of last year. Every sturdy transport worker stands under an obligation to the women and to men like George Lansbury.' When the latter was sentenced to imprisonment, Tillett warned that free speech was endangered by the Liberal government. Under his prodding, the executive of his union issued an appeal for industrial action to protest the infamous 'Cat and Mouse Act', by which hunger-striking suffragettes were released from prison to recuperate and were jailed again as soon as they had recovered. To Lansbury he wrote: 'there is fighting to be done', and he promised to 'have a hand in it'.[28]

In fact, it appears that the rhetoric reflected only superficially Tillett's real views. He felt genuinely indignant about injustice, oppression and exploitation. He was less clear on how to overcome them. Certainly his own conduct belied the violence of his language. He only called for the general strike when there was little likelihood that anyone would follow his advice.

During the dock strikes, Tillett's oratory served a dual role. It vented his emotions and helped maintain rank-and-file morale. During a less tumultuous period, such rhetoric seems mainly to have maintained Tillett's reputation for militancy. He invoked the national strike time and again when there was very little possibility that one would be carried out. Thus he called for one in defence of Mann, when the latter had been imprisoned for his 'Don't Shoot' manifesto to soldiers. Later he invoked the national strike when Lansbury was in jail for having aided the suffragettes. However, when the prospect of a general strike became real, as in the 1913 Dublin transport workers' dispute, Tillett opposed it.

The famous Dublin transport workers' lock-out of autumn 1913 characterized the bitterness and violence of the entire period of labour unrest between 1910 and 1914. Before it was finished five labourers had been killed, thousands injured and 656 strikers arrested. Its leader was James Larkin, by all accounts a man of immense energy, determination and oratorical gifts. He was in many respects a figure much like Tillett. 'I have got a divine mission, I believe, to make men and women discontented', he once told a Manchester audience. By the summer of 1913, he had succeeded to the extent that almost the entire general workforce of Dublin had joined his Irish Transport Workers'

Union.

On 3 September some 400 Dublin employers responded to various of Larkin's provocations with a lock-out affecting 15,000 men. Two days earlier, Larkin, who was being sought for arrest on charges of sedition, had managed to address a rally from the windows of a fashionable Connolly Street hotel, owned by William Murphy, whose Tramway Company workers were already on strike at Larkin's command. The latter's arrest sparked a riot which did not entirely subside until the following day. Two strikers were killed; 200 police and 400 citizens were injured.[29]

Just as the news from Dublin appeared in the press, the British Trades Union Congress convened its annual meeting in Manchester. In response to an appeal for aid by representatives of the Irish Transport Workers' Federation, Sexton of the Liverpool dockers moved that the government should 'institute a rigid inquiry into the conduct of the police'. Tillett, who supported the motion, commented upon its 'mild, not to say guarded' language, and demanded the release from prison of Larkin and his confederate James Connolly. 'I do not want to exaggerate the position', Tillett claimed:

> but it is clear that the man who has the pluck to strike, must have in mind the right to have firearms, and the right to use them. (Cheers.) War has been declared upon the workers and if we pass resolutions of this kind, we must stand by them . . . This exhibition of Czardom is something we will fight against, even if it is sedition and civil war to do so.

The delegates seemed to agree. Many viewed the events in Dublin as the climax to a series of brutal provocations carried out by the employers and military and, indirectly, the government. 'It will be necessary that we have a revolution of force', C.B. Stanton of the Miners' Federation declared. Robert Smillie demanded a general strike in support of the Dublin workers, adding that 'it is our duty, legal or illegal, to train our people to defend themselves'. Nevertheless, the Trades Union Congress merely sent a deputation, headed by Arthur Henderson, to investigate Dublin conditions and to confer with the Employers' Federation. Spurned by that organization, the committee recommended financial support for the strikers. The sum of £5,000 was immediately despatched to the Irish Transport Workers' Union; before the dispute had ended an additional £90,000 was contributed.[30]

This was a far cry from what the Dublin strikers, Larkin and militant

British trade unionists had demanded. Released on bail, Larkin paid a flying visit to London to drum up support. His appeal, however, took the form of a violent attack upon the Labour Party and moderate trade union officials. He demanded sympathetic strikes, even at the risk of breaking signed agreements. Syndicalists throughout England were ready to oblige. During September, railwaymen in Liverpool, Birmingham, Crewe, Derby and Sheffield spontaneously refused to carry goods destined for Dublin. Certain officials of the National Transport Workers' Federation thought transport workers would soon be out as well. 'The rank and file . . . say fight', Robert Williams reported in the *Daily Herald*, predicting even more militant action in the near future.

> Unless we have assistance of a strong, resolute and defiant character for the outraged workers of Dublin, we must appeal direct to Caesar . . . Far better to risk our all on some worthy object, than to be invited ever closer to an age-long servitude. Remember, workers, remember, officials — 'Those conquer who believe they can'.[31]

By contrast, Tillett's advice to the rank and file was distinctly *sotto voce*. He had been at the fore when the aim was to secure Larkin's release from jail, and to frame a protest resolution at a TUC conference. He drew back, however, at the prospect of direct action in which his own organization might participate. Instead, he called for the convening of 'a National Conference . . . of the Trades Union Congress and General Federation of Trades, together with the national Transport Workers' Federation . . . We must settle by honest and satisfactory means the strike. We must ensure fair play between the parties.'[32]

As would soon be revealed, he played a double game throughout the affair. By calling for a special conference, Tillett distinguished himself from the conservatives who preferred to ignore Larkin. Yet any meeting of the TUC was unlikely to take action in which Tillett's own organization could be expected to participate. He was occupying two positions at once. When Larkin, who had been pardoned by the government after his sentence of seven months' imprisonment provoked a groundswell of protest, bore his 'fiery cross' to England in search of support, his first stop was Manchester's Free Trade Hall, filled with an overflow crowd of 20,000. He shared the platform with another British trade unionist, Ben Tillett. Larkin's speech has been characterized as having 'left everything precariously up in the air'; Tillett, however, although reiterating his desire for the calling of a 'great national council' rather

than sympathetic direct action, indulged in another patented display
of incendiary rhetoric:

> There was no alternative in the future but that the workers them-
> selves must arm. He knew there were detectives present from Scot-
> land Yard ... They could take their report to [the Home Secretary
> Reginald] McKenna. He only wished that McKenna would come out
> at the head of the police and then, given the chance to arm them-
> selves, there would be no more McKennas.

Tillett enjoyed attacking the Home Secretary and knew it strengthened his reputation with the militants to do so. Moreover, it was safe. He
had indicated no specific path for the strikers, nor said anything which
committed his own organization to action; and he had learned over the
years that the government preferred his fulminations to prosecuting
him for sedition and making him appear as a martyr. On the other hand,
if an emergency meeting of the trade union movement was held, as
Tillett demanded, it would almost certainly refuse to sanction a general
strike. Yet it was for such a meeting that Tillett continued to call, all
the while maintaining a high level of violent oratory. When, on 18
November, the parliamentary committee of the TUC agreed to convene
an extraordinary TUC session in three weeks' time (9 December), the
aim was to short-circuit Larkin's appeals for sympathetic strikes. Tillett,
who appeared with Larkin again the next day at a mammoth rally at
the Albert Hall, affected to believe that the TUC meeting could have
been convened within three days. Still regarded as a member of the
militant camp, the role he was about to play was entirely misappre-
hended.[33]
Meanwhile, Larkin, with three weeks to rouse the country, had been
given more than enough rope to hang himself. By appealing directly to
the rank and file for sympathetic strikes, he hardly endeared himself to
the leaders who would meet on 9 December. He made matters infinitely
worse by personally attacking the trade union officials and Labour
Party members whom he supposed to obstruct him. His language — and
targets — were uncannily reminiscent of Tillett's outbursts twenty years
earlier. But when 9 December finally dawned, it was Tillett himself who
moved:

> That this conference deplores and condemns the unfair attacks made
> by men inside the trade union movement upon British trade union
> officials; it affirms its confidence in those who have been so

unjustly assailed . . .

This from the castigator of Hardie, Snowden, MacDonald, Henderson and countless others![34]

His motion ensured that personalities would be debated rather than the issue of how best to aid the Dublin strikers. Speaker after speaker rose to denounce Larkin for attacking British labour leaders. Utterly unintimidated, Larkin replied by launching a dramatic and defiant counter-attack. The result was entirely predictable: Tillett's resolution was carried almost unanimously. Another resolution pledging financial support passed too. But the crucial decision was taken when the delegates voted to reopen negotiations with the Employers' Federation. This implied that there was a limit to the generosity of the TUC. When the employers refused to accept even minimal terms from the union, the strike was doomed, as trade union funds were almost exhausted. On 11 February 1914 the lock-out was ended by the employers, who had conceded none of the men's demands.

There would appear to be two explanations for Tillett's conduct during this episode. First, and perhaps most significant, he probably believed that the Dockers' Union was not prepared for another strike. It had, after all, struck twice during the last two years, and had sustained a crushing defeat only eighteen months before. No doubt the union treasury was relatively empty, and no doubt too Tillett feared that the men did not possess the financial resources to sustain another period of enforced idleness. From Tillett's point of view, then, he was only being realistic in opposing a general strike in 1913. At the same time, however, he was indicating, perhaps unwittingly, how little he really cared for syndicalist doctrine which, after all, envisioned the general strike as the probable trigger of a working-class revolution. Clearly that is not how Tillett saw it. The general strike, like any other industrial dispute, would aim at wresting concessions from the employers. Tillett's attitude presaged that of the TUC general council some thirteen years later, in 1926.

The second possible explanation of Tillett's unexpected attack on Larkin is based upon intangibles. He may have proceeded from motives which were not entirely clear even to him. Throughout his career, Tillett complained that he was treated like an outcast. Yet he was too proud and too combative to cease acting in the manner his critics found offensive. In 1913, Tillett was presented with an opportunity to disassociate himself from a man whose very words might have come from

Tillett's own lips. In rejecting Larkin, perhaps Tillett was rejecting that part of himself which accounted for his isolation from the solid centre of the labour movement.

The reaction of the English pro-Larkin forces to Tillett was quick and fierce. 'The Northern Division *Daily Herald* League (representing 250 paying Leaguers) views with disgust the betrayal of the workers by their leaders at the Memorial Hall Conference', began one letter of protest to the *Daily Herald*:

> further they call upon Mr Ben Tillett to explain why he moved a vote of confidence in the leaders, seeing that in all his previous actions and articles he had been against official leaders.

'The rank and file are particularly disgusted with Mr Ben Tillett's action in adopting the role of castigator to Mr Larkin', another *Daily Herald* reader wrote. The editors confirmed that the majority of letters they had received were from 'rank and filers . . . wondering whether the dockers' leader was a Quixote or a catspaw . . . or whether he was fairly reported at all'.

Tillett despatched an angry telegram to the journal — 'Very much resent unfair statement today's issue' — yet his arguments to justify his actions were lame. The resolution, he claimed, was really an appeal for unity, but the anti-Larkin forces had made 'treacherous use' of it. Immediately after the Congress he had attempted to re-establish his position with the militants: 'There must be direct action if that is imperative', he wrote on 11 December, now that there could be none. This time the objective result of his conduct belied the militant rhetoric. As the letters condemning him continued to pour into the offices of the *Herald* (which continued to print them), Tillett responded gracelessly: 'If the armchair rebels will get out and do some real work for Dublin we might win.' To this gratuitous attack the *Herald* responded with good humour: 'All of us have been fighting for a long time now, and you know that in Tudor Street we have not got a solitary arm chair!'[35]

Had he done irretrievable damage to his reputation as a militant? Ironically not. Within a few months, Tillett was calling — amid cheers — for a national transport workers' strike in defence of South African miners, notwithstanding the fact that such action was again entirely out of the question. His criticism of the Parliamentary Labour Party continued unrelentingly. His annual report to the Dockers' Union called for 'revolutionary political agitation', and reasserted his conviction that 'all the great successes achieved have been promoted by industrial mass action, right up to the demand for a national strike'. Tillett's reaction to the outbreak of the First World War, however, permanently ruined his reputation with the left. The war deprived him once and for all of the opportunity to disappoint the advocates of 'direct action'.[36]

Notes

1. See, for example, George Dangerfield, *The Strange Death of Liberal England* (Capricorn Books, New York, 1961), in which it is argued that 'the great unrest' corresponded to a deep-seated malaise in the British soul, and was essentially a rejection of Liberalism; Elie Halevy, *The Era of Tyrannies* (Anchor Books, Garden City, NY, 1965), on the other hand, maintained that it was a rejection of parliamentary democracy and presaged the 'era of tyrannies' – the inter-war years; Henry Pelling, *Popular Politics and Society in Late Victorian Britain* (Macmillan, London, 1968), held that it was primarily an economic struggle for higher wages, and had no greater significance; a view shared by R.V. Sires in 'Labour Unrest in England, 1910-14', *Journal of Economic History*, vol. 15, no. 3 (September 1955), pp. 246-66.

2. For a somewhat disappointing discussion of syndicalism in Britain, see Robert Holton, *British Syndicalism, 1910-14* (Pluto Press, London, 1976).

3. Webb Trade Union Collection, Section B, volume 105, item 15, 'Copy of Report submitted to the International Transport Workers' Federation' by Robert Williams. For a detailed discussion of the National Transport Workers' Federation, see Gordon A. Phillips, 'The National Transport Workers' Federation', unpublished DPhil thesis, University of Oxford, 1968; International Transport Workers' Federation Papers, no. 87, Tillett to Herman Jochade, 10 December 1910. Its first annual general council meeting was held in Liverpool on 1 June 1911. Sixteen labour organizations attended: Dock, Wharf, Riverside and General Labourers' Union; National Seamen's and Firemen's Union; National Union of Shop Stewards; General Railway Workers' Union; National Amalgamated Union of Labourers; National Coal Porters' Union; National Amalgamated Union of Enginemen; Labour Protection League; United Order of Labourers; Amalgamated Society of Watermen and Lightermen; National Amalgamated Union of Labourers of Great Britain and Ireland; Amalgamated Stevedores' Labour Protection League; Amalgamated Protective Union of Engine Drivers; National Union of Gasworkers and General Labourers; London Carmen's Union; and National Union of Dock Labourers.

4. Phillips, 'National Transport Workers' Federation', p. 81; J. Lovell, *Stevedores and Dockers, a Study of Trade Unionism in the Port of London, 1870-1914* (Macmillan, London, 1969), p. 157. I have relied primarily on Lovell for the account of the following events.

5. The Port of London Authority was established in 1908. It replaced the old Joint Dock Committee. Under metropolitan control, it permitted two workers' representatives on its executive council; Lovell, *Stevedores and Dockers*, p. 154; see Dock, Wharf, Riverside and General Labourers' Union, *Annual Reports*, 1900-10; Lovell, *Stevedores and Dockers*, p. 146; Tillett, *Dock, Wharf, Riverside and General Workers' Union: A Brief History of the Dockers' Union commemorating the 1889 Dockers' Strike* (London, 1910), p. 3; Phillips, 'National Transport Workers' Federation', p. 66; *Justice*, 17 December 1910; Tillett quoted in

Alfred M. Gollin, *The Observer and J.O. Garvin, 1908-14* (Oxford University Press, London, 1960), pp. 329-30.

6. *Justice*, 8 October 1910; *Daily Herald*, 16 April 1914; J. Ramsay MacDonald Papers, Public Record Office, 30/69/51/21, Tillett to MacDonald, 29 June 1911; in his biography, *Ramsay MacDonald* (Jonathan Cape, London, 1977), David Marquand argues that MacDonald did not want the Labour Party associated in the public mind with the 'great unrest' which he regarded as a temporary breakdown in an essentially stable system, see p. 147.

7. Tillett, *History of the London Transport Workers' Strike, 1911* (London, 1912), p. 13.

8. Lovell, *Stevedores and Dockers*, p. 179.

9. International Transport Workers' Federation Papers, no. 87, Tillett to Herman Jochade, 27 May 1910; Tillett, *History of the London Transport Workers' Strike*, p. 36; Burns Papers, Add MS 46333, diary entry, 9 August 1911.

10. *Justice*, 12 August 1911; Public Record Office, HO 45/10649, 21 July 1911, Manifesto to the Home Secretary & President of the Board of Trade and the Permanent Officials of both State Departments; International Transport Workers' Federation Papers, no. 87, 'To District Branch Officers and Members – London Section'; Public Record Office, HO 45/10649, Tillett to Secretary and Members of the Labour Party, 17 July 1911.

11. Tillett, *History of the London Transport Workers' Strike*, pp. 13-17.

12. International Transport Workers' Federation Papers, no. 87, Tillett to Jochade, 31 July and 19 August, 1911.

13. Pelling, for example.

14. For Tillett's speaking engagements, see *Justice* and the *Daily Herald*, especially during autumn 1911. For more on the *Daily Herald* itself, see George Lansbury, *The Miracle of Fleet Street* (Labour Publishing Co., London, n.d.), and p. 28 for his description of Tillett.

15. *The Times*, 24 May 1912; a deduction corroborated by H.M. Hyndman, who wrote soon after the dispute had ended that Tillett was 'outvoted and overruled on the 1912 strike'. H.M. Hyndman, *Further Reminiscences* (Macmillan, London, 1912), p. 470.

16. *Dockers' Record*, September and February 1912.

17. *Daily Herald*, 7 June and 11 June 1912; *The Times*, 10 June and 12 June 1912; Burns Papers, Add. MS 46285, diary entry, 12 June 1912.

18. *The Times*, 8 July 1912; *Daily Herald*, 9 July 1912; *Daily Telegraph*, 25 July 1912.

19. *Daily Herald*, 17 June 1912.

20. International Transport Workers' Federation Papers, no. 87, National Transport Workers' Federation Special Meeting of Executive Council; Tillett to Jochade, 29 June 1912.

21. See, for example, Lovell, *Stevedores and Dockers*, p. 200; Phillips, 'National Transport Workers' Federation', pp. 107-9.

22. International Transport Workers' Federation Papers, no. 87, Tillett to Jochade, 22 June 1910; Tillett to Jochade, 14 January 1911.

23. Public Record Office, HO 223 877/65, 'Notes of a Deputation of London Disputes Committee to S. of S.'

24. *Daily Herald*, 21 June and 8 July 1912.

25. *Daily Herald*, 20 July 1912; John Burns Papers, Add MS 46334, diary entry 4 June 1912.

26. *Daily Herald*, 23 August 1912; see also *Justice*, 17 August 1912; and the *Dockers' Record*, June 1912 for essentially the same argument; *Daily Herald* 31 July 1912, 17 September 1912 and 20 August 1912.

27. *Daily Herald*, 17 September, 21 October 1912, 9 October and 24 June

1913; *Justice*, 5 October and 2 December 1912.

28. *Daily Herald*, 19 November 1912 and 18 April 1913; Transport House, LP/PRO/13/11/174, Tillett to Ramsay MacDonald, 27 January 1912; *Daily Herald*, 12 May 1913, 3 July 1913 and 26 July 1913; George Lansbury Papers, London School of Economics and Political Science, vol. 7, fol. 35, Tillett to Lansbury, 15 September 1913.

29. *Manchester Guardian*, 15 September 1913; Emmet Larkin, *James Larkin* (MIT Press, Cambridbe, Mass., 1965), pp. 122 and 126.

30. *TUC Annual Report,* 1913, pp. 67-70.

31. *Daily Herald*, 15 November 1913.

32. *Daily Herald*, 15 November 1913.

33. Larkin, *Larkin*, pp. 144-5; *Manchester Guardian*, 17 November 1913.

34. *Justice*, 13 December 1913.

35. *Daily Herald*, 15-17 December 1913.

36. See, for example, *Daily Herald*, 9 March 1914 and 16 April 1914.

9 THE AGITATOR AS PATRIOT, 1914-18

I

The outbreak of the First World War smashed, among other great illusions, the one that the workers of Europe would refuse to fight each other at the command of their rulers. The Socialist International, built up painfully over the years, was pledged to oppose war between nations or, failing all else, to transform such a catastrophe into war between classes; it was shattered irretrievably in August 1914. After some internal wrangling, the German Social Democrats voted the war credits; French and Belgian socialists rallied to defend their invaded borders; British trade unionists and socialists marched unprotestingly to the trenches.[1]

In every belligerent nation, however, there were dissidents, albeit an embattled minority. In Britain, a tiny minority in the Labour Party, including Ramsay MacDonald, most of the Independent Labour Party, a section of the British Socialist Party, and George Lansbury's Herald League opposed the war from its inception. They were joined by a high-powered group of Liberals, 'trouble-makers' in A.J.P. Taylor's apt phrase, many of whom soon formed their own ginger group, the Union for Democratic Control. Tillett, notwithstanding his reputation as a dissident, his connection with Lansbury and his ties with the syndicalists, would have nothing to do with these critics of government policy. Rather, he sided almost immediately with the patriotic faction in the British Socialist Party — and with the vast majority of labour leaders who supported the war.[2]

Tillett's position between 1914 and 1918 was seen by many as a complete repudiation of everything that he had previously stood for. Though a professed internationalist and proponent of class warfare, he opposed all strikes and echoed the cry that the only good German was a dead one. A long-standing critic of the Labour Party leadership, in 1917 he finally entered Parliament as a Labour representative. Having broken with the rhetoric of Marxist internationalism and class struggle — which was not altogether easy for him, as will become evident — he was able to articulate chauvinistic and patriotic sentiments which he had hitherto generally repressed. Those surprised by Tillett's position during the war, however, misunderstood the complexities and ambiguities of his earlier attitudes. In fact, despite his identification with the left wing of the

175

labour movement, his wartime stance was a logical culmination of his past history.

Throughout his career, Tillett's internationalist declarations served to obscure an ugly streak of chauvinism. Occasionally, however, it broke through the surface, as in his early opposition to Jewish immigration into the East End, his ill-judged remark about 'hare brained . . . continental revolutionaries' at the founding conference of the Independent Labour Party in 1893, and his agitation in 1896 against the employment of foreign seamen, which was explicitly racist. Later, his anti-Semitic lapse during the January 1910 Swansea electoral campaign against Sir Alfred Mond suggests that the mature Tillett, no less than the young agitator, continued to pander to popular prejudices.[3]

A willingness to accept the trappings of British power and authority accompanied them. Tillett's attitude towards the Crown, for example, was not what might have been expected from a revolutionary socialist. 'He was neither a Republican nor a Monarchist', he remarked on one occasion, 'but he regarded King Edward VII as a man and as a great peace maker and appreciated his services to the nation.' Upon Edward's death, he 'breathed his deep feelings of sympathy with the Royal family', and went on to deliver a form of eulogy: 'In the person of the late King they had one of the sanest political forces that had helped to govern the country.' Even during the bitterly fought 1912 dock strike, when class divisions were clearly drawn, his attitude towards the Crown was ambiguous: 'the men had not enough food in their bellies to raise a cheer for the King', Tillett warned, as the monarch prepared to visit the East End. The implication was, however, that under normal circumstances, Tillett would volunteer as cheer-leader. Then, too, Tillett was an imperialist, at least to the extent that he occasionally faulted the government for failing to acknowledge its obligations to British settlers in Africa and the Antipodes.[4]

Despite his many declarations that the working man had no country, Tillett was sufficiently patriotic to wish to see Britain the supreme world power. Thus, he viewed Germany and the United States as rivals that his country must defeat in peaceful competition for trade. In return for this willingness to identify his own interests with Britain's, Tillett seemed to expect a quid pro quo from the government when he dealt with foreigners. This was perhaps most apparent during his brush with the Belgian authorities in 1897, after he had tried to bring the Antwerp dockers into an International Federation of Dock, Wharf and River Workers. Tillett demanded from the British Foreign Office protection and representation in a suit for damages against the Belgian government which had briefly imprisoned him. Thus, surprisingly, the internationalist shared the presumptions of Lord Palmerston.[5]

This streak of patriotism and nationalism could not fail to affect even Tillett's most cosmopolitan statements. Take, for example, his position on the question of naval preparedness. 'The last election was Chinese labour', Tillett wrote in May 1909 for *Justice*, 'this election will be "Dreadnoughts".' Tillett explained at numerous rallies throughout the country until literally the eve of war that his concern was with the 'Breadnoughts' of England instead. 'Dreadnoughts are the symbol of craven incompetence and greed', he once wrote, 'and can be neither defence nor hope of national stability.' As usual, however, his next sentence revealed the ambiguity of his position: 'The international fighting machines are in homes and industry.' Was Tillett's opposition to the naval race, then, merely tactical? Did he oppose it because he believed there was a better way to ensure England's supremacy? In September 1912, at the height of his reputation as an advocate of the international proletarian revolution, he wrote: 'So long as we are in need of a Navy, we of course want the best; the best gun, the best armour plate.' These, he thought, the Admiralty would provide; his point of departure with them was their failure to maintain decent conditions for the men: 'My Lords, when will you waken to the fact that the "lower deck" is your fighting force, and that you need to have splendid men to form splendid crews?' Tillett returned to this point in the pages of the *Daily Herald* on 11 September: 'One man at a gun may turn the whole tide of battle . . . and yet the Admiralty have no person on the Administration who cares a hang for the men.' He did not question the need for naval armaments, then, so much as he doubted their effectiveness in maintaining British supremacy. Rather, a better-treated lower deck would enable Britain to dominate the world.[6]

In like manner, Tillett opposed the 'armour rings' which in his opinion had gained ascendancy over the Liberal government, and were inexorably driving towards war. Workers of all countries, he insisted, should combine to defeat the evil machinations of these international capitalists. When the London-based 'Armour Rings, Shipbuilding Rings and Gunnery Rings' threatened to desert the metropolis, however, Tillett accused them of 'lacking a sense of patriotism'. Whether or not war occurred, the removal of these firms to more profitable locations caused 'serious distress . . . among a thousand families in the Canning Town area'. In sum, Tillett's opposition to the construction of Dreadnoughts was not unqualified; he actually approved of building them when the jobs of his union members were at stake.[7]

It is necessary to dwell upon such examples of Tillett's chauvinism, nationalism, opportunism and ambiguity, not only in order to make sense of his position during the war, but also because his professions in favour of international working-class solidarity and revolution were both frequent and fervent. They began, literally, at the outset of his public career. For example, in an address (delivered almost certainly in 1890) to the Dundee dockers entitled 'The "Help Yourself Gospel" or the New Trades Unionism', Tillett explained that war was a device used by the governing classes to divert public attention from social questions. 'But if these bondholders want to fight,' he cried, 'let them get an army out of Piccadilly'. During the South African War, Tillett was a strong pro-Boer, though ill health curtailed his activities on their behalf. During the five years before August 1914 his reputation as an ardent supporter of internationalism and the international strike to avert war was confirmed. The 1913 annual general council meeting of the National Transport Workers' Federation saw a full dress debate over the issue. Tillett himself moved the resolution:

> In the event of international war being imminent . . . we recommend a general stoppage of work among all transport workers who are engaged in the transportation of troops and munitions of war.

His supporting remarks adhered to the Marxist position laid down by the left wing·of the Second International. 'What difference would be the lot of the [English] workers if they were governed by the German or French Government?' Tillett asked. 'There was no distinction between the German worker and the English worker.' The response of the assembled delegates was favourable. Only Sexton of the Liverpool dockers was opposed, and even he confessed his 'entire agreement with the general principle of the resolution'.[8]

The question of international action against war was linked with a domestic campaign in which Tillett participated as well. This had to do with both the nature and composition of the army. Never a pacifist, Tillett sided with Hyndman and Quelch of the British Socialist Party in favour of a citizens' army, against the anti-conscriptionists in the Independent Labour Party. In 1909, when the TUC voted against conscription, Tillett responded angrily: 'So the flapdoodle of hysterical goody goody peace is accepted.' His reasoning was simple: a population devoid of military training and weapons could neither resist governmental tyranny nor carry out a revolution. In addition he believed that an army of conscripted workers would be unlikely to break strikes.[9]

Tillett often argued that the only war which workers should wage was the class war. This, in addition to his advocacy of the international strike in case of war, and his opposition to the construction of Dreadnoughts (ambiguous though it was), established his credentials as an internationalist. His connection with the International Transport Workers' Federation enhanced it. In early 1914, when Robert Williams, who represented the National Transport Workers' Federation of Great Britain in the International Transport Workers' Federation, argued in favour of withdrawing from the international organization, Tillett firmly opposed him. Invited to Germany during this period, Tillett was manifestly impressed not only by the extent of German trade union organization, the success of the Social Democratic Party, and the hospitality of its leaders, but also by the German workers' ostensible commitment to international peace. He attended a socialist meeting in Kiel, the German naval centre. In retrospect, he could discern that 'the ominous signs of a great international war were quite evident'. Before August 1914, however, the situation had appeared quite the opposite:

> The German workman is quite alive to what a class war means and what international embroilment means. I wish I could say the same of every one of our . . . men in this country.[10]

Tillett may have been wrong about the Germans, but his misgivings about the English were well founded. As the international crisis heightened in early August 1914, public opinion grew enthusiastic for war. At first, Tillett set his face against it. He loyally supported the British delegates to the International Socialist Bureau — Arthur Henderson and Keir Hardie — who demanded that Britain should remain neutral. On Sunday, 2 August, he took part in the famous anti-war demonstration in Trafalgar Square. Beatrice Webb remarked in her diary that it was a pathetic gathering, yet it passed a resolution bristling with defiance:

> That this great meeting calls upon the citizens of London to express their deepest detestation of the international war that seems to be on the point of breaking out, protests against any step that may be taken to support Russia, either directly or indirectly in consequence of any understanding with France; urges the workers to unite to prevent their respective Governments from engaging in war, and the British Government to confine itself to bring about the peace.

Speakers addressed the crowds from three platforms headed by Hardie, Lansbury and Hyndman. The chairman of the British Social Party was heckled by a 'number of brainless and irresponsible youths [who] kept up a chorus of inane interruptions'. Tillett, the next speaker, drowned them out. 'We don't want to sing "Rule Britannia" nor [*sic*] "God Save the King" so much at this juncture. What we want is to sing "God Save the People".'[11]

The British government declared war on Germany at eleven o'clock at night, on Tuesday, 4 August. Until the last moment, Tillett continued to advocate neutrality. The Dockers' Union executive had met in an emergency session on Monday, 3 August: the next day, Tillett sent copies of the resolutions passed to the presidents of the Miners, Transport Workers and Railwaymen − that is, to the leaders of the Triple Alliance − and to the chairmen of the Labour Party, TUC and General Federation of Trade Unions. To the Triple Alliance, Tillett proposed action against the war. There can be little doubt that he wanted to raise the spectre of a possible general strike. 'Will you . . . call together a National Joint Conference of the three Executives at once in order to make a protest and arrange such organization as we may deem fit for the execution of our wishes?' Tillett asked.

> The purpose and power of our alliance can be made felt, and our membership helped to realize the grave necessities of the occasion and their own sacred responsibilities in preventing war and demanding the neutrality of England. If there is to be an alliance between countries, let that alliance be confined to the workers of each country who have no quarrel with each other.

Tillett was less explicit in his communications to Henderson of the Labour Party, Bowerman of the TUC and Appleton of the General Federation of Trade Unions, confining himself merely to 'an earnest appeal for an immediate National Conference of Trade Unionists and Labourites'. Again, however, it is certain that he hoped such a gathering would find some means of pressuring the government to keep out of the war.[12]

At this juncture, Tillett's health again broke down. It had been particularly bad since the dock strike in 1912 'which very nearly killed me'. In March 1914, his doctors had recommended complete rest for twelve months, and he spent April and May in a hospital. It was, he wrote, 'my usual breakdown . . . Neuritis, asthma, and the Lord knows what'. Released in June, his efforts to keep Britain from entering the war probably contributed to his relapse. In any case, the government's decision to intervene occurred simultaneously with his breakdown. Without suggesting that Tillett's behaviour during the next few months was determined by ill health, it is not inconceivable that his emotional response to events after 4 August was somewhat influenced by it.[13]

The patriotic reaction to Britain's declaration of war was overwhelming. Those who had demanded that Britain keep out of the conflict wavered; many found reasons to support intervention. Many of those who remained opposed nevertheless discovered ways to compromise. For example, on 10 August the editors of the anti-war *Daily Herald* wrote:

> In times of industrial disputes, whether we agree with the fight or not, we stand by those who are suffering and help them. We must do the same now . . . It is therefore the duty of every Trade Unionist, Socialist, Syndicalist, and all other persons who are opposed to the principle of war to at once take steps to alleviate the distress which is bound to arise.

This position enabled them to maintain contact with the vast pro-war majority, but it left them with a dilemma. Did one help or hinder the ment at the front by sending them weapons, by agitating for better conditions at home, by criticizing the government? This was to become the crucial question for moderate opponents of the war. Evolutionary socialists like Lansbury never managed to resolve it, but Tillett did. The nationalist groundswell touched a deeper chord in him than Marx had ever reached. He used the argument in favour of alleviating working-class distress as a bridge to the pro-war side.

He did not, however, traverse it in one giant step. Following Lansbury's line, his first move was to take up the case for the rank and file of his union and their families. 'I want you to see our side of the business', he wrote from the 'Bristol Healthatorium' to Lloyd George, who had not yet made public his own position on the war.

> Our people who go to the front are breadwinners; will the State protect them as the State has protected the Bankers and Shipowners and the Credit of the Country? The well-to-do man's son leaves no question of bread and food behind for his family, and I want you to give a lead.

At a special meeting of dockers and dockers' wives held on the evening of 2 September at the Customs House Branch of his union, Tillett expatiated on this theme:

> Every family of those who go to the front must be guaranteed a competence and food. The breadwinner who gives his life demands the price of his risks and sacrifices, and that price is the maintenance of the children and the women who are left behind.

His antipathy to the British ruling class, however, seemed to remain intact. 'There are six to ten million of human beings in this country who could not be worse off if the Germans or the most brutal savage was in Government and in ownership', he asserted in a letter, also of 2 September, to Lloyd George. 'Have you ever asked yourself what they [the dockers] have to fight for?' he queried the Chancellor one week later. 'I wonder if a German invasion could make their position worse!'[14]

Tillett was willing, however, to suspend judgement on this vital question for the duration: 'But for all that we must fight', he had concluded in his letter to Lloyd George. Like Lansbury, he had determined to support the men who did the fighting, and their families on the home front; unlike the editor of the *Daily Herald*, however, Tillett concluded that it was his duty, therefore, 'to rouse our Countrymen to the fate of the Country'. Here was an offer which Lloyd George could not refuse. He promptly arranged an interview for the dockers' leader with H.J. Tennant, parliamentary secretary to the War Office, 'about the valuable services which you could render the Government'. The meeting apparently proved successful, for afterwards Tillett waxed rhapsodic. Class conflict was not inevitable. The war would generate a 'new relationship between the classes . . . a new spiritual sense of being . . . a closer bond of fairer, sweeter human ties of friendship. The last time I spoke with you', Tillett continued his correspondence with Lloyd George:

> was in Cardiff and against the war in Africa. I shall be glad to stand with you on a platform, justifying this terrible war imposed upon us by the brutality of Germany's ruling and sordid class.

He was willing to organize a 'Dockers' Brigade' and to tour the country as soon as his health permitted.[15]

In the meantime, he was far from inactive. 'This is neither a period for regrets or [*sic*] whining, but a time for action all around', he exhorted the rank and file of his union. His first goal was the formation of a 'Citizen's Army', organized into units of one thousand and drilled daily by ex-solidiers. Unemployed dockers should be set to work erecting earthworks and land defences wherever necessary. The north and north-east coast, which was open to invasion in his opinion, should be protected by the dockers, which would free the Territorials and regular military forces for continental duties. To his former German colleagues in the International Transport Workers' Federation, Tillett forwarded a résumé — in translation — of his patriotic labours; to his old friend, the American trade unionist Samuel Gompers, he despatched a lengthy justification of his attitudes. They may serve as an index to his confusion at the time. On 7 October 1914, Tillett proclaimed his support for the war, but with reservations.[16]

'I am still an internationalist, Gompers', he explained. He did not blame Germany's workers for the war; rather it was their 'Prussian oppressors . . . driven to panic fear' because 'our German comrades have been copying and even improving some of our best examples'. Moreover, Tillett did not believe that there had been equality of sacrifice in Britain since the war began. 'The rich classes for whom the war is being waged', he charged:

> are so mean that they have subscribed just a little over a million to the Prince of Wales fund . . . in the majority of cases the employers are shouting patriotism and sticking at home while the fighting is being done for them.

In addition, Tillett was disgusted by all manifestations of the anti-German hysteria now gripping the country. 'Dear Mr George,' he wrote again to the Chancellor, after rampaging mobs in London's East End had sacked local shops owned by people with German-sounding names: 'Can you bring this English hun business to a stop?' And in a letter to Reginald McKenna, the Home Secretary, he added that spy hunts and internment camps 'did not play the British game'.[17]

Despite this relatively sober (and, for Tillett, transitory) approach to the war, there were certain popular atittudes which he already shared. For example, he believed the stories about German atrocities in Belgium: 'the brutality shown to the Catholic Institutions,' he wrote to Gompers: 'the sack of Louvain, Rheims, Brussels, on top of the worst oppression and bullying, the vilest rule of nations has ever known [*sic*] — is proof that we had to take a hand and a big fist in this fight'. He believed that Germany's aim was world domination, and that the balance of power had to be maintained. The defeat of France, he lectured Gompers, would mean 'the German capitalist esconsed [*sic*] opposite our coast, with every outlet for further aggression in trade and a military sense'. Finally, and this became the basis for his conduct between 1914 and 1918, Tillett believed that British troops must be supported simply because they were workers. 'Whatever peculiar view of war a worker may have', he explained to the docker rank and file:

> there can be no question whatever . . . that the workers in numbers are directly responsible for 24/25 of the fighting units, and any action in retarding supplies, ammunition or hospital arrangements acts directly on men of their own class.

It was on this basis that he parted company with Lansbury.[18]

Yet his doubts remained, and his disclaimers continued. He was not yet comfortable in his new role as supporter of the government. 'The State has never previously taken the workers' leaders into its confidence', he conceded in an article for the 5 September *Daily Herald*:

> There are at least five to ten millions of working class folk in slum and starvation who could not be worse off by a German invasion . . the State will not countenance a Citizen Army. All these contentions are true; but nevertheless there is need now to protect the United Kingdom against invasion, against being reduced as a World Power, and greater than all these considerations is the claim the wounded and dead of our own class have upon our kinship, our sympathy and our share of the fighting.

His *Twenty Fifth Annual Report* to the Dockers' Union, written late in 1914, seems an even less wholehearted assertion of the pro-war position: 'All good citizens fight to lessen the tragedy of war.' He considered himself free to criticize the government, which he claimed 'had entirely failed in (a) refusing to nationalise the food supply; (b) refusing to nationalise the munition supply; (c) and refusing to nationalise the material resources of the country'. Nor did he hestitate to join with such anti-war figures as Lansbury, Sylvia Pankhurst and Robert Smillie to agitate for these reforms, or to protest against the Russian government's persecution of trade union organizers.[19]

The turning-point came in the spring of 1915. His health had not improved during the winter. On 4 March, a reporter for *Justice* noted that he was 'not looking well'. By April he was on his way to southern France to recuperate. The journey may have been undertaken at government expense, for in March 1914 Tillett had informed Lloyd George that he was in debt. Did someone in the War Office (Tennant perhaps) calculate that a glimpse of the invaded country would dispel Tillett's lingering doubts and arouse his martial spirit? In any event, that is what happened. On 17 April he watched French soldiers marching toward the front. Impressionable, pugnacious, nationalistic, he was moved deeply by the scene. 'I have never hated war so much as now', he confessed on 12 April 1916, in what was to be his final article for the *Daily Herald*:

> It is so terrible, so real, so near in France that one wants all the loyalty and courage of the Allies to be supported in energetic effic- iency, that the things we stand for shall hold place and power and crush the militarism which has so brutally fostered this war.

Following a six-week convalescence, he journeyed to the front itself. This further excited his combative instincts. 'What I have seen', Tillett wrote immediately afterwards, 'has convinced me that . . . henceforth [we] . . . have only one business — the war.' Shocked by the devasta- tion, Tillett concluded that the men in the trenches needed more and better weapons above all. The justice of the Allied cause became almost secondary; although he now believed in it implicitly, his deter- mination that British workers should not be thrown into the trenches without proper training and equipment seems to have been paramount. All the patriotic embellishments followed: dissent at home, no matter how it was expressed, threatened the safety of the men in the trenches and therefore should be curtailed; reports of German atrocities should be given wide circulation in order to maintain the Allies' fighting spirit; the entire German nation, not merely the Prussian Junker class, was responsible for the war. When he was at the front he had pledged before the survivors of a gas attack at Ypres that he would help 'the workers . . . understand as you understand that here is the greatest war England has ever known . . . she fights for the liberty of the world'. Returning to Paris, he wrote an article for the French socialist journal *Humanité*: 'We must organize all the resources of our nation . . . the menace of the terrible power of the Prussian brute [must be] destroyed forever.' He would devote the next three years to this object.[20]

II

Tillett's views on the war paralleled those of the British working-class as a whole. The Labour Party had quickly joined with the Liberals and Conservatives in a political truce. By the Treasury Agreements and Munitions Act which made them legal, trade union leaders had almost unanimously accepted the suspension of all practices which might impede the war effort. Tillett returned from the front in time to endorse these developments at the 17 June 1915 annual general council meeting of the National Transport Workers' Federation at Plymouth. He moved:

> That this Annual Meeting . . . heartily welcomes the cooperation between the Government and organised labour for the purpose of accelerating the output of adequate munitions of war. It further approves the scheme to avoid all factious disputes during the War by means of compulsory arbitration, and pledges itself to assist the Minister of Munitions to the utmost of its ability . . .

He was preparing to stump the country on behalf of this programme.[21]

Tillett's seeming volte-face did not go entirely unchallenged at the conference of the National Transport Workers' Federation. Some of his old friends were appalled by it. Three years earlier, recalling the 1911 strike, Tillett had extolled the role of William Godfrey of the National Union of Vehicle Workers: 'More power to you William, and may your cheerful voice keep its courage until the greater call is made.'[22] Now, despite the patriotic atmosphere of the conference, Godfrey rose to remind Tillett of his earlier ideals.

> He wanted to take exception to the statement that this was a people's war. There never was a people's war and never could be under capitalism. Tillett had taught him that and now he was preaching the opposite . . . Tillett knew this war was being waged in the interest of the owning class, but the owning class did not fight it; it was the working-class . . . Wars were Kings' pastimes, and soldiers were Kings' playthings. That was another thing that Tillett had taught him, and he would like Ben Tillett to go down to Canning Town and say what he had said there that day. Let Tillett tell these people that this was a people's war . . . he would appeal to Tillett not to throw over the class he had worked for and to which he belonged, to hobnob with the class they were fighting.

The counter-attack was vigorous. James Sexton of the Liverpool dockers rose in Tillett's defence. 'Ordinary capitalist war they were all against', he insisted:

> but he heard from nobody − not even the opponents of the war − any evidence that would place the war in that category. If ever there was a justification for taking up arms, if ever Great Britain went into a war with clean hands, this was the occasion.

When Harry Gosling, chairman of the conference, forced Godfrey to retract portions of his speech, Tillett's vindication was complete.

Leaving Plymouth, Tillett embarked on a whirlwind speaking tour. He had conceived the notion of delivering his message from music-hall stages throughout the country. Within three weeks he had done so 40 times, within sixteen months, more than 600 times. A typical Tillett lecture, entitled 'A Message from the Trenches: or How to Win the War', was described by Harry Beswick, a reporter for the *Clarion* newspaper:

> With a table of 'props' before him consisting of shells and bombs and grenades and other missiles, Ben gives a graphic description of the pluck and endurance of our splendid boys fighting for civilisation in France and Belgium . . . taking a villainous looking sword bayonet, he holds it aloft . . . 'Tell the Conscientious Objector' he cries 'that a wound made with this devilish instrument can't be healed . . . I'd like to rub it across a pacifist's soul . . . ' Ben tells his horrified audience 'as I stand here as a man' how the Huns have crucified our lads − nailed them to a cross, poured petrol on them and burned them alive . . . Bayoneted babies, disembowelled their mothers . . .

He was now in touch with Lord Kitchener and General French, and often concluded his meetings by reading aloud from their letters to him. Not everyone responded approvingly, but this merely raised his ire: 'I find there are a number of soreheads . . . who assume both a cowardly and critical attitude towards the men at the front', he reported to Lloyd George.[23]

At the 1915 annual TUC he had delivered a more reasoned defence of his pro-war position and of his support for the Liberal government which once he had been foremost in attacking. Germany, he asserted, was bent on world domination. British soldiers, the vast majority of whom were workers, must be able to defend themselves against 'Hunnish' atrocities, and consequently 'any feeling at this moment expressed against the war . . . weakens the morale of the men'. In addition: 'if we should lose in the struggle, we shall lose more than any other country'. The 'five to ten million . . . who could not be worse off by a German invasion' no longer figured in his thoughts. Rather, he stressed the gains made by British trade unionists and socialists over the last quarter century, particularly the rights of free speech and combination which must be protected: 'We cannot allow the Germans to take from us the liberties we have so hardly won.'[24]

Such sentiments placed Tillett, for perhaps the first time in his career, squarely in the mainstream of labour movement opinion. For once his old enemies in the Independent Labour Party — MacDonald, Glasier and Snowden — who to varying degrees opposed the war, were the outcasts. Tillett must have enjoyed this reversal immensely. Even better, his villains were now the villains of respectable society and the vast majority of his countrymen. Now even his wildest rhetoric was acceptable, his most horrific appeals attainable. He demanded that workers be given guns, that conscientious objectors be imprisoned, that dissident newspapers be censored, that air raids be launched against German civilian centres, and they were. If before the war he had laboured under a sense of impotence, it was gone now. His extravagant language no longer stood in his way. He mixed with the Duchess of Marlborough and Lord Rhondda; and Cabinet Ministers like Hayes Fisher, President of the Local Government Board and H.A.L. Fisher, President of the Board of Trade. He was friendly as well with important military leaders like General French. He had heard the Lord Mayor of London, Sir William Dunn, compliment him on having 'laboured well in the cause of Empire', and the dockers 'on having such a man as Ben Tillett' to lead them. This was heady stuff for someone who had complained at intervals throughout his career that he did not want to be considered a pariah by everybody outside the labour and socialist movements. In this respect, the years 1914-18 must have been a period of fulfilment for him[25]

They were years of fulfilment in another and more fundamental sense as well. For once he could openly acknowledge the cautious, conservative outlook which before the war he had usually disguised. Take, for instance, his attitude toward revolution. Though a self-proclaimed 'revolutionary socialist' before 1914, in fact none of Tillett's activities had been revolutionary. With the advent of war, his actual fear of revolution became evident. A confidant of Lord Kitchener during the early months of fighting, he understood early on that casualty lists, high prices and short food supplies would unleash incalculable forces on the home front. Pointing to the lampposts outside the War Office, Kitchener is said to have predicted that he and Tillett would both be hanging from them 'before this thing is over'. Tillett's response was not recorded, yet it seems likely that he agreed. So long as the war lasted, fear of revolution was his constant preoccupation. 'Nothing but loyalty has kept our country from insurrection and riot', Tillett wrote in December 1914, long before this question had begun to agitate other reformist labour leaders. 'That this may never happen is my fervent prayer . . . '26

The war also enabled Tillett to acknowledge openly his loathing of all forms of industrial conflict. Previously he had been circumspect, but now he frankly opposed all strikes. 'We will not advise a stoppage unless forced to by the brutal conduct of employers', he declared in March 1915. Three years later, he was more emphatic:

> Any trade unionist, leader or member, who grossly abuses the trust of our fighters by willful dislocation of production, trade or transport, commits a sin against which every fighter will cry. Every mother and dependent will curse those who are guilty of nothing better than assassination, while their comrades are in death-grips with an enemy who has shown neither honour or [*sic*] scruple, as witness the murderous outrages on the high seas, the torture of prisoners and . . . fiendish cruelty . . .

He even hoped to extend the wartime industrial truce indefinitely. On 10 December 1916 Tillett met with thirteen other trade union leaders and twenty-five prominent businessmen to form a National Alliance of Employers and Employed. The aim was to continue the policy of class collaboration after peace had been restored. 'War between Capital and Labour in this country . . . would be a calamity only less terrible in its consequences than victory by Germany', the chronicler of the meeting recorded in the new organization's short-lived journal. 'Happily for the future of British industry', he continued optimistically:

> there are men on both sides sufficiently far sighted and patriotic to feel that a determined effort must be made to overcome the prejudice, narrowness of view, self interest and ignorance on which those on either side who predict industrial war rest their case . . .

Before the war, Tillett might have harboured these sentiments, but he would never have allowed his name to be associated with those who stated them publicly. The war permitted him to do so.[27]

Tillett had not, however, abandoned his former ideals. What had changed most dramatically was not his own world view but that of the governing authorities who, for the first time, were made to realize their dependence upon the British working class. Quite simply, the war could not be won if labour ceased to support it. The government, especially after Lloyd George had become Prime Minister, recognized the new balance of forces in British society which the war had produced. Even in late August 1914, Lloyd George had sensed it. He wrote to Tillett:

> It is very difficult to gauge what the actual effect of war under modern conditions will be upon either capital or labour, but one thing is already perfectly obvious − it must effect a revolutionary change in the relations of the State to both.

It was the role of trade union leaders during the war (Tillett among them), to encourage the government to act upon this acute perception.[28]

As numerous historians have observed, labour proved successful in this endeavour. Government-mandated war bonuses raised unskilled workers' wages to heights undreamed of before 1914. Workers' representatives were consulted as never before upon industrial and political matters. One of them, Arthur Henderson, was brought into the select War Cabinet. In those crucial industries which the government took over for the duration of the war, labour leaders participated with government officials and the employers in regulating hours, wages and other working conditions. Thus British trade unionists took advantage of the conditions created by the war in a manner entirely unforeseen by the revolutionaries of the Second International. They did not utilize them to make a revolution, yet for a time it seemed as though they would, in partnership with the government, significantly reform the bases of British capitalism.

Tillett's activities in this regard were typical of other reformist trade union leaders. He set himself against agitation, but was determined to reap the reward for his loyalty. The smooth functioning of dockland was considered essential during wartime. Tillett was prepared to do his best to maintain labour peace on the docks, but only for a price.

And he received it. During the war the first serious attempt was made to reform the casual labour system. Tillett himself, along with Gosling, Sexton, Williams and a new man, Ernest Bevin, were appointed to the Port and Transit Executive Committee which was established in 1916 to oversee, among other things, conditions of dock labour. Local committees, on which the dockers were represented by men of their choosing, were also founded to deal with individual ports. Perhaps most satisfying of all, from Tillett's point of view, government arbitration was now mandatory in any dispute between dockers and employers. Ironically, then, it was during the horror of the First World War that much of Ben Tillett's reforming vision was actually fulfilled.[29]

III

The war enabled Tillett to achieve two more long-standing goals: election to the House of Commons, and acceptance in the Labour Party. In this latest assault upon those two citadels, he approached from the right wing. Once successful, however, he moved towards a safer middle position, thereby demonstrating even in wartime his old penchant for manoeuvre and politicking.

He had belonged before the outbreak of hostilities to the national executive of the British Socialist Party and had expected to stand at Northampton as a candidate for the British Socialist Party in the next general election. The outbreak of the war, however, produced a schism in the party leading to its virtal dissolution. Tillett signed a patriotic manifesto with other 'old and active members of the Social Democratic Party', including Hyndman, Belfort Bax, Victor Fisher and Will Thorne. Nevertheless, the majority of the party remained opposed to the war effort; at its 1916 annual conference, the minority, Tillett among them, seceded to form a National Socialist Party. He does not appear to have played a significant role in the new body, although he remained on friendly terms with its leaders. As late as 28 March 1918 he was billed to speak for Hyndman at a National Socialist Party rally at Burnley.[30]

Tillett flirted with other patriotic labour organizations as well. In April 1915, the Socialist National Defence Committee was founded during a meeting at the home of Victor Fisher. On 21 July, Tillett took part in its first London demonstration, along with such pro-war socialists as Hyndman, Cunninghame Graham, Crooks, Thorne and H.G. Wells. Anti-war hecklers were ejected by soldiers whom Fisher had hired to act as stewards. Tillett, his impressions of the front perhaps vivid in his mind, delivered 'the most brutally vulgar' speech of his career, one unsympathetic observer recorded. 'He taunted the "skunks and cowards"', according to a more friendly journalist present at the meeting:

> he goaded them, he lashed and slashed and gashed them with flaying
> scorn, he mocked them, he reviled them, he laughed at them . . .
> 'in a strike I am for my class, right or wrong; in a war I am for my
> country right or wrong . . . I have seen a child's golden silken tuft of
> hair with blood and brains upon it, and you dare come here and
> interrupt?'

Yet Tillett does not appear to have joined either the British Workers'
League that emerged from the Socialist National Defence Committee,
or the National Democratic Party which contested the khaki election in
1918 as the British Workers League's final reincarnation. Perhaps he was
put off by the virulent anti-Semitism of its founder, Fisher, or by the
latter's connections with Lord Milner and the various plutocrats who
funded the organization, although, given Tillett's own views and
recent associations, that seems improbable. Most likely, Tillett calculated that with the eclipse of MacDonald, Snowden and Hardie, the
Labour Party was still the most effective vehicle for advancing his views
and career.[31]

The death of Sir William Byles, the Liberal MP for North Salford,
provided him with an opening. Tillett had enlarged his basis of support
beyond transport workers by attaching himself to the patriotic
majority. The war had provided him with the opportunity to transcend
his old reputation as a fire-eating agitator. Invited now by the local
branch of his union to make the contest, Tillett won it easily.

His campaign programme was scarcely different from that of the
Coalition candidate, Sir Charles Mallet. Both stood for vigorous prosecution of the war, although Tillett's enthusiasm was perhaps greater
for 'air raid reprisals on a large scale', which he regarded 'as a duty of
the nation to be supported by every true Briton'. Perhaps more significant, he succeeded in creating an image as the advocate for both the
uniformed and civilian rank and file. He attacked the war profiteers,
whom he blamed for the growth of revolutionary feeling in the country, and the government for diluting the workers' beer. In addition, he
had written to Sir Edward Carson and Lord Derby in conformity with a
TUC resolution, urging a 200 per cent increase in pay for soldiers and
sailors. Still, according to a local journalist, Tillett owed his victory to the
manner in which his Coalition opponent — a professional politician
from London rather than a local man — was 'foisted' on the constituency.[32]

He owed his success primarily, however, to his new identity as a moderate and patriotic labour leader. 'I hear', a writer in the *Clarion* reported approvingly on 9 November 'that Ben Tillett is quite a "safe" man today, and that he has shed all that Tower Hill wildness which made him the terror and horror of all respectable people twenty years ago.' In Tillett's words: 'He had no desire to go to Parliament as a stormy petrel.' Thus the opposition he might once have anticipated failed to materialize; F.W. Wheatcroft, a Conservative ex-councillor of North Salford, remarked that Tillett's victory was 'rather popular' even at the Carlton Club, a Tory citadel.[33]

The triumph was widely regarded as a vindication for patriotic labour. Tillett received messages of support from Hyndman, Havelock Wilson, the National Socialist Party and Fisher on behalf of the British Workers' League. He had received no encouragement from the Labour Party as such. The only Labour Member to speak for him was James O'Grady, who belonged to the British Workers' League as well. As *The Times* put it, Tillett's platform was hardly one on which 'Mr Henderson would care to stand'. Henderson had replaced MacDonald as leader of the Labour Party. Like his predecessor, he was an old enemy of Tillett's. Yet the Dockers' Union leader was prepared to seek accommodation with him in order to secure, finally, the place he had sought in the party since its inception.[34]

He had begun fence-mending at least one month prior to his election, at the annual TUC in 1917. There he had taken a position midway between the supporters and opponents of the Stockholm Conference. This was a proposed meeting, to be held in neutral Sweden, where allied, non-aligned and enemy socialists could discuss labour's war aims. The government forbade British delegates to attend by denying them passports. When, despite this, they attempted to embark, members of the Sailors' and Firemen's Union, acting under orders from their leader J.H. Wilson, refused to hoist anchor. Simultaneously, Arthur Henderson, a Cabinet Minister as well as chairman of the Labour Party, protested against Lloyd George's decision. He was publicly humiliated for his pain. This was the famous 'door mat' incident, so called because Henderson was forced to wait in an ante-room while the Cabinet discussed his conduct. It led to his resignation, and to a quantum leap in working-class discontent with the government.

When the TUC met, J.H. Wilson defended his role in the affair with tales of German atrocities. 'And yet some of you', he concluded breaking into tears, 'would be content to meet these men! You would take the bloodstained hands of murderers within your own.' Tillett followed in a speech chiefly notable for listing further examples of German bestiality:

> I have been in villages where the demented old mother has had her daughter outraged and murdered because she resisted, and her child stripped naked and its brains battered out, and the body of the child afterwards hung up by the feet to the door as a lesson to other women.

Yet he concluded by supporting the proposed conference. He had not finally attained a broad-based popularity in order to lose it by being associated in the public mind with a die-hard like Wilson.[35]

He was no sooner elected to the House of Commons than he set about weakening his connections with the patriotic labour organizations and political conservatives who had supported his campaign. Although his attitudes towards the war, its opponents and industrial unrest remained similar to theirs, he had decided that his prospects were brightest within the Labour Party. Though technically an independent, he soon demonstrated his willingness to take the party whip, and to speak for the party outside Parliament. This involved first a change in attitude towards the 'most exclusive club in Europe' itself. On 21 January 1914, he had written of the House of Commons in the *Daily Herald*: 'the whole atmosphere is corrupt, is nauseating, is vile; and only the great and true can keep their souls undefiled and their enthusiasms heart-high'. Within a few weeks of his election, however, his mind had changed. The House, he announced at a victory celebration in Lower Broughton, was:

> the best ground for the development of one's genius . . . He must say that everyone in the House had treated him very kindly and with the utmost courtesy . . . He had offers of assistance from all and sundry — sons of Earls and sons of Knights — all manner of people had been very kind to him.

Next came a change in attitude towards the Labour Party which 'whatever its defects . . . is still representative of the good, bad or indifferent of our aspiration, and our own Dockers' Union is more or less the responsible pioneer'. Finally came the attack upon those in the British Workers' League who hoped to found an alternative party based upon patriotic labour:

I am very much in sympathy with the resentment shown by this party to the wire pulling and the unscrupulous underhand work of those who are at present wagging the tail of the Labour Party, and I think the best way to fight these creatures is from the inside, where they have cuckoo-like planted themselves as politicians.[36]

His attitudes by now were a confusing mixture of patriotism, chauvinism and genuine sympathy for the men in the trenches and their families at home who bore the brunt of the war. He was capable of contradicting himself almost within the same breath. At the 1918 TUC, for example, he supported a resolution moved by A. Henson of the Sailors' and Firemen's Union against peace by negotiation. As he reasoned, 'however fiendish you may be, you could never match the wickedness, the cowardice and the dastardly character of the German's cunning'. Earlier in the day, however, he had given a lengthy speech in support of J.H. Thomas's resolution that called in part for peace negotiations 'immediately the enemy either voluntarily or by compulsion evacuates France and Belgium . . . I am not one of those who will forever and ever, amen, stand up against the German workman', Tillett declaimed. Or, in another demonstration of inconsistency, despite his professions of loyalty to the Labour Party, he openly attacked J.R. Clynes, the Food Controller and a Labour Member, for failing to take a strong stand against war profiteers. Thus, perhaps, he was able to persuade himself that he remained a critic and gadfly within the labour movement.[37]

IV

Ironically, just as Tillett had finally crowned his ambition to enter Parliament as a respectable Labour Member, public opinion began to shift. The agitation which had marked pre-war England during the 'years of great unrest', and which Tillett had helped to lead, re-emerged, gradually at first, then with increasing vehemence, so that by November 1918 unofficial strikes were sweeping the country. A variety of factors were responsible, among them inflation, food shortages, high casualty lists and the example of the Russian Revolution.

Transport workers in particular turned away from their initial patriotism. As early as 5 March 1915, an emergency meeting of the general council of the National Transport Workers' Federation protested against the Treasury Agreements, and eight months later, the executive of Tillett's union passed a resolution condemning the Munitions Act for 'reducing workers to slavery'. As always, disaffection among the leaders reflected rank-and-file unrest. In 1916, a strike of major proportions in the London docks was averted at the last moment. By 1918, a national transport workers' strike seemed likely, with Liverpool, Hull, Bristol, Glasgow and London the centres of discontent. Opposition to the war itself began to surface as well. In October 1916, the Dockers' Union executive council, like Tillett, had been unabashedly pro-war. By May 1917, however, war weariness and the influence of anti-war agitation were apparent, and during the summer the Dockers' Union executive moved further left: 'We deplore the war and will gladly cooperate with the workers of the Allied and Central Powers. We are of the opinion that the organised trade union movements of the countries concerned in this horrible war should be consulted at once on terms for a speedy settlement of the war.'[38]

The former militant who had made a career of lambasting the workers' representatives in Parliament for abandoning their constituency fought to keep the lid on labour's growing disaffection. Tillett's maiden speech in the House of Commons, delivered on 17 December 1917, struck the note he would sustain until the Germans were defeated.

> There is serious starvation in this country . . . There is great danger in these [food] queues . . . discomfort is growing and it is serious. It is a discontent which does not merely affect the workers and the poor of our towns, but it affects the men in the trenches . . . I do not wish to see a convulsion of feeling between the labourers and employers.

At the Haymarket Theatre, one month earlier, he had pointed where such discontent would lead. 'He wanted to sound a strong note of warning against the pacifists in our midst. We had seen what they had accomplished in Russia.' And in a long public letter to Gompers, he asserted that those in favour of an early peace were 'engaged in collusion and cooperation (conscious or unconscious) with the German propaganda' and, since they could 'buy a hall for £15,000 whereas before they could not raise 15 pence', they were presumably paid agents of the enemy. Later that summer he came out against the members of his union who were demanding higher wages: 'Strikes such as we have had only delay victory as they delay the coming of peace.'[39]

During the war, many of its supporters and opponents inside the

British labour movement had frequently promised each other that they would reunite when peace came. Henderson has been credited with keeping the Labour Party intact by refusing to purge the Independent Labour Party; from the other side, Lansbury, writing in the anti-war *Herald*, affirmed Labour's overriding unity of purpose, 'although some of us are divided in thought because of the war'. In fact, the post-war re-emergence within the Labour Party of such pacifists as Mac-Donald, Snowden, Clifford Allen and Lansbury himself, reveals a great deal about the character of their anti-war activities, and about their pre-war orientation. Nothing they had done between 1914 and 1918 was essentially different from their earlier moderation and reformism; consequently, once the war was finished, they could resume their former places.[40]

For Ben Tillett, however, the Great War was a watershed. Essentially, he too had been a reformist before 1914, but he had posed as a revolutionary. Adept during the pre-war years at camouflaging his objective role as a trade union negotiator and arranger of compromises with violent rhetoric — which no doubt reflected a sincere hatred of injustice and oppression — he was unable after 1918 to shed his wartime image as an industrial conservative and political moderate. Unfortunately for him, and perhaps for other patriotic labour leaders, the immediate post-war years were tumultuous. He could not become again the scourge of capitalism and the government, however much he wanted to. There were personal reasons for the eclipse of Tillett's career as well: his health was bad; and a younger man, Ernest Bevin, had already proved to be a formidable rival within his own union. Above all, however, the war had revealed Tillett's true colours. These were applauded so long as British workers had bowed to the necessities of the national effort; but with the resurgence of internationalism and labour militancy in the period that followed the war, these qualities were reviled.

Notes

1. For more on the Second International, see especially James Joll, *The Second International* ((Weidenfeld and Nicolson, London, 1955); Julius Braunthal, *History of the International* (Praeger Press, New York, 1967) vol. 1; and G.D.H. Cole. *A History of Socialist Thought: The Second International* (Macmillan, London, 1957).

2. For the British anti-war movement, see H.M. Swanwick, *Builders of Peace* (Swarthmore Press, London, 1924), a rather slim account of the early years of the Union of Democratic Control; and the more scholarly work by Marvin Swartz,

198   *The Agitator as Patriot*

The Union of Democratic Control (Clarendon Press, Oxford, 1971); also Peter Stansky (ed.), *The Left and the War* (Oxford University Press, London, 1969); and James Hinton, *The First Shop Steward's Movement* (Allen and Unwin, London, 1973), which unlike Swartz's work, deals with working-class disaffection.

3. See, for example, Tillett's testimony before the 1888 Lords' Committee on Sweated Industries, *Parliamentary Papers* (1888), vol. XXI, p. 136; and Ben Tillett, 'Our Naval Weakness', *National Review*, vol. 27 (March-August 1896), pp. 872-80.

4. *Dockers' Record*, June 1908; *The Times*, 9 May 1910; *Daily Herald*, 9 July 1912; *The Times*, 8 August 1911.

5. Ben Tillett, 'The Alleged Industrial Invasion of England by America', *Independent* (New York) vol. 53 (1901), pp. 3073-6.

6. *Justice*, 12 June 1909; *Daily Herald*, 11 September 1912.

7. TUC, *Annual Report*, 1914, p. 98; Transport House, LP/PRO/13 Tillett to National Executive Committee, 3 February 1913. For more on opposition to the construction of Dreadnoughts and arms rings, see Gerald H.S. Jordan, 'Pensions not dreadnoughts: the Radicals and Naval Retrenchment', and Clive Trebilcock, 'Radicalism and the Armament Trust', in A.J.A. Morris (ed.), *Edwardian Radicalism* (Routledge and Kegan Paul, London, 1974), pp. 162-79 and 180-201 respectively.

8. National Transport Workers' Federation, *Annual General Council Meeting*, 1913, pp. 31-5.

9. *Justice*, 11 September 1909.

10. International Transport Workers' Federation Papers, no. 87, Tillett to Jochade, 24 March 1914; Ben Tillett, *Industrial Germany* (n.d.), printed by the Daily Herald Printing and Publishing Society; the sections of this pamphlet originally appeared as separate articles in the *Daily Herald* during 1912.

11. See Merle Fainsod, *International Socialism and the World War* (Doubleday, Garden City, NJ, 1969), p. 32; *Daily Herald*, 3 August 1914.

12. *Daily Herald*, 5 August 1914.

13. Burns Papers, Add. MS 36285, Tillett to Burns, 30 June 1914; Tillett to Burns 12 May 1914.

14. Public Record Office, T 172/980, Tillett to Lloyd George, 24 August 1914. Lloyd George may have flirted with the idea of leading the 'pacifist' wing of the Liberals in opposition to the war. He did not publicly support British intervention until 19 September in a speech at Queen's Hall; Public Record Office T 172/980, Tillett to Lloyd George, 2 September 1914; T 172/980, 'News Bulletin from the Dock, Wharf, Riverside and General Workers' Union', 3 September 1914; T 172/980, Tillett to Lloyd George, 2 September 1914; T 172/980, Tillett to Lloyd George, 4 September 1914.

15. Public Reord Office, T 172/980, Lloyd George to Tillett, 4 September 1914; T 172/980, Tillett to Lloyd George, 9 September 1914.

16. *Dockers' Record*, 12 August 1914; Public Record Office, 'News Bulletin from the Dock, Wharf, Riverside and General Workers' Union'; International Transport Workers Federation Papers, no. 87, 'The European Crisis', by Ben Tillett.

17. Public Record Office, T 172/980, Tillett to Samuel Gompers, 7 October 1914; T 172/980, Tillett to Lloyd George, 27 October 1914; T 172/980, Tillett to McKenna, 27 October 1914.

18. T 172/980, Tillett to Gompers, 7 October 1914; Dock, Wharf, Riverside and General Labourers' Union, *Annual Report*, 1914.

19. *Justice*, 4 March 1915; *Daily Herald*, 23 January 1915.

20. Lloyd George Papers, House of Lords Record Office, C/8/6/1, Tillett to Lloyd George, 19 March 1914; *Justice*, 17 April 1915; *The Times*, 10 June 1915.

21. National Transport Workers' Federation, *Annual General Council Meeting*, 1915, pp. 49-50.

22. Tillett, *History of the Transport Workers' Strike 1911* (London, 1912), p. 52.

23. *Clarion*, 17 November 1916; *The Times* 22 June 1915; Lloyd George Papers, D/18/20/1, Tillett to Lloyd George, 9 July 1915.

24. TUC, *Annual Conference*, 1915, pp. 323-5.

25. *The Times*, 3 July 1917; *The Times*, 13 July 1916; Dock, Wharf, Riverside and General Labourers' Union, *Minutes of Triennial Delegate Meetings*, 1917.

26. Francis Countess of Warwick, *Afterthoughts* (Cassell, London, 1931), p. 222; Dock, Wharf, Riverside and General Labourers' Union, *Annual Report*, 1914.

27. *Daily Herald*, 20 March 1915; *East London Advertiser*, 12 October 1918; *Industrial Peace*, October 1917.

28. Public Record Office, T 172/980, Lloyd George to Tillett, 25 August 1914.

29. Public Record Office, LAB 2/121/IC 1940/1917, Tillett to Askwith, 23 May 1917 is typical; see also LAB 2/124 files. For dock labour during the war, see Noelle Whiteside, 'The Dock Decasualization Issue, 1889-1924', unpublished PhD thesis, University of Liverpool, 1976.

30. *Justice*, 28 January 1915; see Walter Kendall, *The Revolutionary Movement in Britain* (Weidenfeld and Nicolson, London, 1969), pp. 94-104; and H.W. Lee and W. Archbold, *History of the Social Democratic Federation* (Social Democratic Federation, London, 1935), pp. 237-45; *Justice*, 27 January 1918.

31. *Justice*, 12 August 1915; *Clarion*, 30 July 1915; for more on patriotic labour, see John O. Stubbs, 'Lord Milner and Patriotic Labour, 1914-18', *English Historical Review*, vol. 87 (October 1972), pp. 717-54; and A.M. Gollin, *Proconsul in Politics* (Blond Press, London, 1964).

32. *The Times*, 29 October 1917; *Justice*, 8 November 1917; *Manchester Guardian*, 30 October 1917; this was one of his main themes during the war. See, for example, the *Dockers' Record*, November 1916; *Manchester Guardian*, 29 October 1917; *Salford Reporter*, 10 November 1917.

33. *Manchester Guardian*, 30 October 1917; *Salford Reporter*, 10 November 1917.

34. *Salford Reporter*, 2 November 1917; *British Citizen and Empire Worker*, 10 November 1917; *The Times*, 5 November 1917.

35. TUC, *Annual Conference*, 1917, p. 80.

36. *Salford Reporter*, 8 December 1917; Dock, Wharf, Riverside and General Labourers' Union, *Annual Report*, 1917.

37. TUC, *Annual Conference*, 1918, pp. 244 and 208.

38. 'When the national leaders of Trades Unionism declared in favour of avoiding disputes for the duration of the war, they anticipated that the trading and possessing classes would similarly refrain from taking advantage of the nation's urgent and paramount needs. That these interests did not warrant the confidence placed in them is now a matter of common knowledge.' Webb Trade Union Collection, Section B, volume 105, number 19; *Daily Herald*, 29 January 1916; for more on this, see Public Record Office, CAB 2/127/IC 244/1918, Robert Williams to Askwith, 16 April 1918. This box deals with dock labour unrest during the latter half of the war, and with the efforts of the National Transport Workers' Federation to contain it.

39. *The Times*, 12 November 1917 and 20 July 1918; see also the *Dockers' Record*, October, November and December 1918.

40. Mary Agnes Hamilton: *Arthur Henderson: A Biography* (William Heinemann, London, 1938), p. 97; *Daily Herald*, 10 November 1917.

10 ONE OF THE 'OLD GUARD', 1918-23

I

During the immediate aftermath of the First World War, economic conditions were favourable to British labour. Europe was starved for British exports, and consequently British workers found employment producing them. Prices rose during the period, but wages kept pace: by the end of 1920, prices were 176 per cent higher than in 1914, but wages averaged 170-180 per cent above their pre-war level. The boom ended suddenly, however, in 1921, and with it ended labour's prosperity. European markets could again be fed by European industries which, devastated during the war, were not recovering. In Britain both wages and prices dropped precipitously, and unemployment shot up. In November 1919, it had amounted only to 353,000, but in January 1921, there were 1,213,000 unemployed. Two months later the figure had reached 1,664,000; and by May over 2,500,000 people could not find work. Throughout this period organized labour had been extremely active. First the unions sought, successfully, to take advantage of the boom; then they attempted, less successfully, to protect their members from the slump.[1]

For the last time in his career, Ben Tillett attempted, during this seesaw battle, to play a central role in labour affairs. Ill health plagued him, the bulky figure of Ernest Bevin loomed ever larger in both the Dockers' Union and the National Transport Workers' Federation, threatening to eclipse him entirely; above all, the connections he had formed during the war, and the reputation he had earned as a staunch defender of the government, discredited him with a working class angrily determined not to return to pre-war conditions. Despite occasional flashes of his former fire, these were obstacles Tillett could not overcome. For three years he fought a losing battle; however, his day on centre stage was done.

Tillett must have chafed at his ill health and loss of influence, for the years 1918-1921 marked a particularly turbulent era in British labour history. Viewed by some historians as a continuation of the great unrest of 1911-14, its class antagonisms were, if anything, more severe, for British workers who had been told they were fighting a war to save civilization now expected to reap their reward. On the average, twice as many working days were lost per year through strikes during the later period, and unlike those of 1911-14, some of them were politically motivated. This is significant because it was widely held that working-class willingness to bring industrial weapons to bear on political matters was a prerequisite to revolutionary action. In particular, many British workers opposed Allied intervention in the Russian Civil War.[2]

At the centre of the storm during these years was the Triple Alliance of Miners, Railwaymen and Transport Workers. Founded in 1914 so that the three organizations could co-ordinate industrial strategy, its members had wrested an important concession from the government during the war when mines, railways and transport were state-controlled. Each Triple Alliance member now negotiated a national settlement for its rank and file. Moreover, in 1919 they agreed not to settle with the government until they had first consulted each other. Thus the threat of a Triple Alliance strike hung over Britain from the war's end until Friday, 15 April 1921, when the Lloyd George government finally called labour's bluff.[3]

When health allowed, Tillett participated in the events surrounding and leading up to 'Black Friday', though usually as an advocate of industrial peace rather than direct action. The war had set the seal on his outlook and role in the labour world, despite occasional gestures which he made to the left. He had become, finally, one of the conservative 'Old Guard' who, when he was not reminding younger labour leaders of his past militant deeds, enjoyed warning them against the bolsheviks and hotheads in the movement.

Tillett's performance in the 1918 khaki election confirmed his position on labour's right wing. Taking advantage of a temporary patriotic resurgence, he vied with his Liberal opponent, I.W. Roe-Ryecroft in attacking 'the instigators of this holocaust, the Central Powers [who] must make full reparation for their murders and crimes, their bestial rapine, spoilation [*sic*] and the blighting of the countries attacked'. Standing this time as an orthodox Labour candidate for North Salford – in 1917 he had campaigned as an Independent Labour man and supporter of the coalition – he nevertheless managed to attract Conservative support by attacking the Liquor Control Board. His old enemies Henderson, Snowden and MacDonald, fared less well. Only patriotic Labour men like Sexton, Thorne, Havelock Wilson, James O'Grady and Tillett himself were successful in Lloyd George's 'coupon' election.[4]

These were the men who constituted labour's 'Old Guard'. During the war, they had favoured the industrial truce as a temporary measure. Within weeks of his re-election to Parliament, however, Tillett indicated that for him, at any rate, the Armistice made no difference, the industrial truce should continue. 'There is greater need of national unity now', Tillett explained in his annual report to the union, and went on to attack the advocates of direct action within the Triple Alliance. Two months later, despite another relapse in health, he continued in the same vein. 'There is seething discontent', he wrote to *The Times* on 26 February 1919:

> but to have our grievances mishandled by a set of vicious anarchists in sympathy with, or in pay of, the Central Powers, would be the limit of stupidity and credulity . . . Labour has most to gain by a class loyalty, by patriotism, by love of country, and all that industry, power, wealth, comfort and happiness mean is wrapped up in patriotism . . . Strikes, uncertainty of action, limited and vicious circles of action, can only result in greater gains to the capitalists.

'You have played the game in war and must play the game in peace', Tillett warned a restive rank and file in March 1919.[5]

During the winter of 1918-19, with Tillett offering tirades against direct action from his sick-bed, the miners nevertheless voted by a six-to-one majority for a national strike to enforce their first post-war demands — reduction of the working day from eight to six hours, and a 30 per cent wage increase. The government offered a Commission of Inquiry instead, and the miners, sure of their case, accepted. On 20 March 1919, Bonar Law, speaking for Lloyd George, accepted 'in spirit and in letter' the findings of the Interim Report of the Sankey Commission, which had recommended acceptance of the miners' main demands, including nationalization of the mines. Of the three organizations belonging to the Triple Alliance, only the Railwaymen remained at loggerheads with the government. A deputation to Whitehall, threatening a Triple Alliance strike on behalf of the National Union of Railwaymen, was enough to reopen the stalled negotiations.[6]

Labour had demonstrated its power. Two weeks later it expanded its post-war offensive in a manner which Tillett must have found particularly disturbing. The Triple Alliance had officially extended its demands from the industrial to the political sphere. It now called upon the parliamentary committee of the TUC to convene a special conference to consider four demands: the withdrawal of British troops from Russia; the withdrawal of the conscription Bill before Parliament; the release from prison of all conscientious objectors; and the raising of the blockade against Germany. When the parliamentary committee refused to call such a conference, the Triple Alliance passed by a vote of 27 to 11 a motion to ballot its members on the question of a national strike to support the four political demands. Tillett voted with the minority.

He vehemently opposed national action for political, or indeed any, demands. Typically, however, he discovered an indirect method of doing so at the annual council meeting of the National Transport Workers' Federation at Swansea on 5 and 6 June. There he success- fully proposed a resolution which appeared to be a plea for democracy within the Triple Alliance:

> That this Annual General Council Meeting instructs the Executive, when in Conference with the Triple Alliance to refrain from com- mitting the Unions affiliated to the Federation to strike action with- out a ballot vote being taken of the Unions concerned.

As Robert Williams pointed out, Tillett's resolution would tie the hands of the Triple Alliance, which needed to move with 'lightning rapidity' if national action was to be effective. The Dockers' Union general secre- tary, however, remained adamant. 'We don't want Lenins and Trotskys', he declared in a speech which went on to castigate those who mini- mized the importance of the Federation through 'reckless action or arro- gant assumption that presumes to represent the feelings of the rank and file'. In a speech supporting Tillett's motion, James Sexton dem- onstrated that arrogance was not limited to one side: 'Some of the rank and file I know who talk about running the country could not run a potato machine.' He put his finger, however, on the crux of the disagreement between the supporters and opponents of direct action on a national scale. 'Suppose we succeeded in a National Con- ference in deciding to fight the Government, and suppose we won, where would that lead us? . . . And suppose the Government won? Your organization would be so disillusioned and demoralised that it would take half a century to build up what you have today.'[7]

Three weeks later, at the annual conference of the Labour Party, Tillett demonstrated again how to fight the militants while seeming not to. At the conference of the National Transport Workers' Federation he had pretended to oppose them because they did not want to take time to consult the rank and file. Now he claimed, untruthfully, that middle- class leaders of the Labour Party were the foremost advocates of the national strike. Rising to oppose a resolution introduced by Councillor R.J. Davies of the Manchester and Salford Labour Party, calling for an end to British intervention in Russia, and a special conference of the Labour Party executive and the parliamentary committee of the TUC to decide the best way to enforce this demand — that is, the national strike — Tillett argued that '99% of the delegates there represented Trade Unions. Less than 1% had undertaken to suggest a responsibility they were not able to meet themselves.' Continuing in this vein, Tillett warned:

> When they wandered blindly into revolution led by the professional politicians and the middle-classes, who had gouged out the eyes of Samson, it was the middle-classes and the professional politicians who benefitted — it had been the workers who suffered.

It was, however, Robert Smillie and Frank Hodges of the Miners' Federation, Robert Williams of the National Transport Workers' Federation, and John Bromley of the Locomotive Engineers and Firemen, not the 'middle classes and professional politicians', who pushed through the resolution. Tillett had hoped by his speech to perpetuate the wartime split between the left and right wings of the Labour Party that had, for a time, corresponded roughly to a class division between wealthy supporters of the Union of Democratic Control on the one hand, and patriotic workers on the other. Pacifism and industrial militancy, however, did not necessarily appeal to the same people. His effort to tar the direct actionists with the anti-war brush failed.[8]

Tillett still posed as a rebel, claiming in his speech that 'he had been a direct actionist for 35 years', but he entered a caveat to revolution which could be used to block any call to arms.

> If a blind sacrifice was to be made — he did not say it would not have to be made — . . . it should be organised and fully understood. There must be a scheme, there must be a reason, and there must be hope and a chance . . . They should not allow their Samsons to be massacred.

Who would quarrel with such sentiments? By denigrating the militancy of the rank and file (during a period of exceptional working-class unrest), Tillett seemed to place his own commitment to revolution beyond question. In fact, he had carried into the 1920s the same argument he had used to oppose a national dock strike in the 1890s: the enemy was too strong.

He was, however, still capable of appealing directly to the left. Speaking at Anderton's Hotel in London to the re-called Triennial Meeting of the Dockers' Union, he declared, 'Now the war is over, and we have saved our land, for God's sake don't merely save it for the capitalists . . . You are asked to take part in the great movement toward revolution.' Introducing a resolution which demanded the special conference of the parliamentary committee he had opposed twice before, Tillett explained his turnabout by arguing that the previous resolutions would have permitted irresponsible politicians to shape events. 'We have to be our own saviours', he contended.[9]

Later in the year, when it was time for his annual message to the Dockers' Union, Tillett played the left-wing card again. At the Labour Party conference in June he had bitterly attacked the Russian Revolution, asserting that 'no life was sacred, no personal liberty or property was stable'. Now he claimed that the new regime would 'advance civilisation to a standard of freedom and equality which only dreamers and enlightened rebels have conceived in the past'. As for the war he had so enthusiastically supported, its 'one great lesson [was] that all wars are waste and suicide'.[10]

Tillett's overriding aim throughout this period was to break the power of the direct actionists in the labour and socialist movements and thereby ensure against a revolutionary attempt which he was sure would fail. In order to do so he had to remain friendly with the numerous lesser trade union officials who were sympathetic to the militant position. This explains his seeming oscillations. Above all, he hoped to keep the levers of action in the hands of trusted, conservative trade unionists. It is inconceivable that after some thirty years as an opponent of revolution he could become — and only for a moment — a champion of working-class insurrection. That this was where the advocates of direct action were headed during the extraordinary period following the war was apparent to all. As Harry Kay, the Dockers' Union financial secretary, expressed it at the Triennial Delegate Meeting: 'Direct Action meant a national strike, and a national strike meant revolution.' Ernest Bevin agreed: 'We know what it means. We know what is involved.' (Bevin had attacked Sexton for fearing the results of revolution at the meeting of the National Transport Workers' Federation on 5 and 6 June.) And on 23 July, at a special Triple Alliance conference called to consider the general strike, since it was evident that the parliamentary committee would not budge, Tillett opposed national action, because: 'If there is to be any action of a determined nature, we can easily border, and we cannot merely border, upon revolution.'[11]

That his fears were shared by a majority within the Triple Alliance emerged at the 23 July meeting when it voted 182-45 to postpone balloting its members on the national strike. This proved to be the signal for which the government had been waiting. Almost immediately Lloyd George rejected the Sankey Commission suggestion to nationalize the mines, despite his earlier promises to accept its recommendations as binding. Two weeks later the TUC would only agree to help launch a publicity campaign on behalf of the miners: 'The Mines for the Nation'. For the moment direct action was repudiated. The 'Old Guard' had scored a victory: labour's post-war offensive had been blunted. Tillett, however, was not present to join in the celebrations. His health had failed again.

Throughout most of 1920, illness forced Tillett to curtail his public activities. Chosen on 30 December 1919 as one of three representatives of the National Transport Workers' Federation to the Shaw Inquiry (in many ways the transport industry's equivalent to the Sankey Commission), it was Bevin who brilliantly put the men's case, winning for them a minimum daily rate of 16s, and for himself the popular title 'Dockers' KC'. Tillett attended the hearings, though he took no significant part in them. His energies, such as they were at this point, were devoted to parliamentary affairs, perhaps because Bevin's star was so obviously ascendant in the union. On 12 March, Tillett successfully moved the second reading of his Blind (Education and Maintenance) Bill in the House of Commons. There was virtually no opposition. This does not appear to have encouraged him to play a more forceful role at Westminster either. He framed no more bills there, and indeed rarely even spoke. Poor health seems the most likely explanation.[12]

On 10 May 1920 a team of London dockers refused to load the *Jolly George* with munitions for Poland in her war with Russia. They looked to Bevin, not Tillett, for support. Was this because the latter disapproved of industrial action for political purposes, or because his illness had removed him from the scene? Whatever the reason for Tillett's failure to participate in either the *Jolly George* incident, or the ensuing Councils of Action campaign (which Bevin led) against British intervention in Russia's affairs, it signified a further erosion of his position in the labour movement. At the 1920 Triennial Delegate Meeting of the Dockers' Union held in Plymouth, he was reduced to a lame attempt to link himself with Bevin in the 'Hands Off Russia' campaign. In a remarkably inconsistent speech, he tried to justify his position in the last war by blaming it upon 'the sense of gluttony on the part of the German nation as a whole, not merely the Junkers', while simultaneously asserting that British workers must never fight again. There would be no war with Russia. 'The democracies of the future will not be led and misled by all the great engines of public opinion, the great Press, the great Pulpit, the great Platform, the great Parliament . . . ' He was silent, however, when it came time to discuss the *Jolly George*; and it was Bevin who moved the resolution congratulating the dockers who had refused to load it. Tillett's attitude towards class strife had been revealed earlier in the proceedings, during his welcoming address to the delegates and the mayor of Plymouth. 'After all,' he began:

> so long as the capitalist system exists there must necessarily be friction. I do not want that friction to be other than orderly, well disciplined, common sense friction, where the workers will recognize to the full their sense of responsibility, not merely to themselves and their families, but to the system under which they are working and their State.

So much for his revolutionary pronouncements of the preceding year. Turning to the mayor, Tillett delivered himself of thirty years' accumulated wisdom in the labour and socialist movements:

> if the capitalists will take one word from me, the capitalists owe not merely the success of the war to the general trade union movement, but the capitalists of the country owe the maintaining of their industries to that success of the trade union movement.

The ideology of the 'Old Guard' had perhaps never been so baldly stated. The government of Lloyd George, at least, understood the uses to which such representatives of labour could be put.[13]

Throughout the summer of 1920 the possibility of national action by the miners grew. 'The Mines for the Nation' campaign had failed to move the public, even though the government was realizing large profits from high coal prices, while refusing to raise miners' wages. An August ballot showed more than two-thirds of the miners in favour of a strike, and 25 September was set as the date to down tools. Once again the leaders of the Miners' Federation of Great Britain approached the Triple Alliance seeking support. On 1 September, at a meeting of the executive committees of the Miners' Federation of Great Britain, the

National Union of Railwaymen and the National Transport Workers' Federation, Tillett successfully moved the motion backing the miners' demands: 'That this Conference declares that it is satisfied that the miners' claim is based on justice and equity'. As usual, however, he was opposed to direct action and hoped to avoid it.[14]

It has been cogently argued that for many of its founders the attraction of the Triple Alliance lay not in the industrial power it could wield in confrontation with the employers, but in the control it allowed trade union leaders to exert over militant sections of the rank and file, and in the prospect of bloodless victories its very size made possible. If this was true in 1914, how much more so in 1920, when former sabre-rattlers like Tillett obviously feared to draw the sword from its scabbard. A speech delivered to the Triple Alliance three weeks later, which ostensibly supported the proposed strike, more clearly reflected his sentiments. 'I hope there will not be a fight.' Tillett confessed:

> because it will not be an ordinary fight but might easily mean a revolution . . . [the government] are in possession of complete machinery for the purpose. They have road transport waggons and an army of drivers; they have the Army itself and the other armed forces of the Crown ready, and they have . . . their skeleton railway service . . . and the Press . . . a hireling Press, a suborned Press, a malign and hostile Press obtaining both money and information from the Government . . . This is the nearest thing to a revolution and we have to face the consequences of such an event.

His 1 September resolution must, then, have been a bluff.[15]

In 'the person of the Prime Minister, however, the Triple Alliance confronted a master of the bluffing game. Lloyd George must have understood that Tillett and others in the 'Old Guard' might talk about the general strike in order to keep their left-wing happy, and in order to frighten the employers, but would actually oppose calling one. Shrewdly, Lloyd George proffered the bait, another independent inquiry to consider the miners' demands. Tillett swallowed it, hook, line and sinker. 'At this eleventh hour', he said:

> and speaking as an old fighter (I dare say if it comes to a fight we shall take our place in it) I suggest that we ought to exhaust every avenue that . . . the politicians of the Government have indicated . . . the Miners' Executive should accept the challenge thrown out by the Government and ask . . . 'what tribunal are you prepared to

offer us?' . . . it would mean suspending their notices, but at times like this great courage is necessary . . .

And when the militants demurred, demanding instead that the strike vote be taken, Tillett burst out:

I am anxious that this resolution should be defeated. It is ungracious, it is unwise, it is an error, nay it is more, it is a crime (cheers). If you commit that crime you are dishonouring the men, women and children of the future labour movement.

With their allies wavering, the miners backed down and agreed to postpone the strike for one week.[16]

Three weeks later, on 16 October, the miners finally struck alone. On 21 October, the National Union of Railwaymen belatedly voted to join them unless negotiations between the Miners' Federation of Great Britain and the government were resumed in two days. A meeting of the National Transport Workers' Federation, also on 21 October, however, did not recommend sympathetic action. The 'Old Guard' among transport workers seemed temporarily ascendant.

Secure in the knowledge that the transport workers would not come out, Tillett sought now to end the miners' strike. He had become acquainted with Lord Beaverbrook, the Canadian-born millionaire, former Cabinet Minister and principal proprietor of the *Daily Express*. The latter's role in the contest between the miners and the government is shadowy; it may have been negligible. His sympathies, however, can be imagined, for at the time Beaverbrook was a close friend of both Lloyd George and Bonar Law, and a Conservative supporter of the Coalition government. Moreover, he was a firm believer in free enterprise. Nevertheless, on 22 October, the day before the National Union of Railwaymen was scheduled to come out in support of the miners, Tillett elected to confide his hopes to him and suggest a plan for ending the strike. Enclosing a note 'which is drafted by Frank Hodges [the miners' chief spokesman] and affords a basis of settlement', Tillett admitted to having 'worked damn hard to avert this strike'. Although 'matters [were] pending', he thought that the 'rail strike will be averted' and urged Beaverbrook to meet with Hodges to discuss matters. The meeting took place, Robert Smillie making a third to the party. Beaverbrook 'spent hours with them trying to understand their point of view'. Whether he succeeded, the terms Hodges had framed and Tillett had forwarded were remarkably similar to those which

Lloyd George now offered the Miner's Union in an attempt to head off the scheduled walk-out of the National Union of Railwaymen. They became the basis for the settlement reached between the miners and government on 3 November.[17]

Despite Tillett's best efforts, the coal crisis did not disappear. The settlement of 3 November was merely a truce. There was, however, a six-month lull, during which he was primarily concerned with his health. Though he 'escaped pneumonia by the slightest margin of accident and chance', his 'pulmonary troubles' were enough to incapacitate him, in November and December 1920, and then after a month of activity (mainly office work for the Dockers' Union) again until April. On 27 January he informed the union 'that it might be necessary for him to lay up', and on 16 February he was writing Beaverbrook from a nursing home in Brighton about 'congestion of the lungs on top of my ordinary asthma'. He suffered from eczema as well. Nevertheless, by 10 March he was healthy enough to attend a meeting of the emergency committee of the Dockers' Union, though he admitted to being 'very weak and rather depressed'. Despite another relapse of two weeks' duration, he rallied in April to participate in the next chapter of the struggle between the miners and the government. This time the role of the Triple Alliance was decisive. The failure of the National Transport Workers' Federation and the National Union of Railwaymen to come out in support of the miners has been accounted one of the great 'betrayals' in British labour history. What was Tillett's role in the complex series of events which concluded with 'Black Friday'?[18]

Between 1918 and 1921 Lloyd George played a hand of limited strength with consummate skill. His government weathered labour's offensive of 1919 and retreated from the threat of war with Soviet Russia. One by one the state-run industries were returned to private ownership, and on 31 March 1921, the government announced that it would return the mines to their former owners as well. Lloyd George must have judged that the trade slump would weaken working-class resistance to decontrol. Moreover his government had pushed through an Emergency Powers Act during the last coal dispute which empowered the state, under certain broadly defined conditions, to assume almost dictatorial powers. There were, no doubt, members of his Cabinet, and of Parliament, who were now sufficiently confident to relish a decisive trial of strength with the organized labour movement. There were, too, elements on the other side determined to avoid one.

The events surrounding 'Black Friday' (15 April 1921) have been analysed in detail elsewhere. They can be summarized briefly here. With the government declaration of decontrol on 31 March, the mine-owners announced wage-cuts that in some sections amounted to 50 per cent.They would not negotiate on a national basis, but by district. Here they aroused resentment among transport workers and engineers as well as among miners, for national agreements were considered the touchstone of their wartime advances. The attack upon the miners was seen as the prelude to an attack upon the other members of the Triple Alliance. It was on this issue that the three members agreed to stand. Strike orders were issued for Tuesday, 12 April. The miners, who were already manning picket lines, agreed to send safety men back to the pits so that the mines would not be flooded. This vitiated the pressure upon the owners, who were able to withstand a long strike (as they soon demonstrated) so long as their property was safe. The return of the pit-men was Lloyd George's precondition to resumed negotiations between miners, owners and government. The National Transport Workers' Federation and the National Union of Railwaymen pressed the miners to concede this point, and the Miners' Federation of Great Britain did so in order to maintain good relations with them. The resumption of negotiations led to a postponement of the strike order. On Wednesday, 13 April, the Triple Alliance set a new date — 10.00 p.m. on Friday, 15 April. Numerous other unions agreed to come out simultaneously, the most important being the Associated Society of Locomotive Engineers and Firemen. In addition, the National Joint Council of Labour, made up of the executive committees of the Labour Party, the Parliamentary Labour Party and the TUC, resolved to support the strike. With such force massed on either side, the outcome could not be predicted. Had it occurred on 15 April, as scheduled, and not in 1926, after five years of unemployment and demoralizing set-backs for the labour movement, it might have succeeded. Inaction in 1921, however, was almost as dam-aging to labour as was the General Strike half a decade later.[19]

On the evening of the 14th, Frank Hodges, secretary of the Miners' Federation of Great Britain, addressed a meeting of back-benchers in the House of Commons. Great controversy surrounds that session, during which, in answer to a question, Hodges is supposed to have stated that the miners would accept a temporary settlement on a district basis. Though Hodges later denied making such a concession, Lloyd George immediately dashed off a letter offering to reopen negotiations on this question. The miners, meeting the next morning, considered and rejected the Prime Minister's communication. But the damage had been done. Morning newspapers announced that the strike had been called off. Leaders of the other two members of the Triple Alliance, many of whom had not been present at Hodges's speech the previous evening, were besieged with telegrams and telephone calls asking whether the reports were true. 'Get on t'field. That's t'place', Herbert Smith of the miners bluntly told the delegation of the National Union of Railwaymen and the National Transport Workers' Federation, which came seeking clarification. Confused by the turn of events, resentful of the brusque treatment meted out to them by the miners, above all fearful of confronting a government armed with the Emergency Powers Act when their own counsels were so divided, the railwaymen and transport workers voted, with only three dissentients, to call off the strike. As might have been expected, Tillett sided with the majority.

Only part of his role during this sequence of events can be pieced together. The Dockers' Union executive council met almost daily during the first two weeks of April. Tillett could not attend all the meetings, for his health was still precarious. In fact, once the crisis was past, he left immediately for special treatment at Harrogate, and then for the milder climate of Aix-les-Bains in France. From 7 to 9 April, and perhaps at other points during the two hectic weeks preceding 'Black Friday', Tillett was incapacitated by 'bronchial attacks' and took no part in events. He intervened at two decisive moments, however. The first was after Hodges's speech at the House of Commons on Thursday night. 'Tillett got on the 'phone and bucked him up.' This suggests that Tillett supported Hodges's compromise offer to Lloyd George (assuming, of course, that one was made). In other words, despite having made several statements supporting action during the Triple Alliance meetings, Tillett was seeking a means of avoiding the strike before the decision to call it off was taken. Then on Friday at the National Union of Railwaymen and National Transport Workers' Federation meeting, he sided with the majority against the direct actionists. 'The position is truly hopeless,' he said. 'We have lost the chance of a generation, the chance of a century.'[20]

Later in the summer, Tillett attempted to explain his position to the Dockers' Union executive council. 'It would have been sheer calamity to have gone on with that movement . . . ' he began. His justification for inaction was familiar: 'I am no less a revolutionary now than ever I was, but I am not a revolutionary in theory. I want brains put into the business.' He catalogued the difficulties facing the Alliance: 'In Scotland Yard there are details and schemes to deal with any industry. The Government has prepared with minute care . . . to deal with every form of incipient revolution.' The Alliance, however, had made no such preparations.

> During the negotiations I was anxious there should be a plan. I asked whether they had any sort of plan, and let me say with great regret, until the penultimate evening of the Alliance's decision to support the Miners and declare a National Strike, there was not a scintilla of organization to feed the miners or ourselves in the event of the strike.

Under such conditions, Tillett continued, the Prime Minister was 'cock-a-hoop', believing that an opportunity to crush the Triple Alliance had finally arisen. Hodges's proposal on the night of the 14th, however, pointed the way out of the trap set by Lloyd George: as soon as it was made 'most of the important members of the Coalition determined that Downing Street would have to come to heel'. How did Tillett know this? Was he in touch with Beaverbrook again? Did he play a double game by maintaining the contacts with the government which he had established during the war? With whom was he sitting when Hodges delivered his speech? He was not with James Wignall, the other Dockers' Union MP present that evening. Was he, perhaps, closeted with high-ranking Conservatives and government officials devising schemes to head off the strike? This is not so unlikely as it might first appear; there is evidence to suggest that from 1923 he was receiving annual subsidies from the Conservative Party. Were they for services rendered in an earlier period? At any rate, his opposition to the national Triple Alliance strike is clear.[21]

Once the threat of direct action had been surmounted, Tillett took the lead in organizing other, more limited, forms of support for the miners. This now appears to have been a reassertion of his militancy, once truly militant action could no longer be taken. As a member of the Dockers' Union executive council he headed deputations to the National Transport Workers' Federation and the National Union of Railwaymen, arguing that they should refuse to handle coal during the miners' strike. He successfully recommended that the Dockers' Union should contribute £10,000 to the miners' strike fund, and wrote to Fred Bowerman of the TUC in order to drum up additional financial support.[22]

Amid the bitter recriminations that followed 'Black Friday', Tillett's attempt to shore up his dwindling reputation with the militants must have appeared doomed to failure. On 22 April, the Dockers' Union emergency committee read one angry protest after another from the union's district secretaries. The Ipswich communiqué may be taken as typical: 'All members were solid for the strike. The withdrawal of the arrangement to strike was interpreted by the men as weakness and resolutions protesting were sent to each Union concerned.' Of nine messages received, only that from the Somerset and Dorset branch supported the executive. The entire district committee of London resigned in protest. At the annual general council meeting of the National Transport Workers' Federation in June, the assault upon the leaders continued. Jack Jones MP asked suspiciously whether 'private negotiations' behind the scenes had produced the débâcle. Did he suspect that Tillett had participated in them? No names were mentioned, and Bevin denied that any 'deal' had been made. Meanwhile Tillett had reversed direction again. 'I honestly regret that decision on the Friday night,' he told the assembled delegates of the National Transport Workers' Federation. 'I do not believe that all 100% of our men would have come out; but I do believe we could have had the majority . . . because they would think it was right.'[23]

II

Amazingly, Tillett's twists and turns could not destroy the affection and respect with which the older generation of Dockers' Union officials still regarded him. Their support for him was manifested when his long simmering rivalry with Bevin finally surfaced, over the latter's plans for amalgamation of the various transport unions, including the Dockers' Union, into one giant organization. Tillett called upon this reserve of goodwill among the veterans in order to secure a leading position in the embryonic Transport and General Workers' Union. His hopes were not to be realized. There was no place for him in Bevin's plans.

Tillett had recruited Bevin into the Dockers' Union in the spring of 1911. From Bristol's district organizer to national organizer to assistant general secretary, the former carter's ascent was rapid. During the war, while Tillett barnstormed for the government, Bevin applied himself to the more mundane task of running the union, gaining a reputation as a tough negotiator and an able organizer. He excelled at the administrative tasks Tillett had always despised. Ill health prevented Tillett from reasserting himself once the armistice was signed. Moreover, Bevin's political views were in better accord with the times than were Tillett's. A younger man, he took no part in the last spasm of chauvinistic patriotism during the khaki election, and played a leading role in the campaign against war with Russia. Above all, he established a national reputation during the famous Shaw Inquiry. Later Tillett was to claim that he had been instrumental in helping Bevin to prepare his case. If so, Bevin's most distinguished biographer Alan Bullock, makes no mention of it. By 1921, there can be no doubt that Bevin's mastery in the Dockers' Union was complete. Tillett, although still his nominal superior, was a lesser force.[24]

Amalgamation with other transport workers' organizations had been a goal of the Dockers' Union since its inception. All plans had foundered, however, upon the unwillingness of autonomous organizations to sacrifice their independence of action. The establishment of the National Transport Workers' Federation in 1911 had been a compromise: it brought over thirty unions into one organization, but it preserved their separate identities. It took Bevin to conceive and then put through a plan for amalgamation, which both preserved the autonomy of its constituent parts while unifying them under a single command. This was achieved with a double structure, based on geography at one level, and trade at the other.[25]

In March 1920, Bevin launched his amalgamation campaign. Tillett was ill at the time, and there is no evidence that he participated in the preliminary meetings. Throughout the summer Bevin attended to the details, organized the subcommittees to implement his proposals, drafted a tentative constitution. By December, delegates from unions representing Britain's dock, waterway, road transport, clerical and general workers approved his amalgamation scheme and he submitted it to the rank and file. Some 550,000 ballots were printed and distributed to the members before Christmas. It was at this point that Tillett first commented publicly. He was ill and pessimistic. (The first miners' strike had ended a month before.) He was not prepared to stand against the plan, although he thought that 'in all probability there will have to be complete reorganization of even the scheme now propounded'. His real objection was revealed at the start: 'there are vested interests that must not be ignored'. He was referring to himself.[26]

He worried that his position was being undermined by the young, forceful men in the labour movement, Bevin and Robert Williams in particular. 'I am proud to be an old'un', he told the December amalgamation conference. And again, this time at an executive council meeting of his union: 'some of those who had done the gutter work might not be very clever, but they had experience and understanding that some of the young ones could not have'. On 11 May 1921, Bevin presided over the meeting that officially established the Transport and General Workers' Union. It would not commence activities until 1 January 1922. Provisional officers were elected to prepare for New Year's Day during the interim period. Tillett had hoped to be the union's provisional president. But he withdrew when Bevin, the new union's general secretary, intimated that there were already too many dockers holding high positions in the fledgeling organization. The presidency was filled by Gosling of the Lightermen's Union instead. Tillett was resolved to make the post his own once the provisional period ended.[27]

Ill during May and much of June, Tillett again went to recuperate at Aix-les-Bains. Aside from his usual chest problems, his legs were troubling him; he could not walk. Still, he returned to London in mid-August to make his bid for a post in the new amalgamated union. 'Somebody may say some claim a vested interest', he conceded before the August executive council meeting of the Dockers' Union.

> That is the wisest thing I have heard. I have invested forty years of my life in the movement. I am not ashamed of that, or of any of the officers of this Executive who want to be careful. I do not want the Committee when at meetings to accept willy nilly this that or the other.

He was drifting towards opposition. Sentimental attachment to the Dockers' Union that he had founded thirty years before stood between him and the new organization. Jealousy, too, must have influenced him, for he had been unable, despite decades of agitation, to push through an amalgamation plan. Still, he knew that amalgamation would strengthen the workers in their dealings with employers, and he had not yet despaired of attaining the presidency of the amalgamated union. His quarterly report to the Dockers' Union executive council in November reflected his indecision. 'With regard to amalgamation', he asserted, 'things are in too nebulous and transitory a stage at this moment to offer any definite opinion on machinery and method.' His resentment at the general trend, however, was apparent. 'I have not been privileged to take part in most of the activities since my return to health ... There may be useful years left for me to work with you and for you.' Actually, he had attended the amalgamation conference in Leamington during the third week in September, though played no significant role in the proceedings. But his complaint held true in general terms. He had not been a member of the inner circle that framed and pushed through the amalgamation scheme.[28]

The hour of his defeat was near at hand. Sometime during the last week in November he learned that his name would not appear on the ballot for the presidency. He had been nominated by old members of his union, but Gosling, the other candidate, would not stand against him. If Gosling withdrew, his entire union and others were likely to secede from the Transport and General Workers' Union in protest. They believed that the Dockers' Union already dominated the new body, since Bevin was its general secretary, and Harry Kay its treasurer. The entire amalgamation scheme was jeopardized at the eleventh hour. As Tillett described it:

> It comes to a man that he must do something for principle. He had to make up his mind that in the interest of the greater organisation he should retire.

The vehemence with which he proclaimed his altruism belied its reality. Tillett was bitter and did not scruple to hide it; in the process he contradicted his assertions of his own magnanimity. 'He had a right to the Presidency', he told an extraordinary conference of Dockers' Union district secretaries, convened on 9 December in order to learn from Tillett himself why his name had been left off the ballot. But 'he had been jockeyed and elbowed out of' it. Gosling and Bevin had forced him to retire. Yet, he warned, they had not seen the last of him. 'Not even the futile enmities of the pygmies, nor the sordid and brutish ingratitude we have met, can take away our vision,' Tillett promised in his last annual report to the Dockers' Union.[29]

'If he were left alone against the world he would fight', Tillett had defiantly vowed at the 9 December meeting. In fact, the fight had been taken out of him. All the district secretaries of the old Dockers' Union lamented Tillett's failure to secure the presidency of the Transport and General Workers' Union. They delivered a series of moving tributes to the founder of their union. 'The leaving of Tillett's name from the ballot was rending their hearts', Brother Charles of Swansea told the meeting, expressing the common sentiment. There was nothing, however, that they − or Tillett − could do. There is a rumour that Tillett threatened to desert the Transport and General Workers' Union, taking the Dockers' Union with him. Little credence can be attached to it. He no longer had the energy or the will to execute such a plan. In any event, a position was created for him in the union, 'International and Political Secretary', perhaps to forestall such an eventuality, more likely to satisfy the dockers and district secretaries who had demanded with one voice that 'those who have done so much shall be rewarded'.[30]

III

Tillett's moment on centre stage was over, although he continued to be active on the periphery. He held his seat for North Salford in the House of Commons until 1924, and from 1922 to 1926 he presided over meetings held by Labour Members who belonged to the Transport and General Workers' Union. He was returned to Parliament again in 1929, but his interjections in the House were rare. As he confessed at one point: 'I am the rottenest politician in the world. I don't believe I was made for it.' He lost North Salford for the second time in the 1931 débâcle and did not stand again. He was also a member of the TUC General Council from 1921 until 1929, when as chairman of the TUC he delivered the welcoming address to the annual conference at Belfast. There is no evidence, however, that he played any significant role in the Council, even during the General Strike. Predictably enough, he supported the General Council decision to end it. Rather, his time after 1922 was increasingly spent travelling and attending labour conferences in Britain and on the Continent. Representing the TUC, he journeyed to Russia twice and to the Ruhr in 1923. Occasionally he spoke for the Transport and General Workers' Union as well, but his differences with Bevin were too great, and his energy level too low, for him to threaten the latter's predominant position. In 1935 he lent his name to an organizing drive among boxers, but the union formed was not successful. When in London, he was an habitué of the Trade Union Club, where, 'small, wizened, loquacious, with bright bird-like eyes', he liked to recount his triumphs of the previous century and 'explain to all who would listen how Bevin, the man he had "found and made" had pushed him to one side'.[31]

During this twilight period of his career, Tillett seems to have strengthened his connections with the Conservative Party. He corresponded frequently with Beaverbrook, and also appears to have been on good terms with Bonar Law. In October 1923, he met Stanley Baldwin, the Conservative Prime Minister, and promised him that he would 'fight communism' during the winter. Communist dockers in London had successfully carried out a wildcat strike that year, and it is probable that Tillett hoped to crush them. Baldwin consulted J.C.C. Davidson, Chancellor of the Duchy of Lancaster, who in turn contacted Sir Reginald Hall, Conservative Member of Parliament for the West Derby division of Liverpool and principal agent of the Conservative Party. Tillett had apparently asked for money: 'The Prime Minister wondered whether you thought it might be worthwhile sending for him. There is just a chance he might do business.' Hall got in touch with Sir Stanley Jackson, the party chairman, whose response was revealing: 'Jackson might be prepared to make a special grant of £1,000 if [the] PM decides it', Hall reported to Davidson, 'but he feels as I do that we can't encourage all the derelicts . . . ' Tillett's stock was low on all fronts. His twists and turns had led him finally to a cul-de-sac. Even if the Conservative Party did bail him out, and Davidson's papers are silent on this, it is safe to say that after 1921 the former working-class militant had literally expended his credit.[32]

He was still friendly with his old comrade-in-arms, Tom Mann, despite the latter's membership in the party which Tillett had promised Baldwin he would fight. They often attended theatres and pubs together. 'To see them come out of Henekey's in the Strand', Harry Pollitt, the Communist leader, recalled twenty years later, and 'arm in arm, wend their way to Charing Cross Station giving some coppers to every flower girl, match seller and what have you . . . was a sight for the gods'. By now, Tillett had acquired a reputation as a lavish spender (of Conservative funds?) and a heavy drinker. He was overheard at the House of Commons singing 'Blow the Man Down', and by one account attended the 1922 TUC at Southport 'a little blind if you know what I mean'. He arrived in a similar condition at the funeral service for Mann in 1940. Yet he delivered a eulogy which Pollitt considered to be 'the most beautiful wording and phrasing I have ever listened to . . . It was unforgettable, and despite the sadness of the occasion, those present walked out of the crematorium as if they were already living in the kind of land and that William Morris wrote about.' At least his gift for oratory never deserted him.[33]

During the last fifteen years of his life, Tillett chafed at his relative inaction and impotence. 'I am pensioned off and isolated', he complained to Beaverbrook in 1933, and to Lloyd George, who had similar complaints:

I am feeling the bitterness of Old Age and the shuffling 'Elbowing out of it' which comes to those who are not wary of those they help, and for whom they secure a tenure they never sought for themselves.

Eventually misanthropy compounded the bitterness. 'The other day I was talking to my daughter', Tillett told a meeting of Women for Moral Re-Armament in 1940:

'If I was God Almighty,' I said, 'I would eliminate the whole human race. Such a wonderful world! What a mess we have made of it! What swines we are!'

Yet the Second World War roused him. 'You inspire me to the old enthusiasms of loyalty and devotion', he gushed in 1941 to Beaver-brook, then the Minister of Aircraft Production.

I would take your message to the Industrial centres, to America, to any zone of war, across ocean or sea or land, for I am virile and hearty and would take any cynic, in Open Air, or anywhere.

He was, at this time, 81 years old. Two years later, on 27 January 1943, he died.[34]

Notes

1. All figures taken from G.D.H. Cole and R. Postgate, *The Common People* (Methuen and Co., London, 1968), pp. 556-60.

2. See, for example, James Cronin, *Industrial Conflict in Modern Britain* (Croom Helm, London, 1979); during 1919-21, 40 million working days per year were lost through strikes; during 1911-13, 20 million working days per year were lost through strikes.

3. For a useful account of the pre-war Triple Alliance, see G.A. Phillips, 'The Triple Industrial Alliance of 1914', *Economic History Review*, 2nd ser. vol. 24 (1971), pp. 55-67.

4. *Dockers' Record*, November 1918 and November 1916; *Manchester Guardian*, 6 December and 12 December 1918; his margin of victory was 12,079 to 4,135.

5. Dock, Wharf, Riverside and General Labourers' Union, *Annual Report*, 1918; *Dockers' Record*, March 1919.

6. For a detailed and sympathetic treatment of the miners' movement during this period, see R. Page Arnot, *The Miners: Years of Struggle* (Allen and Unwin, London, 1953).

7. National Transport Workers' Federation, *Annual General Council Meeting*, 1919, p. 75; G.A. Phillips, in 'The National Transport Workers' Federation', unpublished DPhil thesis, University of Oxford, 1968, argues that Tillett's resolution meant that 'direct action could only be taken after prolonged, perhaps prohibitive delay'. National Transport Workers' Federation, *Annual General Council Meeting*, 1919, p.77.

8. Labour Party, *Annual Conference*, 1919, p. 158.

9. Dock, Wharf, Riverside and General Labourers' Union, *Minutes of the Recalled Triennial Delegate Meeting*, 1919.

10. Dock, Wharf, Riverside and General Labourers' Union, *Annual Report*, 1919.

11. Phillips, 'National Transport Workers' Federation', p. 456, quoted from the Triple Alliance Delegate Conference, 23 July 1919, p. 13.

12. For a detailed account of Bevin's arguments before the Shaw Inquiry, see Alan Bullock, *The Life and Times of Ernest Bevin* (William Heinemann, London, 1960), vol. 1, pp. 120-33.

13. Dock, Wharf, Riverside and General Labourers' Union, *Minutes of the Recalled Triennial Delegate Meeting*, 1920.

14. Arnot, *The Miners* p. 245.

15. *Triple Alliance Delegate Conference*, 22 September 1920, p. 14.

16. *Triple Alliance Delegate Meeting*, 23 September 1920, pp. 26 and 45.

17. The date is tentative. The letter is merely dated 'Friday', and was mistakenly placed in the '1921 File' of the Beaverbrook Papers, House of Lords Record Office. But the letter deals with the 'Datum Line' strike of 1920, and must have been written on Friday, 22 October of that year. A.J.P. Taylor, *Beaverbrook* (Hamilton Press, London, 1972) is the best biography of that man; see p. 180 for Beaverbrook's letter to 'a friend in New York', on the meeting with Smillie and Hodges.

18. Beaverbrook Papers, Tillett to Beaverbrook, 16 February 1921; Ernest Bevin Collection, Modern Records Centre, Warwick University, B2/2/18, Dock, Wharf, Riverside and General Labourers' Union, 'Minutes of Emergency Committee, 10 March 1921'.

19. For more on 'Black Friday', see particularly Bullock, *Life and Times of Ernest Bevin*, pp. 143-79; Arnot, *The Miners*, pp. 310-20; P.S. Bagwell, 'The Triple Industrial Alliance, 1913-22,' in Asa Briggs and John Saville (eds.), *Essays in Labour History* (Macmillan, London, 1971), vol. 2, pp. 96-128.

20. Bevin Collection, B2/3/11, Dock, Wharf, Riverside and General Labourers' Union, 'Emergency Committee Meeting, 5 May 1921', Bro. Milford explaining the situation to assembled delegates; National Union of Railwaymen Collection, Modern Records Centre, Warwick University, NUT/3, MSS 127, 'Coal Dispute, Report of Proceedings of Industrial Triple Alliance', p. 69.

21. Bevin Collection, B2/3/33, 'Minutes of Executive Council Meeting, 15-19 August 1921'; see Wignall's account in the Bevin Collection. For more on the possibility that Tillett was receiving Conservative subsidies, see below pp. 218-19.

22. Bevin Collection, B2/3/4; B2/3/1; B2/3/1, Tillett to Bowerman, 18 April 1921.

23. Bevin Collection, B2/3/3, Dock, Wharf, Riverside and General Labourers' Union, 'Minutes of Emergency Committee Meeting, 22 April 1921'; National Transport Workers' Federation, *Annual General Council Meeting*, 1921, pp. 27 and 45.

24. Bevin Collection, B2/4/22, Dock, Wharf, Riverside and General Labourers' Union, 'Conference of District Secretaries, 9 December 1921'.

25. For more on the structure of the Transport and General Workers' Union, see Bullock, *Life and Times of Ernest Bevin*, p. 158.

26. *Dockers' Record*, December 1920.

27. *Dockers' Record*, February 1921.

28. Bevin Collection, B2/3/55, Dock, Wharf, Riverside and General Labourers' Union, 'Minutes of Executive Council Meeting, 19 August 1921'; B2/4/15, Dock, Wharf, Riverside and General Labourers' Union, 'Minutes of Executive Council Meeting, November 1921'.

29. Bevin Collection, B2/4/22, Dock, Wharf, Riverside and General Labourers' Union, 'Conference of District Secretaries, 9 December 1921'; idem, *Annual Report*, 1921.

30. Tillett Collection, MSS 74/6/1/107, S.F. Whitlock to Ian Mackay, 22 January 1951.

31. See, for example, Bevin Collection, B2/3/33, 'Rough Notes of National Docks Group – July 22, 1926 *Coal Dispute and General Strike*. Notes of statements made by Bros. Ernest Bevin and Ben Tillett'; Tillett Collection, MSS 74/6/1/ 31-8 for Tillett and the boxers; Francis Williams, *Ernest Bevin* (Hutchinson, London, 1951), 109.

32. Tillett Collection, MSS 74/6/1/1, Tillett to Beaverbrook, in a letter of 15 September 1928 writes: 'Public life lost a gentleman of honour when Bonar Law died. But you know my regard for him'; Robert Rhodes James, *Memoirs of a Conservative: J.C.C. Davidson's Memoirs and Papers, 1910-37* (Weidenfeld and Nicolson, London, 1965), p. 118 fn.

33. Tillett Collection, MSS 74/6/2/80, Harry Pollitt to Ian Mackay, 21 January 1951; MSS 74/6/2/107, S.G. Whitlock to Ian Mackay, 22 January 1951.

34. Tillett Collection, MSS 74/6/1/12, Tillett to Beaverbrook, 5 April 1933; MSS 74/6/1/54, Tillett to Lloyd George, 29 April 1932; Tillett, *Ben Tillett: Fighter and Pioneer* (Blandford Press, London, 1945), p. 6; Tillett Collection, MSS 74/6/1/19, Tillett to Beaverbrook, 19 October 1941.

CONCLUSION

I

Ben Tillett's emergence as a labour militant occurred during the new unionist era. The young Lib-Lab supporter became an advocate of independent labour representation and of government intervention on behalf of the working class. A variety of factors produced this transformation, but chief among them was the bitter opposition of the employers to his organizing activities. Even at the height of his reputation as a new unionist firebrand, however, he preferred conciliation to conflict. He had assessed the relative strengths of the contending forces in the industrial arena and found labour lacking. The employers commanded bigger battalions, and they were less adversely affected by downswings in the trade cycle.

Thus Tillett sought almost always to narrow, and almost never to widen, those disputes he was unable to prevent. When, as often happened, his tongue outran his real intentions, he always backtracked. His experience in Bristol in 1892 may be taken as typical. Moved by the suffering of the strikers in the city of his birth, and outraged by the employers who had hired blacklegs to break the strike, Tillett made an impassioned appeal for working-class insurrection. Brought to trial for sedition, he escaped imprisonment by demonstrating that no shorthand expert could keep pace with his rapid fire delivery, thus casting doubt upon the transcript of his speech.

The demoralizing string of defeats stretching from 1890 onwards proved crucial in determining Tillett's subsequent evolution. They were responsible for his search for short cuts to the socialist utopia which in happier moments he had come to anticipate. On the political front, successive defeats at Bradford led to his suggestion that labour might have to compromise with the established parties after all. In the industrial world, it was the overwhelming employers' counter-offensive which produced his longing for arbitration.

Thereafter, the ambiguities of his position and his own ambivalence grew increasingly apparent. His hatred of poverty and oppression never faltered, but the methods by which he sought to oppose them were inconsistent. In 1899 he returned from Australia to advocate class peace; in 1907, after a second trip to the Antipodes, he brought back the message of class war. Between 1900 and 1906 he attacked the

Labour Party from the right; thereafter, until the outbreak of the First World War, he criticized it from the left. These oscillations represent the continuing search of a mercurial personality for a realistic standpoint on which to ground its efforts on behalf of the working class. They reflect as well Tillett's need to find a niche, almost any niche, in a labour movement with most of whose leaders he had personal differences.

Ironically, the First World War marked Tillett's liberation. The discrediting of MacDonald, Snowden and Glasier for their pacificism, and the death of Hardie, opened the Labour Party to him, and in 1917 he finally gained entrance to the House of Commons. Now he could be frank about his hatred of strikes. The rhetorical violence which had once placed him beyond the pale was now directed at legitimate enemies, the Germans and traitors at home. The working class could accept this, while simultaneously Tillett entered the respectable society which previously had shuddered at his name. Moreover, his ameliorative vision was finally being fulfilled. Because the government depended upon labour's support to win the war, it intervened in the affairs of the employers. It placed workmen and their leaders, Tillett among them, upon committees which regulated conditions of labour and rates of pay. It established boards of conciliation which, more often than not, found in the workers' favour in order to keep them satisfied during the national crisis. Thus for Tillett, the war years were probably the most satisfying of his career.

With the close of the war, Tillett found himself unable to regain his former leading position in the labour movement. He could no longer pose as a revolutionary socialist, although occasionally he tried, because too many people had heard his pro-government, anti-German tirades. Moreover, in the tumultuous aftermath of the war, he set himself firmly against the Triple Alliance general strike which seemed on the verge of breaking out. With 'Black Friday', Tillett had shot his bolt. There was no place for him in Ernest Bevin's Transport and General Workers' Union which replaced the National Transport Workers' Federation, and with which the old Dockers' Union merged. Embittered and isolated, Tillett allowed his cynicism free rein. He appealed to the Conservatives for funds to fight Communism. From all indications, he died a pensioner of his lifelong enemies.

II

Tillett is not supposed, here, to have been a wholly representative figure. The very fierceness with which he expressed his views, and the rapidity with which he took up first one view and then another and then yet another, however, make him a peculiarly useful figure in British labour history to study. He was in the thick of almost everything, and he was constitutionally incapable of keeping quiet.

His career sheds new light upon certain important moments in the history of the British working class. The scope of Tillett's activities, the range of his contacts, the hyperbole of his rhetoric, above all the process of his conversion to socialist and independent labour politics, analysed here, contradicts those historians who assert that the new unionists differed little from their Lib-Lab predecessors. Ben Tillett's world view was very different in 1893 than it had been in 1887, even if he did not share the millenarian faith of those who believed in the 'religion of socialism'. If Ben Tillett believed in 'Labourism', however, this was a considerable advance over his former views, a point implicitly ignored by those who condemn the 'Labourist' tradition.

A different point may be made with reference to the 1911-14 'great unrest'. A close examination of Tillett's conduct during this period would seem to support those historians who argue that the period did not represent a significant departure in the aims or methods of the British working class. For all his close association with the syndicalists, Tillett continued to think along the lines he had developed since 1889, and these were 'Labourist' in this sense: he generally opposed militant action; he generally thought in terms of better incorporating the workers within the existing system. Yet the significance of the 'great unrest' remains in dispute, even if the nature of Tillett's world view during it is plain. For if Tillett's views during 1911-14 were essentially what they had been during 1900-6, his rhetoric was substantially different. He had, in fact, adopted the language of the syndicalists. That this should have led to a quantum leap in his popularity with the rank and file does indeed suggest a broad change in working-class attitudes. This is a point that historians of the 'great unrest' who dispute its significance have overlooked. Here, then, Tillett's legacy is dubious.

Then there is Tillett's behaviour during the First World War. It helps explain the phenomenon of patriotic labour. In a manner which pre-1914 socialists had hardly anticipated, the British working class, like

Tillett himself, took advantage of the conditions created by war to improve their lot. The government fulfilled some of Tillett's fondest dreams for his class, in order to ensure its support of the war effort.

Examination of Tillett's career would seem, also, to confirm certain generally accepted interpretations of British labour history. Take, for example, the traditional explanation of the origins of the Labour Party. Trade unionists joined with socialists, it is said, after the Taff Vale decision convinced them that the working class needed to fight the employers with their own political party. Tillett's experience bears this out. He himself advocated an independent labour party, mainly as an additional weapon in the struggle with the Shipping Federation. For Tillett, as for the other major founders of the Labour Party, according to Henry Pelling's classic account, the need for independent labour representation did not reflect the growing strength of the working class, but its self-perceived weakness.

III

Despite all the contradictions and reversals, certain of Tillett's tendencies and attitudes changed very little over the years. It is important to take note of them because they help, finally, to place him in a historical context.

First, in spite of Tillett's reputation to the contrary, his distaste for 'direct action' remained constant. He was entirely unprepared for the great dock strikes of 1889 and 1911, and opposed to the other massive dispute in which he played a leading part, the 1912 transport workers' strike in London. In fact, aside from a brief euphoric moment immediately following the success of 1889, Tillett consistently worked to forestall walk-outs. To cite other conspicuous examples: he opposed the Hull conflict of 1893, the London dock strikes in 1900 and 1923, Larkin's appeal for sympathetic action in 1914, and a Triple Alliance strike on 'Black Friday', 1921. He was, throughout his career, an advocate of compulsory industrial arbitration.

Tillett's loathing of strikes and preference for conciliation reveals a fundamental aspect of his outlook hitherto unnoticed. Although he described himself as a revolutionary socialist, he accepted the state apparatus as it was, and wanted only to change its personnel. His hatred of exploitation and poverty were absolutely genuine; but he thought that they would be ended if only the government intervened on behalf of the workers. He wanted the government to restrain the capitalists, not to abolish them. 'The protection which property already possesses the toiler now seeks', he wrote in 1892. He did not foresee that the working class would take control of society, but rather that it would become better integrated within it.

It seems both ironical and surprising that a man of Tillett's instinctive combativeness should adopt so relatively pacific an ideology. Yet he came to it logically. In a country inexorably advancing towards political democracy, it would, perhaps, have been more improbable for a labour leader like Tillett to have turned his back on parliamentarianism. If the state was the workers' enemy, as it indubitably appeared to be during the employers' counter-offensive of the 1890s, then universal suffrage offered a weapon against it at least as plausible as violent revolution.

Tillett fashioned his ideology piecemeal, as a response to his difficult situation as a labour leader. If his prognostications and philosophical musings appear flimsy in contrast with those of William Morris or Friedrich Engels or Eleanor Marx, perhaps that is because, as a trade unionist, his eyes were mainly focused on the near and middle ground. Here, then, is another explanation of his innumerable sudden shifts. As a trade unionist, Tillett's job was to negotiate, to be flexible, to obtain the best possible deal within the constraints of the present situation, and yet to retain a basic loyalty to the rank and file. If Tillett's fiery temperament predisposed him to militancy, then his role as leader of a trade union encouraged him to look for compromises.

The modesty of Tillett's political and social vision may also have been due, partially, to his attitude towards the rank and file. He distrusted it sometimes to the point of contempt. He was continually berating the men: for being too militant or not militant enough; for not following his orders; for not sufficiently appreciating his efforts on their behalf. He wanted to direct the union as if he was a general, and despite repeated declarations of his belief in rank-and-file democracy, he was always an advocate of discipline and authority (though he himself was never very good at following orders).

Thus Tillett was an exponent of 'labourism' to this extent: he viewed working-class interests as sectional; he believed that the gradual accretion of reforms would lead eventually to socialism; and he conceived of socialism in extremely modest terms. 'I have seen a social revolution accomplished in my lifetime', he attested in his autobiography.

It would not do to dismiss entirely, as certain scholars have, Tillett's perhaps complacent view of British labour history. That would denigrate implicitly the positive achievements of Ben Tillett and the 'labourist' tradition with which he is rightly associated. The empirical evidence, which it has been the main burden of this work to provide, reveals the dockers' leader to have been an erratic but irrepressible force in the labour world, whose activities usually brought as much unease and discomfort to the employers as to anyone else. Tillett was an extraordinary organizer and agitator. As a result of his efforts, countless workers were recruited to the socialist and trade union movements.

It would be equally superficial, however, to accept Tillett's role uncritically — as, perhaps, Lord George-Brown did one evening in 1976, and as many historians of the labour movement have done. The general secretary of the Dockers' Union was ambitious to a fault, and often opportunistic. His opinion of the rank and file was low, and consequently his outlook was authoritarian. His vision of socialism remained strikingly incomplete.

This study has attempted to show that for all his inconsistencies, Ben Tillett played a significant part in the history of British labour. His unpredictability makes him interesting; his ubiquity during a crucial quarter century and more, make him important. To examine his experience is to examine that of the working-class movement as a whole.

BIBLIOGRAPHY

Primary Sources

1. Manuscripts and Collections

British Museum, London
Johns Burns Papers
Charles Dilke Papers

London School of Economics and Political Science
Passfield Papers
Webb Trade Union Collection
Charles Booth Collection
George Lansbury Papers
Henry Broadhurst Papers
London Independent Labour Party Papers
Miscellaneous pamphlets, etc.

Modern Records Centre, Warwick University, Coventry
Ben Tillett Collection
Ernest Bevin Collection
Dockers' Union Papers
National Transport Workers' Federation Papers
International Transport Workers' Federation Papers
Transport and General Workers' Union Papers

House of Lords Record Office, London
Lloyd George Papers
Herbert Samuel Papers
Beaverbrook Papers
Miscellaneous printed materials

Bishopsgate Institute, London
George Howell Collection

Nuffield College, Oxford University
Fabian Society Papers
G.D.H. Cole Papers

Public Record Office, London
J. Ramsay MacDonald Papers
Miscellaneous Home Office, Foreign Office Papers

Congress House (TUC), London
Biography file
Miscellaneous pamphlets, etc.

Transport House (Labour Party), London
Labour Party Subjects File
Labour Representation Committee Archive

Labour Party General Correspondence File
Workers War Emergency National Committee File

Transport House (Transport and General Workers' Union), London
Miscellaneous Dockers' Union material

Dock House, London
Miscellaneous newspaper clippings, reports, etc.

Marx Memorial Library, London
Miscellaneous

Hull University, Hull
Dictionary of Labour Biography Files

Boston Public Library
Samuel Gompers Collection, outgoing correspondence letter books (microfilm)

2. Newspapers

Colindale: (consulted systematically)
Bradford Observer
British Citizen and Empire Worker
Cambria Daily Leader
Clarion
Daily Herald
East End News
Eccles Advertiser
Industrial Peace
Justice
Labour Elector
Labour Leader
Labour Union Journal
Manchester Guardian
Salford Reporter
South Wales Daily News
South Wales Weekly Post
Star
Sun
Syndicalist
The Times
Trade Unionist

3. Other Printed Primary Sources

Minutes of Testimony to the Select Committee of the House of Lords on the Sweating System, *P.P.*, 1888, XXI
Report by the Labour Correspondent to the Board of Trade, 'Strikes and Lock-outs', *P.P.*, 1890, LXVIII
Minutes of Testimony to the Royal Commission on Labour, *P.P.*, 1892, XXXV
Minutes of Testimony to the Joint Select Committee on the Port of London Bill, *P.P.*, 1908, X, Appendix 8: Statement of Labour Conditions by Ben Tillett, pp. 677-82
Hansard (for Tillett's speeches in the House of Commons), 1917-23 and 1929-31

Public Record Office
1861 Census, R.G. 9/1734
Minutes of Testimony to the Roche Committee, LAB 2/1040/DPL107/
Minutes of Testimony to the MacLean Committee, LAB 2/1048/

Trades Union Congress
Annual Reports, 1887-1929
Parliamentary Committee Minutes, November 1892-July 1895

Labour Representation Committee
Annual Reports, 1900-5

Labour Party
Annual Reports, 1906-29

Independent Labour Party
Annual Reports, 1893-6

British Socialist Party
Annual Reports, 1912-14

Guild Hall Library
Minutes of Meetings of London County Council, 1892-7

Secondary Sources

4. Works by Ben Tillett

Tillett's Books
Dock, Wharf, Riverside and General Workers' Union: A Brief History of the
    Dockers' Union Commemorating the 1889 Dockers' Strike (London, 1910)
History of the London Transport Workers' Strike, 1911 (London, 1912)
Memories and Reflections (London, 1931)

Tillett's Articles
'The Dockers' Story', *English Illustrated Magazine* (Macmillan, London, 1888-9),
    pp. 97-101
'The Labour Platform: New Style', *New Review*, vol. 6 (Longmans, Green,
    London, January-June 1892), pp. 173-80
'Our Naval Weakness', *National Review*, vol. 27 (Edward Arnold, March-August
    1896), pp. 872-80
'The Alleged Industrial Invasion of England by America', *Independent*, vol. 53
    (S.W. Benedict, New York, 1901), pp. 3073-6
'The Need of Labour Representation' in Frank W. Galton (ed.), *Workers on their
    Industries* (S. Sonnenschein, London, 1896)

Tillett's Pamphlets
Ben Tillett: Fighter and Pioneer (Blandford Press, London, 1945)
A Dock Labourer's Bitter Cry (1887)
The Legislature and Labour (Cardiff, n.d.)
The New Trades Unionism (with Tom Mann) (1890)
Prosecution of Ben Tillett: Speech delivered in Horsefair, Bristol, 18 December
1892 (Bristol, 1893)

Trades Unionism and Socialism, Clarion pamphlet no. 16 (1897)
Is the Parliamentary Labour Party a Failure? (1908)
Industrial Germany (1912)
Who was responsible for the War – and why? (1917)
*The Ruhr: the report of deputation from the Transport and General Workers'
    Union* (1923)
An Address on Character and Environment (n.d.)

5. Autobiographies and Memoirs

Askwith, George. *Industrial Problems and Disputes* (John Murray, London, 1920)
Barnes, G.N. *From Workshop to War Cabinet* (D. Appleton, New York, 1924)
Besant, Annie. *Annie Besant, An Autobiography* (Fisher Unwin, London, 1893)
Blatchford, Robert. *My Eighty Years* (Cassell, London, 1931)
Bottomley, Horatio. *Bottomley's Book* (Odhams, London, 1909)
Broadhurst, Henry. *Henry Broadhurst MP* (Hutchinson, London, 1901)
Clynes, J.R. *Memoirs*, vols. I and II (Hutchinson, London, 1937)
Collison, William. *The Apostle of Free Labour* (Hurst and Blackett, London, 1913)
Hyndman, H.M. *The Record of an Adventurous Life* (Macmillan, New York, 1911)
———*Further Reminiscences* (Macmillan, London, 1912)
Lansbury, George. *My Life* (Constable, London, 1931)
———*Looking Backwards – and Forwards* (Blackie, London, 1935)
——— *The Miracle of Fleet Street* (The Labour Publishing Co., London, n.d.)
London, Jack. *People of the Abyss* (Macmillan, London, 1903)
Mann, Tom. *Tom Mann's Memoirs* (MacGibbon and Kee, London, 1967)
O'Connor, Thomas P. *Memoirs of an old Parliamentarian* (E. Benn, London, 1929)
Rhodes James, Robert. *Memoirs of a Conservative: J.C.C. Davidson's Memoirs and
    Papers 1910-37* (Weidenfeld and Nicolson, London, 1965)
Sexton, James. *Sir James Sexton, Agitator* (Faber and Faber, London, 1936)
Smillie, Robert. *My Life for Labour* (Mills and Boon, London, 1924)
Snowden, Phillip. *An Autobiography*, vols. I and II (Nicolson and Watson, London,
    1934)
Thomas, J.H. *My Story* (Hutchinson, London, 1937)
Thorne, Will. *My Life's Battles* (George Newnes, London, n.d.)
Tupper, E. *Seamen's Torch* (Hutchinson, London, 1938)
Countess of Warwick, Francis, *Afterthoughts* (Cassell, London, 1931)
Webb, Beatrice. *My Apprenticeship* (Longmans, London, 1926)
——— *Diaries, 1912-1924* (Longmans, London, 1952)

6. Biographies

Brockway, Fenner. *Socialism over 60 years: The Life of Jowett of Bradford*
    (Allen and Unwin, London, 1946)
Bullock, Alan. *The Life and Times of Ernest Bevin*, vol. I (William Heinemann,
    London, 1960)
Cross, Colin. *Phillip Snowden* (Barrie and Rockliff, London, 1966)
Gollin, Alfred M. *The Observer and J.L. Garvin, 1908-14* (Oxford University
    Press, London, 1960)
——— *Alfred Milner: Proconsul in Politics* (Blond Press, London, 1964)
Hamilton, Mary Agnes. *Arthur Henderson: A Biography* (William Heinemann,
    London, 1938)
Havighurst, Alfred. *Radical Journalist: H.W. Massingham* (Cambridge University
    Press, London, 1974)

Kapp, Yvonne. *Eleanor Marx*, vol. II (Pantheon Books, New York, 1977)
Larkin, Emmet. *James Larkin* (MIT Press, Cambridge, Mass., 1965)
Leventhal, F.M. *George Howell: Respectable Radical* (Harvard University Press, Cambridge, Mass., 1971)
Marjoribanks, Edward. *Life of Lord Carson*, vols. I-III (Gollancz, London, 1932-6)
Marquand, David. *Ramsay MacDonald* (Jonathan Cape, London, 1977)
Morgan, Kenneth O. *Keir Hardie, Radical and Socialist* (Weidenfeld and Nicolson, London, 1975)
Symons, Julian. *Horatio Bottomley* (Cresset Press, London, 1955)
Taylor, A.J.P. *Beaverbrook* (Hamilton Press, London, 1972)
Thompson, Edward P. *William Morris* (Lawrence and Wishart, London, 1955)
Torr, Dona. *Tom Mann* (pamphlet) (Lawrence and Wishart, London, 1944)
—— *Tom Mann*, vol. I (Lawrence and Wishart, London, 1956)
Tsuzuke, Chuschichi. *H.M. Hyndman and British Socialism* (Oxford University Press, London, 1961)
Williams, Francis. *Ernest Bevin* (Hutchinson, London, 1952)

7. General Secondary Sources

d'Alroy Jones, Peter. *The Christian Socialist Revival, 1877-1914* (Princeton University Press, Princeton, 1968)
Arnot, R. Page. *The Miners: Years of Struggle* (Allen and Unwin, London, 1953)
Booth, Charles. *Life and Labour of the People of London*, vols. 1 and 4 (Macmillan, London, 1904)
Brand, Carl. *British Labour's Rise to Power* (Stanford University Press, Stanford, Ca. 1941)
Braunthal, Julius. *History of the International*, vol. I (Praeger Press, New York, 1967)
Briggs, Asa and Saville, John (eds.). *Essays in Labour History*, vols. 1 and 2 (Macmillan, London, 1967 and 1971)
Broodbank, S.M. Joseph. *History of the Port of London*, vol. 1 (Daniel O'Connor, London, 1901)
Brown, Kenneth D. (ed.). *Essays in Anti-Labour History* (Archon Books, Hamden, Conn., 1974)
Brown, Raymond. *Waterfront Organisation in Hull, 1870-1900* (University of Hull Press, Hull, 1972)
Clegg, H.A., Fox, A. and Thompson, A.F. *A History of British Trade Unionism since 1889*, vol. 1 (Oxford University Press, London, 1964)
Cole, G.D.H. *A Short History of the British Working-Class Movement* (Allen and Unwin, London, 1941)
——*A History of Socialist Thought: The Second International*, vol. 3 (Macmillan, London, 1957)
Cole, G.D.H. and Postgate, Raymond. *The Common People, 1746-1946* (Methuen and Co., London, 1968)
Cole, Margaret. *Makers of the Labour Movement* (Longmans, London, 1948)
Cronin, J. *Industrial Conflict in Modern Britain* (Croom Helm, London, 1979)
Dangerfield, George. *The Strange Death of Liberal England* (Capricorn Books, New York, 1961)
Fainsod, Merle. *International Socialism and the World War* (Doubleday, Garden City, NY, 1969)
Fishman, William. *East End Jewish Radicals, 1870-1914* (Duckworth, London, 1974)
Graubard, S.R. *British Labour and the Russian Revolution* (Harvard University Press, Cambridge, Mass., 1956)

Halevy, Elie. *The Era of Tyrannies* (Anchor Books, Garden City, NY, 1965)

Harrison, Royden. *Before the Socialists* (Routledge and Kegan Paul, London, 1965)

Hinton, James. *The First Shop Steward's Movement* (Allen and Unwin, London, 1973)

Hobsbawm, E.J. *Labouring Men* (Weidenfeld and Nicolson, London, 1964)
—— *Industry and Empire* (Pelican Books, Harmondsworth, 1975)

Holton, Robert. *British Syndicalism, 1910-14* (Pluto Press, London, 1976)

Joll, James. *The Second International* (Weidenfeld and Nicolson, London, 1955)

Kendall, Walter. *The Revolutionary Movement in Britain* (Weidenfeld and Nicolson, London, 1969)

Koss. Stephen. *Nonconformity in British Politics* (Archon Books, Hamden, Conn. 1975)

Lee, H.W. and Archbold, W. *History of the Social Democratic Federation* (Social Democratic Federation, London, 1935)

Lovell, John. *Stevedores and Dockers, a Study of Trade Unionism in the Port of London, 1870-1914* (Macmillan, London, 1969)

Middlemas, R.K. *The Clydesiders* (Hutchinson, London, 1965)

Morris, A.J.A. (ed.), *Edwardian Radicalism* (Routledge and Kegan Paul, London, 1974)

Owen, D.J. *The Port of London, Yesterday and Today* (Port of London Authority, London, 1927)

Patterson, A.T. *A History of Southampton*, vol. 3 (Southampton University Press, Southampton, 1975)

Pelling, Henry. *The Origins of the Labour Party* (Macmillan, London, 1964)
—— *Popular Politics and Society in Late Victorian Britain* (Macmillan, London, 1968)

Phelps Brown, E. *The Growth of British Industrial Relations* (Macmillan, London, 1959)

Poirier, Phillip. *The Advent of the Labour Party* (Columbia University Press, New York, 1958)

Powell, L. *The Shipping Federation* (Shipping Federation, London, 1950)

Pribicevic, Banco. *The Shop Steward's Movement and Workers' Control* (Oxford University Press, London, 1959)

Price, Richard. *An Imperial War and the British Working Class* (Routledge and Kegan Paul, London, 1972)

Richman, Geoff. *Fly a Flag for Poplar* (Liberation Films, London, n.d.)

Roberts, B.C. *The Trade Union Congress, 1868-1921* (Harvard University Press, Cambridge, Mass., 1958)

Saul, S.B. *The Myth of the Great Depression* (Macmillan, London, 1969)

Schorske, Carl. *The German Social Democratic Party, 1905-17* (Harvard University Press, Cambridge, Mass., 1955)

Smith, H.L.L. and Nash, Vaughan. *The Story of the Dockers' Strike* (Fisher Unwin, London, 1889)

Stansky, Peter (ed.). *The Left and the War* (Oxford University Press, London, 1969)

Stedman Jones, Gareth. *Outcast London* (Clarendon Press, Oxford, 1971)

Swanwick, H.M. *Builders of Peace* (Swarthmore Press, London, 1924)

Swartz, Marvin. *The Union of Democratic Control* (Clarendon Press, Oxford, 1971)

Taplin, E.L. *Liverpool Dockers and Seamen, 1870-90* (University of Hull Press, Hull, 1974)

Thompson, Paul. *Socialists, Liberals and Labour: The Struggle for London, 1885-1914* (Routledge and Kegan Paul, London, 1967)

Webb, Sidney and Beatrice. *The History of Trade Unionism* (Longmans, Green, London, 1920)

Woodworth, Arthur V. *Christian Socialism in England* (S. Sonnenschein, London, 1903)

8. Articles and Theses

Alderman, Geoffrey. 'The National Free Labour Association', *International Review of Social History*, vol. XXI, part 3 (1976), pp. 309-36

Anderson, Perry. 'Origins of the Present Crisis', *New Left Review*, vol. 23 (January-February 1964), pp. 26-63

—— 'The Myths of Edward Thompson', *New Left Review*, vol. 35 (January/February 1965), pp. 2-42

Donovan, P.F. 'Australia and the Great London Dock Strike: 1889' *Journal of the Australian Society for the Study of Labour History*, no. 23 (November 1972), pp. 17-26

Duffy, A.E.P. 'New Unionism in Britain, 1889-90, A Reappraisal', *Economic History Review*, 2nd ser., vol. 14, no. 2 (December 1961), pp. 306-19

Nairn, Tom. 'The Nature of the Labour Party (I)', *New Left Review*, vol. 27 (September-October 1964), pp. 38-65

—— 'The Nature of the Labour Party (II)', *New Left Review*, vol. 28, November-December 1964), pp. 33-62

Pattison, C. 'Nineteenth Century Dock Labour in the Port of London', *Mariners' Mirror*, vol. LII, no. 3 (1966), pp. 263-79

Phillips, G.A. 'The National Transport Workers Federation', unpublished DPhil thesis, University of Oxford, 1968

—— 'The Triple Industrial Alliance of 1914', *Economic History Review*, 24 (1971), pp. 55-67

Reynolds, J. and Laybourne, K. 'The Emergence of the Independent Labour Party in Bradford', *International Review of Social History*, vol. 20, part 1 (1975), pp. 313-46

Schneer, Jonathan. 'Ben Tillett's Conversion to Independent Labour Politics', *Radical History Review*, 24 (fall, 1980), pp. 42-65

Sires, R.V. 'Labour Unrest in England, 1910-14', *Journal of Economic History*, vol. 15, no. 3 (September 1955), pp. 246-66

Stedman Jones, G. 'Working-Class Culture and Working-Class Politics in London, 1870-1900, Notes on the Remaking of a Working Class', *Journal of Social History*, vol. 7, no. 4 (1974), pp. 460-508

Stubbs, J.O. 'Lord Milner and Patriotic Labour, 1914-18', *English Historical Review*, vol. 87 (October 1972), pp. 717-54

Thompson, Edward P. 'The Peculiarities of the English', *Socialist Register* (1965), pp. 311-62

INDEX

Amalgamated Society of Dock
  Companies' Servants and General
  Labourers 40-1
Australia, Tillett's trips to 115-16,
  120, 131-2
Aveling, Edward 32, 85, 105

Baldwin, Stanley 218-19
Barry, Maltman 102
Bartley, James 69
Beaverbrook, Lord 209, 213, 218-20
Belgium, Tillett's incarceration in
  113, 116
Besant, Annie 28, 34, 37n5
Bevin, Ernest 190, 218; advocates
  direct action 205; in the
  National Transport Workers'
  Union 206, 214; organizes the
  Transport and General Workers'
  Union 214-17; post-war
  prominence 197, 200; see also
  Union of Dock, Wharf, Riverside
  and General Labourers
binding arbitration, Tillett's
  advocacy of 122, 125, 128, 150,
  226; after his trip to Australia
  116, 117; only way to achieve
  parity with employers 123-4, 226
'Black Friday', 15 April 1921
  210-14, 224
Blatchford, Robert 69, 93, 106,
  108, 120, 144
'Bloody Sunday' 26
Boot and Shoe Operatives' Union 25,
  27
Booth, Charles 8-9, 14, 17, 21n8
Bottomley, Horatio 126-7, 131,
  136, 147n11
Bow and Bromley Institute 24
Bradford: industrial conflict in 68-9;
  Tillett's nomination for
  Parliament 62-3; Tillett's parlia-
  mentary campaign, 1895 108-11;
  Tillett's parliamentary campaign,
  1892 67-76, political platform
  72-3
Bradford and District Labour Union

69, 72, 78n17
Bradlaugh, Charles 24, 28
Bristol 6, 21n3
Bristol dock strike of 1892 80-6,
  89, 93-6, 100-1, 223; causes 80;
  radicalizing effect on Tillett 82-3,
  85; street fighting 84; strikers
  defeated 86; union leaders'
  sedition trial 84-6, 89, 93-4
British Socialist Party 165, 175,
  191; see also Hyndman, Henry and
  Social Democratic Federation
British Workers' League 194-5
Broadhurst, Henry 24, 36n1, 98, 103
Burns, John 85, 111, 136, 160;
  attracted to the Social Democratic Federation 26, 29;
  candidate for Parliament 45-6,
  68, 71; drifts away from the
  dockers' union 96; elected to
  Parliament 79; in the dockers'
  strike of 1889 42-3; in the Hull
  dockers' strike 81, 91-2, 96;
  Liberal cabinet minister 155;
  moves toward the Liberals 129;
  new unionism 58; opposes dock
  strikes in 1890-1, 51-2, 54; tea
  operatives' union 29, 32; tries to
  prevent links between the Trade
  Union Congress and Independent
  Labour Party 102-4
Buxton, Sydney 50

Cardiff dockers' strike 54-5
Carson, Sir Edward 111-12
Champion, H.H. 40-1, 43, 68, 102
chauvinism, Tillett's 176-83, 195;
  advocates a citizens' army 178,
  183; supports the war effort
  183-92, 196-7, 200, is isolated
  after the war 197, 200, moves
  into the Labour Party mainstream
  188-95 passim; versus his class
  feelings 182-4; versus his internationalism 178-83
Clarion 69, 89, 107, 138
Cobden Club 24

236